Spirit

Derek Feldon

Derek Feldon lived in Lancashire, leaving school at the tender age of thirteen with no qualifications. He attended night school three times a week, after a full day's work, for the next nine years.

He served in Palestine as a member of the armed forces for a couple of years and gained wide experience in many branches of industry, from shop floor to management level. At the age of thirty he moved to the Isle of Wight with his family, to take up a teaching post.

Derek is a keen traveller and has visited many countries around the world. Having retired at the age of seventy he now writes as a hobby.

Order this book online at www.trafford.com/08-0521
or email orders@trafford.com

Most Trafford titles are also available at major online book retailers.

Note for Librarians: A cataloguing record for this book is available from Library and Archives Canada at www.collectionscanada.ca/amicus/index-e.html

Printed in Victoria, BC, Canada.

ISBN: 978-1-4251-7671-6

www.trafford.com

North America & international
toll-free: 1 888 232 4444 (USA & Canada)
phone: 250 383 6864 ♦ fax: 250 383 6804 ♦ email: info@trafford.com

The United Kingdom & Europe
phone: +44 (0)1865 487 395 ♦ local rate: 0845 230 9601
facsimile: +44 (0)1865 481 507 ♦ email: info.uk@trafford.com

10 9 8 7 6 5 4 3 2

Companion Book 1

'The Spirit of Adventure'

By Derek Feldon

Is now available at: www.trafford.com/04-0796

Derek and Glenys with Mother Chadra and family, SOS Children's Village – India.

With the sale of this book, a donation will be made to SOS Children – Registered Charity Number 1069204.

The world's largest orphan charity, SOS Children provides a home and family to more than 50,000 children without parents in 125 countries until they are independent.

They care for children regardless of race, nationality or creed & they are non-governmental. The charity is non-denominational and funded mainly by voluntary contributions.

THANK YOU FOR HELPING ORPHANED AND ABANDONED CHILDREN AROUND THE WORLD.

Derek.

Yet again, I would like to thank Petra, my daughter, for the unenviable job of deciphering my hand written notes and typing up the final manuscript.

My love and thanks to Glenys, my wife, for her patience and support – and the endless editing of the script!

Some character names have been changed to protect the identity of the individuals.

Introduction

"I shall not cease to explore,

And at the end of my exploring I shall arrive at where I started from, and,

I shall know that place for the very first time."

I have thousands in fact millions, of ancestors who have gone before me and I don't know who they are, what they did and how they survived. Not one left me a scrap of paper saying 'this is me and this is what I did'. No words of wisdom, no insights on how they thought and no clues as to the wonderful experiences they must have encountered.

I can't remember being told anything beyond my grandparents. I do know that my Great-Granddad, John Smith was the Mayor of 'Talke oth Hill' in Staffordshire. My Granddad Brookes moved from Staffordshire to Lancashire to get work on the coalface in the pits.

Great Granddad Joseph Feldon lived in Chorlton upon Medlock, Manchester and was a bootmaker by trade. My Granddad Charles Ramage Feldon lived in Chorlton-cum-Hardy. He was a foremen patternmaker in a brass foundry.

I was lucky to be brought up in a poor family, who strived to better themselves. Dad was a clever man, full of ideas and innovations. He was strict with our upbringing and was teetotal. He smoked (a habit he had picked up in the trenches in the First World War) and he suffered ill health (due to being gassed in France, which had permanently damaged his lungs and stomach), but he was a survivor. My Mam, well she had a lot to put up with! She became a servant at the age of fourteen; they called it 'Being in Service'. She met Dad in Chorlton-cum Hardy, Manchester, when he came out of the army. They fell in love, and stayed that way through their lives. She was a fantastic Mam. She also knew what real pain and suffering was, but she never complained.

One day you and your grandchildren, may take this book off your shelf and you will enter into My World; My experiences, My challenges, My happiness and My sadness.

"Life Must Be a Great Adventure – Or It's Nothing!"

Derek Feldon

Whatever it is you want to do, do it while you can; For future days may alter things and fate could steal your plan.

Glenys Feldon

Contents

1

It's Custard Wot Makes The Fish Yellow

Bang! The door flew open and hit me right in the middle of the back. I lurched forward, just managing to miss putting my hand down the toilet pan; that would have been a disaster as it was still full of yesterday's misgivings – boy, the smell was enough!

This was my first real job as a self-employed plumber. The landlord of these poor, dilapidated, badly maintained terrace houses had given me the job of repairing all the old lead pipes feeding the rusty cast-iron cisterns overhead, in the outside lavatories.

Peering around the door was a little lad's face, covered in black treacle from the butty he held in his hand.

'Wot you doin' mister? Are yer FETTLIN PET? Cause I'm bursting for a pee.'

Now I hadn't a clue what he was talking about. This was Farnworth's run-down district and they seemed to have a language of their own! When I got home I asked Glenys what 'Fettlin Pet' meant.

'Mending the lavatory,' she answered, as quick as a flash.

Having completed the major alterations to our new house, everybody wanted me to do similar work to their houses. They all had many repair jobs that needed doing, but couldn't get hold of a builder or plumber for love nor money.

I had built up a good reputation for doing these odd-jobs in my spare time and thought it was time for a change from hotel engineering – and this wonderful new business opportunity was just knocking on my door. So, with a deep breath, I handed in my notice to the chief engineer, who was sorry to see me go but wished me luck in my new venture. And that's how it started.

Having repaired all the burst pipes, I was up a ladder repairing and replacing a length of gutter. Now we didn't have scaffolding but I managed to get hold of a pair of ladder brackets. These were adjustable and fitted over the rungs of ladders. Two centre lever brackets extended out to form a platform so that one, or two, planks could stretch from one ladder to the other, very similar to shelf brackets on a wall. From this temporary contraption I could do almost any building alterations required; from new gutters to replacing rotten window frames, from re-slating a roof to pointing a full gable end of a house – marvellous!

This was a warm sunny day, after the thaw of the ice and snow, and I was just sealing off the joints on the gutter. A scruffy young lad was shouting away in the next back yard; his clogs had holes in the toes, his socks draped around his ankles, his breeches were torn in a couple of places, his white shirt was as black as the ace of spades with what looked like bright red raspberry jam wiped down the front, and his hair and face hadn't seen soap for years. Then it began again.

'Eat yer bugger!' he shouted, as he jammed half a loaf of stale bread into a large glass jam jar which was perched precariously on the edge of the scullery stone window sill. 'Yer get nowt else until yer finish this off!'

I shouted down, 'What are you doing, son?' He looked up.

'What the 'ell do yer think I'm doing, I'm feeding t' bloody goldfish. Can't yer see?'

I climbed down the ladder and went into the yard next door. I lifted up the jar, and pressed tightly against the bottom was, (he was right), a goldfish! Dipping my hand in the jar I quickly pulled out the soggy bread.

'You mustn't do that,' I said. 'You'll suffocate the poor fish.'

'Listen, mate. My mam said I had to feed the goldfish some bread, and that is what the bugger is going to git, and if he don't eat it he'll git no bleedin' pudding.' Lo and behold, on the floor there was a greasy black tin with half a jam roly poly pudding complete with a large dollop of deep yellow gungy custard!

I suggested to him that it might not be such a good idea to give the fish the pudding and custard. He looked at me as if I was an imbecile.

'Look mister, 'es got to eat the custard cos that's wot makes 'im a goldfish. Yer see, it's the yella custard what makes 'im yella, and that's true cos my dad sez so – and 'es bigger than you!'

Just at that moment his dad came through the back gate and into the yard. He was a big fella, and I mean BIG, with shoulders like a bull. He was wearing a pair of corduroy trousers, size twelve clogs, a dirty vest showing his bulging arm muscles, and a cap perched on a mass of curly hair. I must admit he was a fine specimen of a tough and rough coal miner; I could smell the beer, before he had fully come through the gate.

'Wot's he done now?' asked the dad 'I'll give 'im wot for!'

'Er, nothing,' I said as the little lad crouched down behind me in terror.

'Nothing? Well, wot yer doin' ere?'

I tried to explain about the feeding of the goldfish.

'Yer not from around these parts, mate, are yer? Yer talk too bleedin' posh to be from around 'ere.'

Before I could reply, the little lad butted in.

'Isn't that right dad? It's the custard wot makes the fish yella.' His dad winked at me.

'That's right son, that'd be a black fish without the custard.' He leaned forward until his bloodshot eyes were about half an inch away from mine, and whispered, 'Lad's not very bright yer see, so I 'ave to humour 'im.' Then in the next breath, 'Do yer want a cup of tea?'

'I'll have to be going,' I said nodding towards the ladder next door, 'but maybe next time.'

'Sure, and if yer ever need any 'elp and a bit of muscle just ask for Big John. I'm always out for a bit of beer money, but don't tell the wife!' Another wink and he was gone.

It was at that moment I became aware of the galvanised tin bath hanging on the wall. In those few seconds I had a flash-back to when I was a lad, standing in our back yard. It's funny, that symbolic bath was always in the same place on the kitchen wall, except of course on a Friday, when it was bath night, then it was on the rug in front of the blazing fire. My mam kneeling down with a huge chunk of carbolic soap and me sitting in the bath with a face towel jammed as tightly as possible over my eyes – boy, that soap didn't half sting if you got it in your eyes.

'Are yer listening to me?' I jumped back into reality as the lad pulled at my shirt. 'I told yer my dad knows everything, and 'es bigger that you. And there's som'at else, my dad said yer might be posh but yer not very bright are yer!'

I stood there for a minute absolutely flabbergasted, and thought what a cheeky young devil this boy was. Then the truth hit me and I started to laugh.

'You're right lad, I've a lot to learn. I've a lot to learn!' and I gently closed the gate behind me.

Putting my bass (canvas holdall) containing my tools, a drum of putty, a tin of red-lead paint and two sets of ladders onto my newly acquired hand cart, I was ready for the long trek home, but then had second thoughts. I went back next door, and as I opened the gate and saw the lad poised over the jar with the baking tin.

'What are yer doin' now?'

'Well, I don't want me fish to go black so I thought I'd give 'im the custard now before the puddin'.'

'How do you fancy a ride on my hand cart to the bottom of the backing?' I asked quickly.

Bang! The tin clattered as it bounced on the stone flags in the yard.

'D'yer mean that, mister?' and he was out of the gate like a flash.

Climbing up the spokes of the large four-foot diameter wheels, he perched himself on top of the ladders.

'Wow! It's like a bleedin' fire engine up 'ere!' And off we went down the backing. Kids appeared from nowhere.

'Can we 'ave a go, mister?' they chanted.

'Tomorrow, maybe. If you're good!'

'Oh, we'll be good!'

The next day they were all waiting; six of the little mites climbed onto my hand cart shouting and cheering for all they were worth, the din echoed back and forth between the narrow backing walls. Bump, bump, bump, they went, over the cobble stones. As soon as I reached the street at the end of the lane I thought they would lead me a right merry dance, trying to get them all off, but I was wrong. They were all quite happy as they climbed down off the cart.

'See yer tomorrow, mate,' they chorused as they ran up the backing, kicking sparks with their clogs on the shiny cobble stones, and then disappeared through their own back gates and into their houses for tea.

I soon built up a reputation as the 'Posh Man'. All the kids would come and chat to me, and some even offered me half of their bubbly gum; they were very generous to me, even if they had chewed it for a couple of days! And I could always get a cup of tea at their house. One of the kid's mams asked me if I could do a flit (removal) for them on my cart. She said it was only three streets away, but I found out it was a 'moon-light flit' as they hadn't paid their rent for weeks and had to move out quickly. I had to say that I was sorry, but I didn't work nights! Phew! That could have really caused a problem with the landlord who passed a lot of work on to me.

It was all downhill from Farnworth to Little Hulton and, with a following wind, I reckoned I could be home and in the house within an hour. I knew my arms and legs would be throbbing with the vibration of a three mile trudge pushing the cart over endless cobblestones, but that's the joy of being self-employed! After a full day's graft I still had to sort the cart out for the early start the following morning.

It wasn't long before Phil, a young lad from Salford, asked me for work as an apprentice. He wasn't the least bit perturbed about the prospect of pushing the hand cart from job to job. Little did I know that soon, very soon, this form of transport would change dramatically.

2

I'm Forever Blowing Bubbles

It was still raining hard. With the key in my hand I opened the front door.

'Dad!' I shouted, but no answer. Funny, I thought, then I spotted the greenhouse door open. Up the path I ran and barged into the greenhouse, and stopped dead in my tracks; there was dad, slumped shoulders, head down, sitting on an old milk crate, sobbing his heart out. He waved for me to go away. I was stunned. I could only remember him crying once before, and that was when I had my last thrashing as a very young boy. I didn't move and he lifted his head slowly. The first thing that struck me was the limp sodden cigarette hanging from the corner of his mouth, wet through from the tears still streaming down his sunken face.

I sat down beside him and put my arm around his thin shoulders. It was then that I realised that he mustn't have been eating anything. Picking up a scrap of towelling off the bench he covered his face. We sat like that for ages until he eventually settled down, completely exhausted.

'What's up, dad? What's it all about?'

Then he poured out all his thoughts and pent up feelings, it was like a dam bursting. 'Oh, son, I'm so lonely. I've never felt so lonely in all my life. Sometimes I think my heart is going to break. I've not slept a wink since ma died. I don't want to go to bed at night, and when I do I just lie there hour after hour staring at the ceiling, thinking and talking to myself. What if I could have done more to help her, should I have done this, could I have done that. Then I start talking to her as if she's still there and I tell her all the things I should have told her over the years. I'm up at two, three, four and five o'clock in the morning. I make myself a cup of tea and light another cigarette, then I sit and cry and cry.'

'Come on dad," I said gently. 'Let's go inside and we'll have a cup of tea.'

'No, no" he protested, 'but I would like to sit and have a cup of tea with you. Sorry. Sorry, son. I didn't want you to see me like this. I didn't know you were coming around today.'

I dashed up the path towards the house just as the heavens opened in a torrential downpour. I made the tea, opened a tin of beans, and toasted a couple of rounds of bread. Covering the tea and beans on toast with a large pan lid I dashed back up the garden path. We sat there in silence listening to the sound of the rain. He drank his tea and downed his toast.

'Ee, do you know, I really enjoyed that, son. I haven't known a cup of tea taste so good for a long time.'

He had calmed down, and looked more like my dad again. The rain was hammering on the glass roof and the water poured off into the gutter filling the water butt up and overflowing in a gushing bubbling stream down from the vegetable patch to the front gate. He looked up at me.

'Do you know, at times, I think I'm going mad. It may sound funny to you, but I think I'm losing my marbles. Yes, I think I'm crackers. I can't sleep, I can't eat. I spend most of the time in a trance and feeling so sorry for myself. Can you understand what I'm saying, son?' The rain still thudded away on the glass and dad talked in a whisper, as if afraid of what he might say.

I brought an old upturned bucket out from underneath

the bench and sat down opposite him.

'Right dad, come on and tell me all about it.'

He looked up an gave me a gentle smile, 'Well, it's like this, you see when you all married and left home your mam and I were quite content and happy to spend the rest of our lives in our dream home. Funny, I never thought she would leave me; I somehow thought we would always be sharing our lives together. When ma died, all my dreams died with her. I often sit and think of all the good times; like when we moved into this house. Do you remember when we filled the garden with gladioli, and the chickens, and your apple tree at the end of the garden? I can still see your ma now, handing out bunches of gladioli to anyone who came to see her. I lie in that big double bed at night and it just seems so empty and cold. We had been through a lot together and I knew that one day this would happen; she suffered so much for so long, it was a blessing to see her go in peace at last. But I do miss her. You know I would never let you sing *I'm forever blowing bubbles.*' Softly he started to sing, '*I'm dreaming dreams, I'm scheming schemes, I'm building castles high. They're born anew, their days are few, just like a sweet butterfly. And as the day is dawning they come again in the morning! I'm forever blowing bubbles, pretty bubbles in the air. They fly so high, nearly reach the sky, then like my dreams they fade and die. Fortune's always hiding, I've looked everywhere, I'm forever blowing bubbles, pretty bubbles in the air* – Well my bubble has gone, just faded away and died,' he continued. 'Your ma was my pretty bubble and she just faded away and died. I'm so lost and lonely without her. So you see son, I think it's time I let go of my past dreams and see what I can do with the rest of my life. I've decided to sell up and move on.'

* * * * *

Eventually dad sold the house and bought a vacuum chimney sweeping business in Altringham, Cheshire. It didn't work out so he gave me the 1935 Morris Van he had acquired.

I sat in the van with my handbook *How to Drive a Car.* In and out of my stable cum garage, clutch in clutch out, hour after hour. Then it was time to go up and down the backing, forward, reverse and so on. Randal, a friend of ours, said it was now time to get on the road. Boy, it frightened the life out of me – no duel controls – and off we went. I soon got the hang of things and put in for my test at Oldham Road in Manchester.

We all sat on a form outside the inspector's house.

'Smith,' the inspector shouted, then he instructed him to read the number plate on an old lorry parked on the cleared bomb site opposite. *Smith* couldn't read it – I couldn't even see it, at that distance! Smith failed and was told to reapply when he had got himself a pair of glasses. Next was a young chap; he had walked past the lorry and made a mental note of the number plate on his way to the test centre.

As soon as they had driven off I was across the site to the lorry. The number plate was filthy dirty. I wrote the number down on a scrap of paper Randal had given me, and shot back to the centre just in time. Out came the inspector.

'Feldon' he barked.

'Sir,' and off we went.

I must tell you about the hill start. We stopped halfway up a steep hill. The inspector got out of the car and placed a box of matches behind and touching the rear wheel.

'Okay, laddy, when you're ready, move forward a couple of yards. If you squash my matches you fail.'

'Don't worry, if I squash your matches I'll buy you a new box!' I said. But the man wasn't amused.

Back at the test centre he asked me why I wanted the van. I told him that I had started up as a plumber and builder.

'Well, son,' he said. 'You're in business. Good luck, you've passed!' I could have kissed him – but the moustache put me off! Randal took off the 'L' plates and threw them in a dustbin nearby, and we headed off to the nearest café for a well needed cup of tea.

On the way home I felt like Stirling Moss. We were clogging along at 30 mph overtaking pedestrians and we even passed the odd cyclist or two. Windows open with the wind in our hair – Oh heavenly bliss, what luxury. I couldn't get home quick enough to take Glenys out for a spin.

Randal said that the blue smoke belching out of the exhaust was caused by burning oil and that a tube of piston seal squeezed in the cylinder head should help. It did, but I still had to put in a pint of oil to every four gallons of petrol. As far as I knew at that time, that was quite normal. Of course, bits and pieces kept falling off, but it is surprising what a length of wire, and old tin can and a tube of exhaust seal can do. There was no question of buying a new exhaust; it would cost more than the van was worth.

One day I was taking, Gladys, Glenys's mum to Bolton. There we were motoring along, not a care in the world. We were just passing Bolton Wanderers football ground when the van suddenly acquired a mind of its own; and believe me when it decided to do something daft it just did it, with absolutely no consideration to me, its master.The van suddenly veered over to the right, shot straight across the road and in front of the two huge black and white shire horses, pulling a dray loaded with barrels of local fine ale. Their heads jerked upwards as we miraculously managed to miss them by a couple of feet – not worried in the slightest, on and on they plodded up the hill. I then began to panic slightly. I spun the steering wheel round and round, but to no avail.

'Crickey!' I said under my breath, not wanting to worry Glenys's mum, as we mounted the pavement with a bump, and drove right across a garage forecourt, past the petrol pumps and directly through the open garage workshop doors.

Enough is enough, I thought, and jammed the brake on as we gently sidled up to the mechanics bench.

'Blooming Heck!' he exclaimed. 'Don't do that. You frightened the life out of me! What's up mate?' I showed him the free-spinning steering wheel. 'Ah! No problem!' and he disconnected the shaft from the steering box, welded the two halves together, reassembled the unit; and we were back on the road in fifteen minutes flat.

The mechanic popped the half a crown in his back pocket and carried on his work as normal. Gladys looked at me.

'Is everything alright Derek?'

'Oh yes, fine!' I replied, attempting a reassuring smile. 'Just a spot of maintenance.'

After dropping Gladys off, I returned safely home back to normality to find Glenys cooking a lovely tea. We didn't have pea soup that night, but we certainly had plenty during the next few weeks – though I must admit I wasn't keen on the flavour...

3

We're Off, We're Off, We're Off In A Motor Car!

A 'Pea-souper' was fog so dense you couldn't see your hand in front of you. Coming back along the main Manchester to Westhoughton Road I crawled along the kerb. Phil had the nearside door open.

'In a bit. Out a bit,' he guided, and so it went on, as we edged slowly home.

Arriving at Wingate Road I turned left, only a few yards more and we would be home. A quick right turn into the backing running parallel with the back of the houses on the main road, then a sharp right turn straight into my workshop yard. Thank goodness for that, our eyes were running and red raw with the strain and fumes from driving in the thick fog.

We got out of the car but found we couldn't get out of our yard as the entrance onto the backing was completely blocked by a large red double-decker bus. I heard a voice from somewhere above.

'Where the hell are we, mate?' The driver of the bus was leaning out of his window.

I shouted back, 'What the blazes are you doing up here?'

'Well,' he replied 'You seemed to know where you were going so I just followed your red tail-lights for the last three miles!'

'Just follow me,' I shouted back and walked on up the backing. I guided him slowly round into the next street and back to the main road.

'Thanks mate,' he yelled and off the bus crawled into the greenish-yellow fog of the night.

But as I turned around, I saw to my surprise, that the bus was being closely tailed by a large transport lorry, which in turn was being directly followed by another bus, then a car, then a horse and cart, and so on! I shot in the house and brought Glenys out to see the amazing spectacle of dozens of vehicles slowly diverting off the main road, down the backing, and back onto the main road again! Not one of them wanted to risk losing sight of the red lights in front of them.

Even after tea we could still hear the heavy drone of engines shunting their way slowly along our backing.

Frank, my brother in law, who now worked for me as a carpenter, and Tommy, the apprentice, and me, had spent one Saturday morning working on four very old cottages stuck out in the middle of nowhere, in the centre of the Moss. Wow! What an experience that was. I decided I needed to go to the lavatory, so off I went through the back door and across the cobble yard to the row of toilets at the back. I popped, rather smartish, into the third one in the row; inside there was a box with a hole in the centre. Trousers down, I settled comfortably over the hole.

Then a chap started coughing; and you name it, he did it. It was just like a symphony orchestra tuning up. Trumpet blowing, drum banging, and of course, the French horn was blasting away! I sat there mesmerised at the din. Then I heard water running followed by a slithering, sliding sound. The stink that met my nostrils was unbearable. I jumped up off the hole in time to watch the whole 'orchestral movement', including torn up newspaper and fags ends, go sailing by along the v-shaped corrugated iron trough! Ugh! It was disgusting! Up came my trousers and out I dashed, only to meet the big fella pulling his braces up. He looked at me, nodded, and disappeared into the next-but-one cottage.

This practice had been completely new to me, so, being the inquisitive type, I decided to investigate the matter further. I found that all four toilets were joined together by the sloping trough, which finished up overhanging a large pit at the end. At this moment a big, fat, round-faced lady appeared out of the end house.

'Oh 'ello, luv! Has that Big John not cindered his sh*te? Ee never does!' And with that she shovelled a spadeful of cinders from the pile round the corner and covered Big John's leftovers.

Seeing the slightly disgusted look on my face, the lady said, 'Before you ask, no, we don't have any drains. The council come and empty every three months in the middle of the night. That's the night to keep the windows closed, winter or summer!'

I had read about the "middens" when I was studying the history section for my sanitary inspector's course, but assumed they had gone out with the ark.

Colliers was the butcher's shop on Longcauseway in Farnworth; now that was a 'rum' job if there ever was one! It was one of those bitter cold mornings, quite a nip in the air, as I slowly clamboured up the extension ladder and stepped on to the roof ladder which we had made out of 2.5 x 1 inch slate battens.

Even before I reached the chimney, I could feel the heat from the old brickwork. I huddled down below the chimney to shelter from the biting cold wind that whipped and howled across the open, exposed rooftops. On inspection, I could see the cause of the damp patches in the bedroom below. All the lead flashings on one side of the chimney had been torn out by the hurricane force winds we had endured over the last three days. Now, I thought to myself, if these are off here I wonder what about all the other chimneys stacks running right down the length of this row of terraced houses. Some had King Crown chimney pots, buff coloured with zig zag crown-shaped tops, and a couple of the expensive 'O-H'-chimney pots (shaped like a letter H), and guaranteed to cure all smoky chimneys.

Sitting astride the long ridge, I waddled my way duck-like, along the full length of the row, stopping at each stack to inspect them. Surprise, surprise; there were five other houses with missing flashings. I made a mental note of the damaged ones.

Well, I thought to myself, that should take care of the next week's wages for the lads and me, as the smell of baking, and hot meat and potato pies, drifted up from Mrs Kirk's bakery next door.

Frank was busy in the backyard trying to mix up a load of mortar with the help of half a dozen small bantam hens, who kept up a constant clucking sound then flew up and, plop, landed right in the middle of the fresh mortar mix. This didn't, however, deter the large old Rhode Island cock who, with a glint in his eye, had other ideas!

Tommy, our apprentice, with his mop of curly black hair, climbed up and down the ladder carrying slates, and rolls of extremely weighty lead. Everything was running like clock-work when Mrs Collier, Doris, poked her head out of the kitchen and shouted.

'Come on lads. There's toast and hot coffee down here! Come on, before it gets cold!' I didn't need telling twice, down the ladder I shot and entered the kitchen to find both Frank and Tommy had already beaten me to it.

The flames in the old stove were roaring around the large, copper pot. Tommy took a swig of the delicious, hot, steam-ing coffee, and suddenly let out a yell.

'Wowee!' Shaking his head he danced up and down.

'What's the matter? Have you burnt yourself?' I asked.

'Na!' he replied, 'that's the best tasting coffee I've ever 'ad in me life!'

Frank picked up his cup and took a mouthful; his cap shot up in the air as he screwed up his eyes, and shook his head, 'Cor! I see what you mean!'

Not to be outdone, I too took a swig of Doris's special coffee. Oh my goodness, it shot right down to the tips of my toes, in fact, I thought I could feel my toenails popping right off, one after the other! By the time I had recovered my senses, my whole body was aglow and tingling.

'Wow! That sure is some coffee!'

This was our first baptism of fire to the Collier's renowned coffee.

Bob, Mr Collier, came in; 'Ready for a top-up lads?' The apprentice's mug was the first one on the table awaiting another offering from the Gods. Bob took a sip of the coffee.

'Well, that won't do you much good! Hang on a minute.' We looked at each other as he poured another half bottle of rum into the already quite potent mixture. 'There, that's more like it!' and our mugs were refilled to overflowing. Frank and I had to sit and drink ours, whilst Tommy paced backwards and forwards in the kitchen, like a cat on hot bricks. Taking a gulp every now and then, he shook his head and muttered to himself.

'Now that's some coffee! Whoa, is that some coffee!'

Climbing the ladder back on to the roof seemed to take ages. It felt more like a tread mill than a ladder. On and on I climbed but somehow didn't seem to get anywhere. Up on the roof, the cold, frosty air soon brought me back to my senses. Frank was killing himself laughing as he watched Tommy attempting to climb the ladder. Up three rungs he went then down he came again; he swore blind that the fourth rung kept bending like a piece of rubber! In the end Frank brought the slates up and Tommy got stuck into mixing up the mortar.

How the job got finished I'll never know, but one thing I do know, is that once you've tasted Collier's coffee, no other coffee will ever taste the same again!

It was time for dinner so we all packed in the van. Tommy lived near me so I dropped him off at his door. Then Frank got out at the Swinton bus stop and I made my way home. Waiting at our gate I could see young Billy Hardman, the ten year old from across the street. He had a bucketful of soapy water in one hand and a large sponge in the other. Before I had even pulled up, Sandra, the little girl from next door, came dashing out through her front door, then Sheila Hancock came running down the street, she was also ten years old and lived in the end house.Two seconds later little Paddy, with flaming bright red hair, came flying around the corner, clinging on to a bucket now only half full, with water shooting about in all directions; his short trousers and shirt wet through.

'Right then! Can we start?' they shouted as I climbed out of the van. I laughed and left them climbing all over the bonnet, soapy water sloshing everywhere, as they started to clean the van ready for tomorrow's day out to the seaside.

Billy was always very helpful in running errands for Glenys, and spent most of his spare time in my workshop. He would have a go at tackling anything, but you never saw him dirty or untidy. His shoes were always shiny, his socks held just below the knee with garters, short trousers with a crease back and front – with no holes or repair patches in them, a pristine white shirt and a smart pullover, and his blonde curly hair cut neat and trim.

Quite the opposite was little Paddy, who lived across the backing; he was a real rum 'un, a real tearaway. His mum and dad were Irish, both lovely people with a grown up family when young "fireball" Paddy made his appearance. He was a smashing kid, and again would do anything for you, but he was a real nutcase! Out of our dining room window, we often used to watch him standing on top of the air raid shelter with a motor tyre tied on the end of a piece of rope. When anyone walked past he would launch the tyre at the middle of their back sending them sprawling across the backing. They would look up stunned and there was no one to be seen! One day, I asked him why he did this.

'Oh, Mr Derek' (that's what he called me), 'I'm just trying to lasso them, but they keep falling down!'

At times he would knock on our door and say to me, 'Can you ask your mother if you can come out and play.' Glenys almost fell over with laughter when I told her.

'Mother! Huh, I'll give him your mother!'

I must tell you about the lovely Hancock family. There was no mistaking the kids, like little Sheila, all her four brothers had big (and when I say big, I mean big) brown, innocent eyes. Whenever I had cause to tell them off, they would just look at me and tears would well up in those lovely eyes and I would finish up apologising for their misbehaviour.

One evening I went to their house to see if Sheila would like to come on a trip with us to New Brighton. I entered the tiny dining room-cum-kitchen. On one side of the chimney breast were two shelves and on the other were three shelves, all with small ladders attached to them, and to my surprise, perched comfortably on each shelf with cushions all around them was a child: one laid out reading a comic, Sheila sitting, legs swinging, over the side doing a spot of sewing, and the eldest lad had a crane made from Meccano and was lowering a pencil case to his brother on the lower shelf. Everyone was happily occupied whilst their mam and dad sat at the table reading the Manchester Evening News! The whole atmosphere was oozing with love and contentment.

The day of the seaside trip was upon us. Sheila, and the other kids from our street, arrived with thick sliced bread sandwiches, piled up with cucumber, jam, marmite, and one had peanut butter (her sister had married a yank from Burtonwood, the American Airforce Base!). I placed the assortment of drinks bottles in a cardboard box; Sheila had Robinson's Barley Water, Billy brought Sarsaparilla, Sandra lemonade and Little Paddy didn't have any drink so he had filled an empty pop bottle with water and, without his mam knowing, poured in half a pound of sugar out of the blue packet – sugar was still on wartime ration so his mam would not be too pleased when she found out! During the progress of the day they passed the bottles around and Little Paddy's drink was the most popular among them all, but by the end of the day it was half full of soggy breadcrumbs from everybody's sandwiches!

They placed their cushions on the two planks that I had screwed onto the wheel arches. Then, with a toot of the horn, we were motoring along the East Lancashire Road towards Liverpool, singing merrily.

'We're off, we're off, we're off in a motor car. Sixty miles an hour and we don't know where we are. Hurray!' I don't know about sixty miles an hour – twenty eight miles an hour maximum was more like it!

As we got to Kirkdale there was a lot of shuffling going on in the back, then Billy shouted out.

'Sandra wants to wee, and she can't wait!'

'Hold on for a minute,' I shouted, 'I'll try and find a public lavatory.' I pulled up at the side of the road and asked a lady who was pushing a pram and walking a dog. She was having trouble with the lead, as it was getting all tangled around the wheels of the pram. She looked up.

'Just round the corner, luv,' she directed, 'Damn dog, it'll 'ave to go, it'll 'ave to go.'

Sandra dashed into the yellow bricked toilet and two seconds later she was out.

'I need a penny for the slot machine on the door!' Oh crickey! Scrabbling though my change I found half pennies, three penny pieces, sixpences, but no pennies. Just then, the dog came flying round the corner pulling the pram behind it, together with the, by now, very harassed young woman trying desperately to hang on to her charges. But, as luck would have it, she had a penny! Sandra was back in the toilet. A few minutes later we heard her shout.

'Next!' and in shot Sheila, then 'Next!' and in went Glenys! 'Next!' in went Billy, then Paddy and finally me – Glenys stood on guard outside, as it was the ladies toilet, but not bad, six wees for a penny!

When we stopped at the entrance to the Mersey Tunnel to pay the toll, the keeper looked into the back of the van and gasped, looked at Glenys and said 'Are they all yours, missus?'

Cheekily I replied 'Yes!'

'God help yer, missus,' the keeper said shaking his head. 'Go on and bugger off, I'm not charging you for that little lot. You deserve it.' And off we went without paying a penny.

The kids thought it was marvellous going down into the tunnel, the noise was deafening as the cars whizzed by us with their lights on. Climbing steadily we came out into daylight. The kids all cheered and started singing, 'Oh I do like to be beside the seaside....'. Sharp turn right and we were nearing New Brighton. Screaming and laughing they tumbled about in the back of the van. Next minute, they all had their swimming costumes on! Clothes were in a pile all mixed up on the floor, among the sandwiches and pop. Knickers, underpants, shirts and blouses were everywhere; but no one cared, we were off to the seaside!

We had a whale of a time building sand castles, paddling, carry buckets of water backwards and forwards for the moat around the castles. The sandwiches were followed by ice creams and lollipops all round, washed down by the remainder of Paddy's 'sugar water' – fantastic! Much too soon it was time to go home. Still wearing wet costumes they all piled in the back of the van again; sand between their toes, in their hair and down their costumes. Their faces were as red as beetroots from the salty air and the sun.

As we came out of the tunnel they started to get re-dressed. Billy's underpants had mysteriously gone missing, along with the odd sock or two, but they were too tired and happy to be bothered. They started up the 'Motor Car' song again, but it soon fell silent. We looked around and saw that they had all fallen fast asleep, lying all over each other, with not a care in the world. We had to wake them up when we got home, and the first thing they asked was 'Can we go again sometime, to that lovely New Brighton?'

'We'll see, we'll see,' I replied, as we half carried them, dragging along their buckets and spades in one hand, and their empty pop bottles, and the odd shoe, in the other hand.

Another time we decided to take Glenys's mum and dad out on a trip to Derbyshire. They had two nice deckchairs complete with cushions in the back of the van – even more extravagance than the two planks the kids had. We had a lovely ride and everything was going smoothly when we approached the top of Snake Pass at Glossop. I changed from my top, third, gear down to second gear and off we went down nice and gentle. After a couple of bends I met the next one which was steep and sharp. I put my footbrake on, but to my horror – "phut" – and the brake pipe broke! I pumped my foot up and down but to no avail, and we started to increase speed at a fair old rate. So I thought I would use my handbrake and change down to first gear. As we slowed I changed to neutral. I thought to myself, don't forget, double-de-clutch, then handbrake on to slow down engine to get into first gear, when there was an almighty crack, as the handbrake cable snapped. We shot off like a rocket, swinging round the bend like lunatics; with Gladys and Guy sliding from side to side, on their luxurious seating, in the rear of the van!

'Don't you think you're going a bit too fast, Derek?' Guy asked nervously.

'No, everything's just fine,' I gasped, as the sweat poured down my face.

When the road levelled out and straightened I slid slowly to the kerbside and stopped. Calmly I said 'I think we'll stop here and have a picnic, while I adjust the brakes a little.' We pulled the deckchairs out and set them out on the grass. I got the primus stove going and Glenys made a welcome cup of tea as I slid under the van with a length of fence wire which I had pinched from the top of a farm gate. All done, and we set off on our gentle journey home.

As we dropped Glenys's parents off at their house, they both thanked us for a lovely day out – I just nodded and smiled, if they had known what had been going on they would have had an absolute fit!

At our house one evening we had a bit of a party with our friends Ken and Margaret Lever. I said they didn't have to worry about the 'last bus home', as I would drive them back later. It was gone midnight, and pouring with rain, and we set off with Margaret in the front and Ken, sitting on a drum of putty, in the back.

Just as we were approaching their house at Moses Gate, Ken pointed and said 'Hey! Look at that!'

Caught in the glow from my headlights, we watched as a wheel whizzed past us and continued its journey down the road and right through the gates of the cotton mill yard at the bottom of their street. We looked around in disbelief, who in their right mind would roll a wheel down a street at almost one o'clock in the morning?! What a stupid thing to do, it could have caused a nasty accident. I pulled up outside their front door. The rain was still lashing down and all the street gas lights had been turned off. Margaret got out and dashed indoors, then Ken attempted to clambour out of the back. Bang! The van suddenly tipped up backwards.

'What's going on?' I shouted out into the rain.

'That bloody wheel was yours!' I heard Ken shout back.

He went inside and returned with a torch that shone like a searchlight; he always did have the latest gimmick! We ran down the street and through the gates of the mill. We found the wheel leaning against the yard wall, with the hub cap still on and, luckily, all four of the nuts rattling away safely inside. Of course, we didn't have a jack, so out came the plank. We found three or four loose bricks from the top of the yard wall, which we used as a fulcrum, with the plank on top and under the van. Ken stood on the plank, and the van lifted up. I whipped the wheel on as quickly as possible and tightened the nuts. Drenched to the skin, I finally jumped in the van and headed back home.

Talking about Ken and his latest gimmicks, we had to laugh. His dad was a grocer and the two of them had just bought an ex post-office van at an auction. It was a little Austin; I think they paid about £25 for it. Ken had obtained a set of car horns which worked off the manifold of the engine, and best of all, they played a tune when switched on. The trouble was they relied on the pressure in the engine to expel the exhaust gas into the horns before they could play. Well, he was passing us one day going up the hill at Moses Gate. He waved and proudly pressed the horn. "Da-da-di-da," it hooted out loudly, then it stopped halfway through the tune – and so did his van. His face went as red as a beetroot as he held up the traffic, waiting for the pressure to build back up in his little engine, before he could move on again. He told us later that he could play the horns going downhill, but didn't have the power in the engine to keep the van going and sound the horns at the same time when he was going uphill!

Our business started to take off and we opened up a shop, workshop and showrooms on Market Street in Farnworth. Glenys looked after the shop and we now had a few tradesmen working for us. Apart from Council modernisation contracts we started working for Geoff Seddon, an architect. He passed some very good quality contracts our way and we had great experience when he introduced us to a client who wanted a bungalow built. We were very proud when the owners moved in, and they were absolutely delighted with their new home. At this time Glenys was expecting our first baby. She was taken into Haslam's Nursing Home one icy, foggy night – and, believe me, that was a night to remember!

4

Don't Worry We Have Never Lost A Husband Yet

Smokey chimney, no problem! I climbed the ladder up into the hayloft above the stable-cum-garage and there, stacked neatly in the corner, was a nice pile of sacks. I took hold of the top one; that should do the job, and lobbed it down through the loft trapdoor. Then, taking the coil of rope off the large hook I laid it out on the floor, thinking it would be amply long enough for the job in hand.

Jack told me that he had lived in the same house for twenty five years and had never had a smoky chimney – and he'd never had the chimney swept.

'Wow! What's the secret?' I asked astounded. He told me that the 'secret' was simple; every three months he lowered a sack containing a brick down the chimney on a length of rope, not forgetting to first block up the fireplace with a sheet of brown paper. Nothing could be easier; I had all the gear, including my extension ladder.

We were having a bit of a do the following day and smoke kept puffing out of the fire opening. Before lighting the fire would be the ideal time to clear the soot from the chimney. As instructed I first cut the strong brown paper to overlap the opening of the fireplace. Licking the strips of gummed paper I sealed the edges to the tile surround. With more gummed strips I also sealed the brown paper to the hearth, making sure everything was secure to protect our new carpet and velvet-covered three-piece suite.

Up the ladder I went and stepped onto the roof tiles. In a jiffy I was firmly wedged at the side of the chimney. Checking the rope was tied securely to the sack, I gently lowered the brick and sack down. Every now and again small puffs of soot shot up into the air; the majority however, was dropping down into the fireplace. I was just thinking how clever I was at saving five shillings by doing the work myself, when the rope suddenly went slack. Had I hit the bottom? Then, whoosh! Soot belched up out of the chimney pot, and I was completely covered from head to toe! The mushroom-shaped cloud of black soot continued upwards and outwards until the whole roof was covered. Funny, I don't remember Jack mentioning this unusual phenomenon!

I pulled the sack back up gently and realised there was no brick in it, just a big hole in the bottom of the rotten sacking.

'Oh, heck!' I shouted and shot down the roof, slipping and sliding down the ladder and into the house, past Glenys, who was in the kitchen quite unaware of the events taking place. In the front room the strong brown paper was all torn to shreds where the brick had come flying down the chimney and ended up in the hearth. Fortunately, for me, the hearth had collected most of the soot, but there was still a thin layer spread over the carpet and most of the furniture.

Two hours later, as I emptied the vacuum cleaner for the third time, things were at last beginning to look normal once again, and do you know there wasn't even a hint of a puff of smoke from our blazing fire at our party the next day.

* * * * *

Glenys had quite a reputation for the fantastic sumptuous strawberry trifles she made. Even friends who didn't like trifle would finish them up with second helpings! They were delicious and out of this world. Somehow I always ended up with the job of whipping up the cream in a large basin with the aid of a trusty fork. The task went on and on, and it took ages before the cream finally relented and solidified enough to form peaks. As the kitchen was very small I had to complete the task in the extension using the cream off the top of the rich, fresh, farm milk.

One day we were having a party for a few friends, and were dressed accordingly in our Sunday best. Glenys was in the kitchen putting the finishing touches to the meal. I was in the extension performing my usual whipping trick when I suddenly spotted my small electric drill. Now that gave me an idea. I found an old fork, and two seconds later had cut it down to size and had fixed it into my drill. Standing over the basin half-full of golden cream, I switched on the drill and the fork whizzed round merrily. I gently lowered it into the cream. SPLAT! I looked, and looked again; the bowl was completely empty. Every spot of cream had disappeared, all gone! I glanced around the extension; we had a beautiful cream-coloured dado line at waist height all around the room – and funnily enough it continued right across my shirt, tie and pullover! I started laughing, and then the boss came in to see what all the noise was about; for some reason she didn't see the funny side of it. Oh well, back to the drawing board, or should I say back to the bowl and fork!

* * * * *

One day, on my way to Salford, I found myself cruising along behind a long trailer carrying huge baulks of timber heading for the docks. The policeman on traffic duty put his hand up, as he mouthed the word 'Stop!' The lorry squealed to a slow halt and I jammed on my brakes. However, my van had other ideas as it skidded forward over the wet cobbles, and the overhanging timber came straight for my windscreen. Thinking quickly I threw myself down across the front seats to the sound of a loud explosion, as glass splattered everywhere above my head. But that wasn't the end of it; the timber carried on through the van, then I heard a loud crunch, as the back doors burst wide open.

I tried to move but found I was pinned between the seat and this huge plank of wood. Suddenly the van started to shake and began rocking from side to side as the lorry driver in front, completely unaware of the situation, began moving his heavy load onwards; with me being dragged slowly behind. He passed the policeman on point duty and continued up the road for another fifty yards, then the lorry accelerated and with a tremendous grinding noise the wood disappeared from above my head. I sat up stunned just in time to see the lorry turning down Cross Lane, towards the docks with my drum of putty firmly attached to the end of the overhanging timber.

I just sat there, completely bewildered, wondering what to do next. I had been on my way to pick up a new bathroom suite from a local builder's merchants, but decided to give up on that idea. I started the engine up, and it seemed to be working okay. After securing the back doors with a butterfly wire wall tie, I set off back the way I had come. Typically, by now it had also started raining heavily, and the wind was forcing the rain through the opening that once used to be my windscreen. Isn't it daft what you do by habit; I automatically flipped the switch to start the windscreen wipers. Zonk! Zonk! Zonk! Away they went without any effect whatsoever; the rain continued to pour in and I got soaking wet.

On closer inspection of the van I discovered that the back doors were dinged beyond repair, as mentioned, there was no windscreen and the top of the bonnet had a rip along its full length. I spotted a new second hand van in Brackley Street, Farnworth; it was a 1946 Austin. I attempted to trade in my poor old Morris van but the best I could get was twelve shillings and sixpence scrap value for the poor old girl.

We had our name emblazoned on the side of the new Austin van. It was fantastic; none of the usual blue smoke bellowing out behind us. It started first time so no more push starts on cold mornings. What luxury! And it was big enough to put the new coach built Silver Cross pram in ready for our new baby…

All that cold December day I was a bag of nerves, with Glenys being in the Maternity Home, and I was dashing about repairing burst water pipes. It was icy and very cold and, just as it was getting nearer to visiting time, down came a blanket of thick fog. After my last job, I shot home and had a wash and changed. I had no time for tea and left the house with just enough time to drive to the Maternity Home which was the other side of Bolton. But I soon realised the roads were rather icy and cars were skidding about all over the place. In some places the fog was so thick it was difficult to see even the kerb.

Frozen, tired, and also feeling rather sick, I eventually arrived at the Home and the Matron met me by the door.

'Where have you been?' she barked, 'Your wife is already in labour and we are expecting her to give birth at any time!'

'Oh, my God!' I muttered as I followed her dazedly into the dark labour room.

'Sit down at this side and just hold her hand' I was ordered. Glenys was moaning and groaning and kept letting out a scream now and again. Terrified, I did as I was told and kept hold of her hot, sweaty hand. Eventually my eyes became accustomed to the low light and the nurse gave me a cloth to mop Glenys's brow. I leaned over and looked – and then I looked again; her hair was jet black! Oh no!

'Nurse! Nurse!' I shouted, trying to stand up, without much luck, as the woman in the bed had a tight grip on my hand. 'Nurse, this isn't my wife!' I croaked, as she came dashing over.

'Of course it is!' she said indignantly, 'Look, it says Mrs Bradshaw on the bed'.

'But, but, my name is Feldon!' I whispered half-heartedly.

'What! Then what the devil are you doing in here! Get out! Get out!' the nurse said, as she shooed me out into the corridor.

I shot into another room, and there was Glenys sitting up in bed.

'Where have you been?' she asked 'You're half an hour late!' I flopped into a chair next to Glenys. The gas fire was blazing; I was getting hotter and hotter, and feeling fainter and fainter! Then wallop – I passed out!

The first thing I heard when I came to was the nurse saying to Glenys, 'Don't worry, we have never lost a husband yet!'

Della Yvonne was born at dinner time on the 3rd December 1952, and all went well (or so I was told, as husbands were not allowed anywhere near when the actual birth was taking place).

Wow! That was certainly a very embarrassing moment, holding hands with a complete stranger in those circumstances. But have you ever wished the ground would just open and swallow you up; I have, and that was one of the most embarrassing moments in my life.

5

Good Day & Thank You Sir!

We have four children; Della born in 1952, Vanda in 1955, Tony, who was born in 1954 – and Petra who made her welcome, but surprise, appearance in 1970.

In 1956 our business was booming. We had eleven men on our books and our order book was full with Council approved conversion contracts. This was to bring old houses up to modern day standards; complete with modern kitchens, bathroom suites, constant hot water, damp proofing throughout and to make the roofs sound and secure.

Glenys looked after our Farnworth showroom whilst I spent my time chasing up the contract work. Overnight the interest rates shot up, the mortgage rates zoomed up to a whopping 15%. Builders' merchants stopped credit buying and Government and Council contracts were cancelled. Practically all building work came to a halt. Money became tight and unfortunately we had to lay off our workforce. Fortunately, however, we managed to sell our workshops and showroom. Then it was time for me to look for a job with a steady income.

I had the good fortune to secure a job in the offices of a large Building Supplies Merchant., as the Chief Estimator for supplying materials for the Lancashire to Yorkshire M62 motorway – this entailed multi-million pound contracts with a 2% profit margin.

It was really scary at the beginning; six telephones were continually ringing on my desk. One phone at each ear, negotiating prices between contractors and suppliers, whilst the red phone and blue phone still rang merrily away (these were direct lines to senior contracting staff). The remaining two telephones were internal connections to our accountants who had the job of monitoring the profit margins on each deal.

My counterpart, Jordan, was well-experienced in making deals with quarries supplying stone, and tile manufacturers in the Midlands, who then supplied millions of quarry tiles to provide damp courses on the bridges spanning large valleys. He had all the time in the world; he was extremely relaxed and spent his time chatting and laughing with the customers. It took me quite a long time to get into the routine and set priorities on each phone call and on each deal. The pressure was really on, and I found it very interesting and exciting – especially if I managed to negotiate a really tough deal, and therefore produce a good profit for the firm – but this wasn't my idea of earning a living.

In the meantime, Eddie and Alf had used their teaching certificates and had left the building industry to take up posts in a Technical College and a school respectively. This got me thinking! They were working from nine in the morning until four in the afternoon, five days a week, three months holiday a year (with pay!), and would also receive a pension when they retired! I tell you what, it didn't take me long to start looking through the paper for vacancies in the teaching profession.

Then, one day on my way home after a particularly hard day of negotiating, I spotted it; "Qualified Plumbing Lecturer required at Bolton Technical College". I had all the right qualifications and a vast amount of industrial experience to back me up. One week later I was called in for an interview at the college. Now that was (yet another) one of the most embarrassing experiences of my life! Even today I cringe at the very thought of it.

I was sitting alongside the other five candidates on the bench in the newly painted green and cream corridor; within a few minutes our clothing began to reek of linseed oil and white spirit, from the open cans set out on the nearby dust sheet spread across the floor. Painters were still at work high up on the planks perched across two trestles. Every now and then a spot of paint splattered at our feet. We all jumped up. Here we were all dressed in our Sunday best attempting to relax, when in reality we were all a bag of nerves; all, that is, except one. Isn't it funny, you always get one cocky devil. He was already in the profession and taught evening classes and decided he would frighten the life out of us, relating his experience of other interviews he had been to and all the questions that we would have fired at us. Again, he was the only one with a nice portfolio, packed with pictures and descriptions of all the work he had done.

The first appointment and interview was supposed to have been at 11 a.m. We all eagerly kept an eye on the large clock on the wall, which slowly edged its way to five past and then, eventually, to ten past, followed by quarter past. By this time I was ready to get up and go home. One of the lads next to me did get up.

'I don't stand a cat in hells chance of getting this job. I'm off back to work' he said. And that was the last we saw of him, dodging in and out of the trestles and slipping and sliding on the dustsheets covering the highly polished floor.

I glanced at the clock for the hundredth time to see that it was now twenty past eleven. We all jumped out of our skin as the old oak door creaked open. Standing in the frame was, looking like something out of a Dickens novel, a little old janitor with thin grey hair plastered down on his shrunken skull, his gold-rimmed glasses perched on the end of his beak-like nose. Much to our surprise he wore a frock coat and pin-striped trousers. With his pointed black shoes highly polished, he looked like a typical undertaker.

He closed the creaking door behind him and pointed, with his bony finger, to each one of us in turn.

'Which one of you is Reynolds?' We all looked at each other waiting for a reply. Utter silence; 'Reynolds, I said!' he boomed, and proceeded to spell it out 'R-E-Y-N-O-L-D-S'. Still no answer. 'You are wasting my time and your time if you can't spell your own name, now stand up Reynolds!' We all stared back blankly. He turned around slowly and opened the huge oak door; again it squealed and creaked as he closed it behind him. We all started laughing.

'So who's Reynolds then?' I asked. The lad with the portfolio said it must have been the lad who went back to work. The door creaked again. We all shrank back against the wall in fear, hoping he didn't call our name out!

Standing in front of us again, and pointing his finger, he said 'Thomas? I don't suppose we have a Thomas here?' At that very moment the old janitor started to glide very slowly away from us, he never moved a leg or a muscle, yet on he went drifting down the corridor. We sat there aghast; it was a bit like a horror movie. We then spotted the two painters way down the corridor, who were pulling away at the dustsheet, in an attempt to cover a new section of brickwork ready to be painted. The janitor stepped off the dustsheet and aimed his bony finger at the painters, who by this time were in fits of giggles.

'You think it's funny? Well just you wait until I tell the Principle!' he threatened. He turned and walked back up the corridor towards us, 'The chairman is not going to be pleased with this delay. So, if Thomas will follow me I will take you to your seat.' The lad next to me stood up. 'These common tradesmen are all the same,' muttered the janitor, as he and Thomas disappeared through the large doorway, 'No class! No class about them whatsoever!'

Ten minutes later they reappeared.

'Thomas you may go, we will be in touch.' Poor Thomas, he was red in the face and completely flustered. He turned to go up the corridor, then the janitor informed him that that was not the way out.

As he passed us he said, 'Never again! I'll stick to me plumbing from now on!' Off he went dodging the trestles and set off running down the corridor to freedom.

The voice spoke once again; 'Will Entwistle follow me.' Entwistle turned out to be the chap with the portfolio. As cocky as ever, he strode through the open door confidently with his head held high.

As the door closed, the remainder of us looked at each other.

'Cor! I wish I hadn't come now!' said one of the lads. I had exactly the same feeling. The other lad was very hot under the collar and was sweating profusely; his nerves had completely got the better of him. Creak! The door reopened, Entwhistle came out smiling.

'Sit there Mr Entwistle', ordered the stern voice. We all looked up, did he say 'Mr' Entwistle? 'Right, Feldon, follow me.' I couldn't move; I felt as though I was glued to the seat. My mind worked overtime; what horrific thing awaits me beyond the thick oak door? I started to shake. Taking a deep breath I made a dash after the disappearing figure of The Voice, nearly knocking him over in the process.

The first thing that struck me when I entered the room was the God-like figure silhouetted against the dome-shaped window at the far end of the room. The oak panelled walls towered above me reaching up to the ornate ceiling. It was as if I had just entered a cold cathedral, or temple, with the high priest awaiting the next sacrificial victim. The Voice pointed to the chair at the end of the long polished mahogany table.

'This is Mr Feldon, your honour,' he announced. After which, as if like magic, he just melted away into the dark background. As my eyes adjusted to the low lighting, I became aware of eight other people sitting, four each side of the chairman, behind the lengthy table. There were six men and two ladies. After a couple of short, sharp coughs the chairman began.

'Ah, good morning Mr, er, Feldon. Please take a seat.' I attempted to pull the large, heavy chair slightly away from the table. It groaned and squealed, much to my dismay, so I left it halfway out and squeezed myself in between the chair and the overhang of the 20ft table, and finally perched awkwardly on the edge of the seat. All eighteen eyes turned to stare at me; not a word was uttered. I waited and waited, knowing I should be saying something, but I didn't know what.

The chairman shuffled his papers. The committee shuffled their papers. I shuffled anxiously on my seat. Then a voice broke the silence. The silhouette directly opposite me at the far end of the table boomed out.

'Well, well, Mr Feldon, and what do you think that you have to offer this college that the other candidates are unable to offer?' Silence again. Oh dear me, how the heck did I know what the other candidates had to offer, especially Entwistle, the Portfolio King. I was completely stumped.

'Er, well, I, er…' I jabbered on talking complete nonsense. I just hadn't a clue how to handle the situation; I was completely unprepared.

One of the robotic ladies spoke, 'Mr Feldon, how would you handle a classroom full of boisterous sixteen year old boys eager to learn a trade? You open the door and the boys, who have just come off a building site, are pushing and shoving each other to get to the front of the class. Just imagine if you walked into that room without any work or lesson prepared! Do you think you could handle that situation?' It was then that I realised that perhaps Portfolio Entwistle knew what it was all about and that this job should actually go to him.

The chairman looked me in the eye and said, 'I don't think we need to waste anymore of your time, Mr Feldon. The teaching profession is not a career you should even be thinking about. Good day, and thank you, sir!' The Voice materialised and touched me on the shoulder.

'This way, sir', with a strong emphasis on the word "sir". Two seconds later I was passing the painters and on my way out of that building.

I was blazing with myself for appearing such a fool in front of that committee, and needless to say I soon received the expected letter thanking me for attending the interview, unfortunately however, I was unsuccessful in securing the position, etc, etc. I didn't get the job but I did learn one thing, and that was "If you don't take control there's always someone who will!" I was more determined than ever to show that stuffy, pompous crowd that I had the ability and determination to become a first-class teacher. I searched the evening papers for teaching vacancies. The next time I went for an interview I would be prepared; I would be the one asking the questions as to what it was that they could offer me! Yes, I would be ready to take on the faceless committee members and the foreboding silhouetted chairman. Always one for a challenge, I began to actually look forward to the prospect of putting my plan into action.

Then on an unforgettable Friday night, an advert in the Manchester Evening News nearly jumped off the page at me. "Urgently required. Experienced Craft Teacher. Send for application form to: The Lancashire Education Committee." I sent off for the forms that very night, and also requested information on the school, along with the headmaster's name. The reply arrived by first class post the following day...

6

Someone Whispered, 'Blow Your Whistle, Sir!'

Knock, knock, knock. Standing outside the old front door I waited. No reply. I tried again; lifting the large black cast-iron knocker, then down it came. Knock, knock, knock. Ah well, I thought, it was worth a try. I turned to walk back towards the gate, when someone said, 'Can I help you?'

Standing there was the gardener who was trimming a substantial holly bush at the far corner of the front garden. He looked more like a country yokel, with his battered straw hat pulled down over his happy smiling face. His shirt sleeves were rolled up and his tatty trousers, tucked into his muddy Wellingtons, were held up with a piece of string instead of a pair of braces.

'Well, yes, thank you,' I said, 'Can you tell me if the Headmaster, Mr Adams of Winton County Secondary School For Boys, is in?' The gardener started laughing.

'Oh yes, he's in!'

'Well, I wonder if I could have a word with him,' I asked, 'I have been knocking for ages on the front door.'

'Oh, he won't hear you knocking, because he's out in the garden.'

'Oh right. Er, could you ask him to spare me a minute then?' He laughed out loud once more.

'Well, young man you are speaking to him – It's me, I'm

the Headmaster!' I couldn't believe my eyes; this chap was quite human! I started laughing too.

'Oh sorry,' I spluttered, 'I thought you were the gardener!'

'Don't worry, young man, I'm that as well!' From that moment Mr Adams and I got on like wildfire. I told him that I was applying for the post of craft teacher. 'Well, come inside,' he said 'and I'll explain what it entails.' After a long chat he suggested that I contact Reg Wilkinson, the Head of the Craft Department. 'He's a nice chap and very easy to get on with. I'll phone him now and see if he can spare you a few minutes. He will be able to help you fill in your application form.'

Five minutes later I was sitting in Reg's kitchen, as he lived just around the corner. I explained that I had never taught before.

'Oh, don't worry about that,' he said, 'I'll teach you all you need to know, and with your wide experience, I'm sure you'll be an asset to the school.'

Then he dropped a bombshell; the vacancy was for a woodwork teacher – I had been under the impression that the post was for a metal work teacher. He explained that there was nothing to it, and that the two workshops opened up into one large room.

'I will demonstrate and take the lessons,' he continued, 'Then you will supervise the class. If you have any problems pass them over to me and we'll sort them out together. How does that sound?'

'Fantastic!' I replied, 'But I've not had the interview yet!'

'Right, let's have a look at the form then. This section is the most important,' he said pointing to "Extra Curriculum Activities" – I didn't even know what that meant!

'So, could you help me out in making scenery for the school plays?'

'Yes, I'd love to!'

'Did you say that you go rambling and climbing?'

I nodded.

'And would you be prepared to go on the annual school trip to the Lake District?'

'You bet!' I replied. And so the conversation went on. We finished up with two extra pages of what I had to offer the school.

I had mentioned to the Headmaster that I had already put in an application for a metal work teacher in Salford. The Headmaster told Reg to get their interviews brought forward. Reg agreed, as he thought we would get along fine. I liked both Reg and Mr Adams from the moment I set eyes on them; they were both down-to-earth, dedicated, experienced teachers. They told me that they liked, and wanted, someone with a bit of initiative and industrial experience.

Outside the interview room at the Town Hall sat five other chaps. I thought to myself, this is going to be difficult, but then I remembered what my dad used to say, 'It's not what you know, it's who you know that counts'. I had met the Head and I had met the Head of Department. I had also seen the school and I had been in the workshops – and, I had seen the curriculum for the next twelve months! I was ready with my portfolio of ideas and experiences. I was totally relaxed and looking forward to the interview.

In I went. The Chairman of Education was at the head of the table, the Headmaster, Mr Adams, was next to him along with seven other members of the board with their notebooks and glasses of water at the ready. As soon as I sat down I introduced myself, and then I took charge; I don't think they knew what had hit them!

I was asking them the questions, like, what had they got to offer me that would entice me to leave my senior post at the firm I was presently employed with. Do you know, only two people actually asked me a question. One was the Headmaster, and other was the Chairman, who finally said,

'If we offered you the post, would you be prepared to accept it and commence employment at the beginning of the new term?' I remained silent for a few minutes, everyone waited with bated breath.

'Yes, I would be delighted to accept the post!' A great sigh of relief came from the rest of the board, and the Headmaster smiled.

The Chairman spoke, 'Would you kindly wait outside, and if the post is offered to you, I would be obliged if you would contact Salford Education Authority with your decision.'

I thanked them for their time, and said I would await their favourable decision. Up I got and left the room.

After all the other chaps had been in for their interviews, I was called back in to be informed that they were delighted to offer me the post, and congratulated me on a first-class interview. I shook hands with each one of them in turn, thanked them once again, and departed a very happy man!

* * * * *

Nobody took the slightest bit of notice when I entered the playground. The din was deafening, over 300 boys tearing around like lunatics. This was my first day at school and I found myself on playground duty!

I spotted one lad spinning around and around whilst his pal hung on for dear life to the edges of his school blazer, faster and faster, then he let go to hurtle at a fantastic speed into space.

Against the wall a dozen boys were playing British Bulldog; one stood against the wall, the next lad bent down and held his waist. The other four lads bent over hanging on to the one in front. Then it started. The other six leap-frogged over their bent backs to land heavily on the first group. The idea was to make the bent over group collapse in a heap on the floor. Five had made the jump, and they were still holding up. Then it was the turn of the burly, big, fat lad. He made his jump; up in the air and, wallop, straight on top of the last bent over lad! His knees collapsed and he went down, the rest then collapsed like a row of dominos one after the other, to the sound of cheering from the jumpers, who by this time were in a huge pile splattered all over the playground.

Across the yard two boys played marbles; they took no notice and kept their concentration, they just kept shooting their marbles across the playground, and a couple of swats were sitting on the floor leaning against the railings copying each other's homework.

This is it; I blew hard on the whistle which gave off a shrill piercing noise. As if by magic, they all stopped dead in their tracks. There was complete silence, nobody moved and nobody spoke. Now I had a bit of a problem, I had been told by the Deputy Head to just walk into the playground and blow the whistle, but he had omitted to tell me what to do next.

All pairs of eyes turned on to me, then a little lad nearby put his hand up.

'Sir, you're new 'ere aren't yer? Well, yer just blow your whistle and we'll all line up!'

So, one more blast of the shrill whistle and, before you could say Jack Robinson, they were all lined up in their various classes, still in total silence. Now, I thought, do I tell them to go in or should I blow this damn whistle once again? Then someone whispered, 'Blow your whistle, Sir!'

I gave it a sharp "peep", and the first line began to walk smartly forward through the entrance door. By the time the last lad had disappeared I was shaking like a leaf. I met Reg in the corridor.

'Right Derek, this is your 4T Class. Let them in but don't let them sit until you are ready. Then mark the register.'

After being instructed, 4T lowered themselves into their seats very warily, weighing me up, as if to say, I wonder how far we can push this new guy!

It was later that I was informed I had been given the roughest, toughest group of lads in the school. It didn't worry me; I had seen and dealt with far worse on the building sites. The boys told me that 4H was the top class. Clever buggers, they said, 'H' stands for 'High and Mighty'! Next class down was 4N (apparently for 'Normal'). Then there was 4T; the other teachers said that the 'T' stood for 'Trouble'!

The bell rang – Brrrrrrr! They all stood up and ambled towards the door.

'STOP!' I yelled. They all froze in amazement and looked around. 'Back to your seats, and sit down!'

'But, Sir!...'

'Quiet, boy!' I barked. 'Back to your stools, and sit.' Mumbling and grumbling they pushed and shoved their way back in and sat down. Turning my head slowly, I made eye contact with every boy, each one staring back in deathly silence. They all looked at each other in confusion, then the boy in the front row put his hand up. 'You, what's your name?' I asked.

'Robinson, Sir. Please, Sir, if we are late for our next lesson we will all be put on detention.'

'Right, Robinson, you will tell your maths teacher that Mr Feldon held you back to learn his new rules. From now on, Robinson, you will be my monitor.'

'Oh, thank you, Sir!' he replied, amidst the cries of 'Ooo, that's not fair, I wanted to be a monitor.'

'Quiet!' I shouted. 'Now put up your hands anyone else who would like to be a monitor.'

Much to my amazement every single boy in the room raised his hand!

'Okay, okay, I'll see what I can do. Right, back row march out quietly. Now the next row.'

They all stood and marched out in an orderly line, one

row after the other. I had told them that I would train them like real soldiers and that the school would be proud of them and would be amazed at their new behaviour.

'Great, Sir! Let's show 'em!' they shouted back.

The next day I had written a list of monitors on the blackboard; funnily enough, the name of every boy in my class was on that list! Robinson was my Register Monitor, he ran errands for me. We also had a Pencil Monitor, a Pen Monitor, a Rubber Monitor, as well as a Paper, a Book, a Blackboard, a Chalk, a Sink, a Soap, a Door (to let visitors in), and a Door (to let visitors out), Monitor. In fact, you name it, we had a monitor for it. They were all thrilled to bits with their responsibilities.One lad piped up, 'Sir, don't give Williams the Rubber Monitor job, 'cause he'll pinch the lot. He's always pinching 'em to make pellets for pea shooters! Peas are banned by the Headmaster, and the Caretaker fella he don't like 'em either, 'cause he 'as peas growing in 'is rose gardens!'

I must admit the rose gardens were a sight to see full of dark red Frenshem roses. At the back end he would cut them right down to about six inches high. I wouldn't have the nerve to do that, but up they would come in the spring to produce an abundance of blooms all through the summer months.

Well, guess who got the job of Rubber Monitor. Yep, Williams! And, do you know, we never had a rubber go missing after that.

Little Smithy was the scruffiest kid in the class. I don't think his neck, face or hands had seen any soap since the day he was born. Ironically, he was the Sink Monitor. He would spend all playtime scrubbing away at that sink until it shone like a new penny – and, so did his hands. He never complained, even when the Ink Monitor washed all the inkwells in the pristine sink leaving behind a blue rim. Every night before leaving school Little Smithy would have that sink sparkling, and even the Caretaker commented on how clean and tidy our classroom had become.

The class used to get through a box of pen nibs a week. The boys would split the top end of the wooden pen and insert paper flights. Using these as darts they would use the school notice board as target practise. Even after just one throw the nib was ruined! They had to hand the old one in to get another. Well, that all changed when Tufty became the Pen Monitor. (He was nicknamed Tufty as his thick, bushy eyebrows turned up at the ends). If we got through even half a dozen nibs in a week he would be complaining that they were wasting 'his' nibs.

Then the first snag appeared. All the boys insisted I gave them a Monitors Badge to wear. I had a quiet word with Mr Adams, the Headmaster, who was taken aback by the proposal, but after explaining about my discipline and reward procedure, was in complete agreement, if I could curb the rowdiness that the class had a reputation for. He handed me the punch machine to make little round lapel badges. Each badge was printed with "Special Duties Monitor". I told the boys to wear them with pride, but if there was any misbehaving in other classes their badges would be taken away from them.

'Don't worry, Sir. We won't let you down!' they all chorused. (Surprisingly, they never did).

Reg had a laugh as all the boys took their duties so seriously. We had the cleanest sink in the school, we never had a ruler or pencil go missing, and the blackboard was washed down at the end of every day. Visitors commented on how nice it was to have the door opened for them and then to be escorted out again by a 'charming young man'. They were a grand set of cheeky chappies; always out for a laugh, but knew just how far they could go. Which to my way of thinking was absolutely fantastic, and, what's more, they were a joy to teach.

I was expected to take other subjects as well as my specialised subject, craft. To my horror, one cold, wet, Thursday morning I looked at the notice board in the staff room; there it was, in black and white, "Mr Feldon to referee the football match between Winton Boys and Cromwell Road Boys".

I went cold all over; I had never played football in my life, let alone referee the game – I didn't even know the rules! Spotting Mr Butterworth, I shot across the room.

'You've got me down to referee this afternoon's football match, well, I'm sorry, but I can't.' I went on to explain my reasons.

'What! You've never played football before? Not even at school?' he asked with incredulity. 'Well, you'll have to manage. I haven't got anyone else to do it, as three of the staff are off sick.'

One thirty came and the register was marked. My class then informed me that they were going down to the field to watch the football match.

'Stop right there!' I said. 'So, who's the best footballer in the class, and knows all the rules?' They all pointed to the same lad.

'Knee Pads' is the best in the class. He plays for Peel Green Juniors on a Saturday!'

'Right Knee Pads', er, I mean Jones.'

'Oh, don't worry, Sir! They all call me that 'cause I'm a good footballer!' he said proudly.

'Do you know the rules well enough to be a referee?' I enquired.

'Of course I do. You ask any of this lot.'

The other lads in the room nodded, 'Yes, Sir, he's the best.'

'Hmm,' I continued, 'I'm not so sure, but how would you like a trial to see if you are the best, and I reckon this afternoon's game would be a good place to start.' And with that, I passed him the whistle attached to loop of green cord.

'Cor, Sir! Do you really mean it, Sir?' he asked, his eyes almost popping out of his head.

'Yes, but I'll be watching your every move, and, if you make a mistake I'll never let you referee another match of mine again!'

In ten minutes flat he had his football gear on – complete with knee pads. I borrowed a black shirt from the PE department and off we went.

The game was a success; Winton Boys won 3-2. Everyone was very impressed with the ref's professionalism.

'Jones,' I said after the game, 'You have done us proud, and I'm very pleased with your expert refereeing.'

'Thank you, Sir. Can I do it again then?'

'Oh yes, I think so – especially when I am on duty!'

Wow, that was a close shave. Like my dad said, 'If you can't do it, there's always somebody who can!' Thanks Knee Pads!

There was, however, one thing I could do well, and that was mountaineering and potholing and it didn't take long before I found myself on the annual school journey to the Lake District. In the meantime, the Winton Boys Adventure Club had become a reality. It's amazing how history has a habit of repeating itself.

7

Oh! Oh! Oh! Jolly Dee, Jolly Dee Fella's!

At Bank End Farm, Jane, the farmer's daughter, brought a huge plate of sandwiches out for the starving lads, as we had done some very strenuous hill walking over Kinder Scout in Derbyshire.

Great discussions were now taking place. I had just told them the tales of Giant's Hole and Satan's Tomb, and all the other caves and caverns we were going to go into: Peak Cavern, with the largest entrance of any cave in England, Speedwell Caverns where we would go by boat underground to the Bottomless Pit, the Blue John Mines and Treak Cliff Caverns, and climb the famous Winnats Pass. They couldn't gobble down their sandwiches quick enough! Then Toothy piped up.

'What are we gonna call our gang?' Toothy was a nice lad, always laughing, displaying the gap where his front teeth were missing! Life was one huge joke to him and there was never a dull moment when he was around. I mentioned the word "Ramblers".

'Nar! That's really soppy!' said Bobbles (he, naturally, was the one wearing the bobble hat!). Someone suggested "Winton Wanderers"; nobody agreed, it sounded more like a football club who didn't know where they were going.

Spiv, who stood at the back, spoke up. He was well-spoken and came from a very good family who lived near the school. He was always well dressed and had a permanent quiff, with a nice straight parting. Even out here in the strong winds not a single strand of hair was out of place.

'I reckon if we are going down those caves this is going to be one of the biggest adventures in all our lives'. Everyone nodded in agreement. 'So as we are all Winton boys, and are going on adventures, how about Winton Boys Adventure Club?'

'Hooray!' they all shouted, 'That's a fantastic name! The Winton Boys Adventure Club; what do you think, Sir?'

'That's great!' I answered. 'And let's take the school motto, "Seek, Strive and Find" and use it as our motto.'

Well that was it, no more arguing. Everybody agreed that we would make every trip an adventure. I told them that if they were tough they would have to come out in all weather, hail, rain, shine or snow, and that they were not to be afraid of getting cold or wet.

'No problem there, Sir, you can count on us, we won't let you down!' they shouted.

Leaving the farm behind us, we continued along the ridge and started the decent towards Castleton. With the Winnets Pass behind us we made our way down and across the field leading to the roadway.

Suddenly the sky darkened and we all glanced up. To our amazement, slowly, very slowly, the huge dark outline of a massive eagle-like bird, wings outstretched, flew down towards us. One of the lads screamed out in fear.

'Look out! Look out! It's coming to get us!' The boys started to run, and scattered in every direction. Down it swooped, talons at the ready. We threw ourselves to the ground as the monstrous bird swept a few feet above us. With our bodies hugging the ground, nobody moved. Then slowly we moved our heads to see if any of our boys were missing. Just a few yards away, lay the motionless body of the exhausted creature, wings outstretched.

Then everyone started to laugh at once, as the bird's head suddenly lifted and a man climbed out!

'Sorry about that chaps. I ran out of thermal lift and had to make an emergency landing. I spotted the field and headed for it when you chaps suddenly decided to cross it! Anyway, do you think you can help me get these wings off and help me to carry them to the edge of the road? Transport won't be long, I've radioed for help. Oh! Oh! Oh! Jolly dee, Jolly dee fellas!'

Well, we got the wings off and carried the glider and wings to the roadside, and then left him to it. What a start to our new adventure club, and "Oh! Oh! Oh! Jolly dee fellas" became the clubs new slang for 'I'm alright chaps'!

* * * * *

Snow, snow and more snow was the forecast for the Peak District. The school workshop was a hive of activity. It was a Friday lunchtime and we, the club, were off on another adventure first thing tomorrow morning.

I had designed a lightweight sledge, with all the shapes and sizes chalked up on the blackboard. The club was divided up into teams, with each team having a specific part to make. The lads were going at it like the clappers, and by the time the bell went for the afternoon session all the parts were ready. I voiced my concerns, as not one of the lads had eaten their dinner.

'Oh don't worry, Sir,' came the reply. 'But can we come back at 4 o'clock to put it together?' I agreed, and in the meantime had a word with the head cook in the school kitchen. As luck would have it, she was the mother of one of the lads in our team.

Dead on 4 o'clock the lads appeared, sleeves rolled up, aprons on, ready to assemble the racing sledge. On hearing someone outside the workshop, the Door Monitor dashed to the door and opened it. In came the cook carrying a jug of steaming hot soup and three loaves of bread, followed by her helpers, who were weighed down with a large tin of treacle pudding, a jug of piping hot custard and some drinks.

The cook made the boys stop work, amidst some protests of 'We haven't got time to eat. It needs to be finished for tomorrow's trip.' Their protests were in vain.

'Sit! Eat! And Shut Up!' ordered the cook, and you didn't argue with her! So all the lads sat, had their soup, gobbled up their treacle pudding, and washed it down with a mug of rich dark cocoa. To the embarrassment of the cook, they then stood up and gave three cheers to the 'best cook in the world'. She blushed, nodded, and shot out of the room followed by her helpers who were laughing their heads off.

'That's the first time she's been at a loss for words!' they giggled.

That weekend I taught the boys Alpine Mountain Craft. It was a bit of a job to get nine boys on my 120 foot length of climbing rope, but they managed somehow, without even tripping each other up. The famous ice axe was rationed to half an hour each boy. They watched each other like hawks.

'Sir, Sir, it's not fair! He's had thirty two minutes with the ice axe, and I only had thirty!' and so it went on.

In an attempt to pacify the unhappy lad I said, 'Don't worry, I'll let you melt the snow in the kettle, and as a special treat, I'll even let you light the primus stove.' But this only led to more problems.

'Hey, that's not fair, Sir!' they chorused.

'Anyway, it's my turn to light the stove today,' another boy piped up. Well, believe me, that stove ended up being lit and re-lit every hour on the hour! And we went through a whole tin of OXO cubes, but at least nobody complained!

* * * * *

In June I joined the staff and lads on the annual outing to Newlands, near Keswick in the Lake District. Previously they had hiked and climbed a mountain or two, or did a circuit around the lake. Having done a lot of climbing in the Lakes, I decided it was time they did a real bit of mountaineering. I told them that tomorrow we would be going on a Mystery Tour. There was near panic stations when they found themselves traversing Striding Edge on Helvellyn. I gave them all (including the staff) a really good taste of mountaineering. By the end of the day, they all admitted it was the best day they had ever had on their annual trip, but thought it would be a good idea to use the next day as a rest day. I suggested we could tackle just two or three peaks the following day, but I was shouted down.

'No, no, no! You can go yourself.'

'Yeah, you can count me out!'

In fact, I decided I would go, together with three lads who thought it was wonderful – and we conquered three more peaks!

Reg Wilkinson, my Head of Department, and my true mentor, said he thought he was getting too old for this type of mountaineering stuff, and in future would stick to the usual fell walking.

Back at Newlands Youth Guest House, which was run by the holiday fellowship, Mr Bowles the warden asked for volunteers to lift a caravan which had run off the road into a ditch. Eric Butterworth, the Deputy Head, assisted by Reg, Ray Blackwell and myself, plus thirty one very eager boys, all turned up to help, much to the surprise of the young couple, who owned the caravan, and their son. On the count of three, we lifted the van up into the air, out of the ditch and carried it bodily to the centre of the road. After hooking his car up to the tow-bar the young man insisted that the warden give all the boys a bottle of pop each, and thrust a five pound note into his hand. Then they drove slowly away to the delighted cries of 'Oh! Oh! Oh! Jolly dee, jolly dee fellas!'

* * * * *

Now then, "caravans", that reminds me about a holiday we had; Glenys and I had been married for just twelve months. Randal and I were queuing up in the chip shop one night. At that time we were both pretty hard up, and couldn't afford a holiday, but you never know what's around the corner – or, perhaps I should say, just at the side of the chip shop! Now that's a good Eggs-Ample if ever there was one!

8

Now That's A Good Eggs-Ample!

Rolling from side to side, Glenys and I were both feeling a bit queasy. Kneeling up and throwing the eiderdown towards the back of the van, I opened the doors and heard Molly shouting.

'Shoo! Shoo! Go Away!' The lightweight caravan, which was attached to the tow bar of our van, was rocking from side to side so hard, I thought it was going to tipple right over, and if that thing went over then so would we!

I hopped out of the van, landing in the long wet grass. There, staring at me with its huge brown eyes, was the biggest, fattest cow I had ever seen, gently chewing its cud and having a rare old back scratching session on the corner of our nice new cream-coloured "ten foot by six foot" caravan!Randall popped his head out of the door. I shouted to him.

'For goodness sake, shift that big fat cow of yours, before we all go over!'

Next minute Molly opened the back window, 'I know I'm pregnant, but I'm not that fat!'

Oh dear me, that started it; we all roared with laughter. Randall jumped down, and stepping around the corner of the van, found himself standing barefooted in a steaming hot cow pat! The cow, obviously realising it wasn't wanted, turned slowly and ambled off down the meadow.

I suppose you might ask what we were all doing in the middle of a field in the heart of Somerset during Farnworth Wakes Week. Well, it all started with fish and chips and a bag of mushy peas...

Let me first take you back a few years. I had just finished my initial army training in Northern Ireland, and I had ten days leave before being posted to my new regiment. By shear luck, my leave happened to coincide with the Bolton holidays, namely Farnworth Wakes Week. This is what we waited all year for, when the fairground came to town. All the folks who couldn't afford to go to Blackpool came to the fair instead, and all the mills and factories closed down for Wakes Week.

A whole gang of us, dressed to kill, descended from the trolley bus and made a bee-line up to Brackley Street, where there was hustle and bustle, lights flashing, loud music, screams and laughter, all mixed with the heady smells of candy floss, chips and toffee apples. The dodgems banged and banged as they hurtled around and collided with each other and the electric blue sparks flew off the metal mesh above. The carousel had beautifully painted horses which galloped up and down on the gold twisted poles, in time to the music of the hurdy-gurdy orchestra. The bright coloured horses carried their riders proudly; kids, mums and dads, uncles and aunties, all singing and laughing at the top of their voices. The Waltzer flew round at terrific speeds making skirts fly up, much to the amusement of the crowds watching. Then there was the Ghost Train, with all its spooky noises; the rattling of chains, followed by moans and groans and ghostly "Whoooa's!" The coconut shy was always crowded with young men determined to win a coconut for their girl friends standing at their sides. Every now and then a loud cheer would go up, as a wooden ball made contact with a coconut and sent it flying off its perch.

We descended upon this island paradise; girls, girls and more girls, all laughing and giggling.

Gordon and I soon spotted two nice girls in a dodgem car. As soon as one became free we jumped in like a flash, paid our money, and were off in hot pursuit of the damsels in distress; the girls car had firmly jammed in a corner.

'Hi, girls! Can we help you out?' we asked smoothly. They smiled and gave us a friendly wave; I was out, and quickly swapped places with Jane who hopped in our car next to Gordon. Audrey clung on to me as we chased the other two around, in an attempt to get them in a corner. We were nearly hurled headlong out of the car as another couple of our gang caught us unawares from behind.

Bang, bang, bang, and so it went on, until the lights flickered and the attendant shouted 'Everybody out!'

Of course, we went on the ghost train; we came out into glaring lights still kissing away to the sound of laughter. As we strolled around, Audrey looked at me.

'You know, Gordon is my brother.'

I nearly dropped through the floor; 'Gordon's your brother?'

'Yes, didn't he tell you?'

'No, he flippin' didn't!' I replied. 'He said he would bring you along tonight, if I brought Jane, who he fancies but didn't have the guts to ask out himself – even though she fancies him too!' A little girl carrying the biggest golden teddy bear I had ever seen came up to us.

'Mister, why don't you win your girlfriend a teddy like mine?'

'Oh yes please!' said Audrey excitedly.

The little girl with the big, innocent, bright blue eyes said 'I won it over there on the Roll-a-Penny Stall, just over there. I won it for just one penny!'

Arriving at the stall, I noticed that all the big teddies hung up had numbers on them which corresponded to the outside corner squares, which were the farthest away from the roll-a-penny chute. Audrey gave me a big squeeze.

'Go on Derek, you can do it!' I gently placed a penny in the slot and down it rolled, finishing up on a line.

'On a line, Sir,' said the stall holder, as he raked my penny towards his bucket, which I could see was half full of pennies. (That's where the term "Raking in the Money" comes from!)

Time and time again I tried. Then, finally, on the sixth attempt I did it – the penny landed right in the centre of a square, without touching the line. Everyone standing around started to cheer.

'Good for you mate!'

'Well done, you've done it!' came the cries.

The stallholder shouted at the top of his voice, 'In the square, Sir, in the square. You're a lucky winner!' By this time everyone was pouring money down the chutes, whilst the stall man raked in the money as fast as he could. 'I'll be with you in a moment, Sir,' he said, and returned with a three inch tall teddy which he passed to Audrey. On seeing her face drop he said, 'Sorry, lady, only the numbers matching wins the big one.'

'It's a rip off!' shouted someone in the crowd. But the stall man was insistent.

'Rules are rules. You get yer number and you win yer prize!'

Just as we were heading over to Gordon and Jane, a lady hung her head out of one of the caravans.

'Sally! Sally! Come and get yer supper!' Along strolled Sally, with the big teddy and innocent eyes.

''Ere you are, Mam,' she said as she handed over her bear. The mother promptly hopped down from the caravan and handed it back to the little girl's dad, on the Roll-a-Penny stall! We just stood there flabbergasted; we were totally and utterly speechless. Then we saw the funny side and started laughing. Audrey decided to call her teddy "On the line, Sir", and hung it up over her dressing table mirror when she got home.

Getting back to caravans, Molly, Randall, Glenys and I were sitting around their dining room table one night chatting away, when Molly, who worked in Glenys's dad's chemist shop, butted in to the conversation.

'Well, we don't want to go to Blackpool this year, have you got any ideas?'

My stomach was rolling and I was getting hungry, so I replied 'How about fish, chips and a bag of mushy peas?' That certainly got the taste buds going. The girls set the table and put the plates in a bowl of hot water to warm them up, whilst Randall and I strolled across the road to Radcliffe's Chip Shop. Parked right next to the chip shop was this brand new Sprite caravan. Whilst waiting for the food to be cooked, Randall got chatting to Mr Radcliffe, and managed to turn the conversation towards the caravan.

'I don't suppose you fancy renting your caravan out to us for a week?' he asked.

'No problem, Randall,' he said, to my surprise. 'As long as you bring it back in one piece; me and the missus are going to Fleetwood at the end of the month.' (I later realised that they were quite good mates, as they both belonged to the Walkden Conservative Club, known as the "Wogden Con. Club" by the locals, which was ten times more covert than MI5!)

Mr Radcliffe gave us the keys to have a look inside – it was a little Bobby dazzler! It had a table and two bench seats at one end, a sink and cooker down the side opposite a small wardrobe, which was one foot square, and a dressing table, with a little settee at the other end. There were cupboards above the sink with sliding doors, and all the woodwork was finished in a light oak effect. Proper posh, you might say. Dashing back to the house, with our by-now-cold chips, we were red hot with excitement!

That was it then – holiday all sorted! He said he would fit a tow bar to his new Vanguard van, then look out Cornwall, here we come! It was no trouble to fit the tow bar, as Randall was the "son" of Howard & Sons Engineers, Walkden. They specialised in making turnstiles for football grounds, and public toilets; they even had Howard & Sons turnstiles at Belle Vue Speedway and Pleasure Park. (Why, even in Cornwall we spotted one at the entrance to the old Victorian toilets in Newquay!).

We had no problem in pulling the caravan as the Vanguard had a powerful engine and we sped down the main 'A' roads. It was getting dark by the time we reached Somerset and encountered the typical narrow winding lanes. It was a bit of a nightmare when we met up with traffic coming in the opposite direction, and we found it took a lot longer than expected. Looking at the map I reckoned we were only about one mile from Edith Mead campsite near Burnham-on-sea. I mistakenly thought that Edith Mead was the farmer's wife, not a place!

By this time, Glenys and Molly could hardly move, they were both expecting babies. Two year old Graham, Molly and Randall's little boy, was asleep on our 'z' mattress at the back of the van. We were all starving.

'Stop! Stop!' I yelled suddenly, peering through the van window into the darkness. 'There, there through that gate!' Everyone looked; we could see the farmhouse all lit up. Nipping smoothly out of the van, I dashed across the road and tried to open the five-bar gate. The catch was rusted away and jammed, with the gate sagging in a sorrowful state. I banged it a bit then gave it my usual back kick, but even that didn't budge it. Randall came to the rescue, and between us, we managed to lift it off its hinges and let the gate topple slowly to one side. We weren't in any mood to be beaten at this stage!

The farmer's wife was a jolly old soul, and made us most welcome.

'Put your caravan over ze other side of ze field and zen come in for a nice cup of tea. I zuppose you are ready for a cuppa!' We thanked her and asked her if she could do us a bit of supper, as we hadn't eaten since dinner time. 'Well, I suppose I could do you zome boiled eggz, if zat's alright. And I've got plenty of 'omemade bread and butter.'

'That would be fantastic!' I replied and off we went to park the van.

It was rough and bumpy across the field and we decided to leave the caravan attached to the van overnight, and sort things out in daylight. All we wanted to do was have something to eat and then drop straight into bed. It was decided, before we started, that Molly, Randall and Graham would sleep in the caravan, and Glenys and I would sleep on a mattress in the back of the van.

It was dark – in fact, it was very dark, as we made our way back across the field to the welcome light of the farmhouse.

'Come in. Come in. Don't just stand zere, zit down and make yourzelves at 'ome.' Her face was red and weather-beaten. She had her sleeves rolled up and was wearing a white pinnie which was tied at the back. On her feet were big black shoes and she wore a black beret perched on the back of her curly black hair. Out came chunks of homemade bread, still warm and smelling delicious, and there must have been about 5lb of homemade butter slapped in the middle of a huge plate. We couldn't wait to get started; grabbing a piece of bread each, we stabbed our knives into the lump of butter, as if there was no tomorrow.

Watching us scoff the chunky bread smothered with

lashings of rich butter, she said 'My goodness! You must be 'ungry, but don't fill yourzelves up, ze eggz will be anozer minute yet.' She poured us all a large mug of tea out of the brown enamel teapot, then went back to her place by the farm stove. She turned back to the table carrying a huge earthenware basin, full to the brim with boiled eggs. 'Now, come on. You must 'elp yourselves. Zey 'ave all got to be eaten, as we don't like wasting food in zis 'ouse!'

The beautiful brown eggs hardly fitted in the pottery egg cups – we used to keep hens during the war, but I had never seen eggs the size of these before. I decided she must be keeping ostriches in the back yard, as they were such whoppers! Our first eggs disappeared rapidly. As if by magic, the shells simply disappeared from the egg cups and a new egg appeared in its place, and, believe me, we soon whooshed that down too! Lo and behold, another egg soon reappeared in the empty cup. Now with the chunks of substantial bread and the first two eggs hardly digested it became a bit of a struggle to tackle the third egg. The farmer's wife was beaming all over.

'I zee you like my eggz! Don't worry, zere is plenty more, where zey came from.' At that, I had visions of this huge (ostrich-like) hen cocking its leg up and eggs simply rolling out one after the other! I started laughing to myself. The others asked what was so funny, so I gave them a pictorial description of the big, brown hen.

'Oh no, you've put me right off!' Molly said.

Eventually the last of the eggs were scraped out of their shells; the farmer's wife appeared again carrying the teapot, and refilled the girl's mugs.

'Now you ladz won't be wanting more tea – I've got a nice bit of real Zummerset Zider for you two.' She emptied the dregs of tea from our mugs then produced a large earthenware jug topped with a wooden lid. 'Try zis for starters,' she said, and started to pour out a nice spot of the old "Zummerset Zider", and she kept going until our mugs were overflowing onto the old pine kitchen table. With that she started giggling, 'Oh dear me! You'll 'ave to excuse me, I don't zink I should 'ave 'ad zat second tankard of me 'omemade stuff! Of course, I wasn't expecting visitors at zis time of ze night! Come now, get it down you. It'll put 'airs on your chest!' With that she patted her chest, just like King Kong. That did it – cough, cough, cough.

Molly turned around and said, 'Cough it up luv, you never know it might be a piano!'

She started giggling again, and we all joined in laughing. Randall took a gulp of the cider and I followed suit. Gee! It nearly blew our heads off! It was more like apple syrup than the watery, weak cider we knew.

We sat back and enjoyed our drinks. When I glanced down I couldn't believe me eyes, there nestled cosily in my egg cup, was yet another big, brown egg.

'Oh, no!' Molly cried, 'I couldn't possibly, I'm already feeling egg-bound.'

The farmer's wife, who I had decided to call Edith, was now acting rather tiddly. She giggled again, thinking the whole egg thing very amusing. She removed the eggs from the girl's plates and put them on mine and Randall's. Putting on a brave face, we managed to force the fourth egg down, but no way could we eat that last one. The minute our Edith turned her back, we whipped the eggs off our plates and stuffed them in our pockets! I must admit, by now the cider was taking effect, and we both felt in a most jolly mood.

'Come on, now lads. Drink up!' and before you could "zay" Zummerset Zider the mugs were once again full to the brim. By this time, the girls were ready for bed, and suggested that perhaps it was time to sort out our sleeping arrangements.

We gulped back the zider, as quick as we could, and,

waving goodbye to Edith, staggered out of ze farmhouse and across ze field.

'Do you know, I zink zat Zummerset Zider is ze strongest zider in ze 'ole world!' Randall said.

I just nodded my 'ead and 'ung onto Glenys, relying on 'er totally to get me back across zat bumpy field. How I got into bed zat night I'll never know! Even more 'z's' followed.... zzzzzzzz!

* * * * *

Another thing I'll never know, is how twelve bridesmaids can suddenly appear overnight in a boys school!

9

Twelve Bridesmaids And Not A Girl In Sight!

It's funny, but as soon as I stepped into Winton Boys School I felt comfortable and at home. I suppose it had something to do with the building and the layout. It had been designed by the same architect as Moorside School, the school I attended when I was a boy. Both schools were built just before the war in 1938. This was the year they both celebrated their coming of age; this was their 21st birthday.

It was very convenient for us, as Glenys was offered a teaching post in the Girl's School attached. Miss Williams, the Headmistress, was a real stickler, and no one, but no one was allowed to cross over the line that separated the boy's school from the girl's school. Our current vehicle was a Bedford Dormobile, with windows all around and seats in the back. I used to pick up our friends, the Hewitt's children, and with ours, drop them off at my old school, Moorside. (How's this for a coincidence? Glenys's Auntie Gwenny, Miss Jones, was the Deputy Headmistress in the Moorside Junior School). Then Glenys and I would continue our journey to our posts at Winton.

I spent the midsummer holiday on the HMI (Her Majesty Inspectors) Teaching Course at Shoreditch Teacher Training College. I achieved a 94% Pass in my final assessment – that was a real confidence booster.

To celebrate the 21 Years of Winton it was decided that we should put on Gilbert and Sullivan's Ruddigore. Reg and I were in charge of building the stage and the scenery. Being an all boys school, I was interested to see how they would tackle the sixteen bridesmaids and fisher girls in the chorus. This produced an amazing challenge to the make up and music department.

We had a bit of a snag trying to work out how the paintings in the picture gallery in Ruddigore Castle were going to come alive. Life-like, full-size paintings were made using the actors as models. The Art Department, under the direction of Miss Roberts, did a splendid job. Behind the paintings on the castle walls we left an opening for the actors to step through when the original paintings were moved. This, on the night, had to be done in a fraction of a second and in complete silence. The lights went off for one second only, and were then switched on again, and in that time the transformation had to be complete. Well, we rehearsed it quite a few times; removing the pictures, and the lads stepping through to take their places. Oh dear me, you should have heard the clattering and banging going on in the pitch black! One lad tripped and flew across the stage to end up flat on his face, whilst another lad got a fit of giggles and collapsed on the floor after he had stepped through.

'Don't worry, it'll be alright on the night… I hope!' said a bright spark from behind the scenes.

On my way home one night I called into Valentines, the scrap metal merchants, to see if they could come up with any ideas for making a silent revolving platform. Hey Presto! An idea for an ingenious contraption was born.

Back at the school, I attached a large plank to the back of the scenery. I then bolted three motor car wheels and bearings firmly onto the plank. Mounting the platform and pictures to the wheels, we now had a perfectly silent turntable. The lads stood back-to-back with their portraits, posing exactly as in the picture. The lights went out, and gently, but swiftly and more importantly noiselessly, we turned the pictures around, and the boys disappeared through the scenery to reappear stage-side as the pictures on the walls of the castle.

On the first night we stood behind the scenes with baited breath waiting for the moment when the pictures were due to come alive. There was not a sound, not a murmur. Then right on cue, all the lights went out, pitch black descended and we did our stuff! The lights went back on, and there was silence in the audience; it had worked, they hadn't spotted the picture switch! Then the characters stepped out of the pictures and there was a huge gasp of amazement from the audience, followed by a terrific roar of clapping as they showed their appreciation of the transformation – Secretly, that was my moment of glory, and I knew then that I had given back to the school a little bit of myself.

The whole production was a complete success, and yes, the sixteen girls appeared, and I couldn't even tell which boys played their parts, the make-up and costumes were so good. This was my first introduction to this land of make-believe, and do you know, I loved every minute of it!

Of course, it was nothing new to Glenys; she was in the Farnworth Operatic Society, but even she was amazed at how an all boys school could tackle a production like that.

The following year we did The Pirates of Penzance. Again, it was a roaring success, but I know that the magic of Ruddigore will stay in my heart to my dying days. (A quick, belated 'thank you' to Reg and all at Winton Boys School, for all the help you gave me which guided me on to a very enjoyable and successful teaching career).

A few months on, one cold February day, the boys had created a long ice slide right across the playground. Queuing up nicely, they took it in turns to dash across the yard and jump on the frozen ice slide. Whoosh! They sped down one after the other, finishing in a pile of flying bodies at the far end. It wasn't my problem; I was sitting comfortably by the gas fire in the staff room, thumbing idly through the latest edition of Teacher's World magazine. Naturally, I focused mainly on the craft section. My attention was drawn to an advertisement, "Urgently Required. Experienced Craft Teacher to take up duties in a modern school. Apply Newquay, Cornwall." I continued looking and immediately below was another advert, "Woodwork Teacher. Required next term. Cowes Secondary School, Isle of Wight."

Crikey, I thought, what do I do? Have I enough experience to apply for a job like that? Feeling really awful after all the help, advice and guidance he had given me, I decided to have a word with Reg.

I can see him now; he looked at me for a few minutes then said, 'Derek, you have all the experience in the world, and could take on both jobs with your eyes closed! You know I don't want to lose you, but to be quite honest, if I had three young children to bring up, I know where I would rather live. But, it is your decision. Go home, have a word with Glenys, and if you do decide to go for it, you'll have my full backing.'

After a night of chatting, we decided we would take a chance, and I filled in the application forms for both jobs. I heard back from both schools and I had two interviews to attend, one on the Isle of Wight and one in Newquay, Cornwall. If I was offered a place, it would be a double blow to Winton, as it would mean they would be losing Glenys as well.

Easter came, and we travelled in our Dormobile down to the Isle of Wight, with extremely mixed feelings, as it would mean leaving all our families and friends behind. But, what a challenge! Would the wish I made at Blackgang Chine, on our honeymoon, come true?...

'I'd like to live in a place like this'....

10

Be Careful What You Wish For, As It May Just Come True!

It was a magical moment as the Red Funnel Ferry, named 'Vecta', eased into Fountain Pier in West Cowes on the Isle of Wight. The crewmen threw their lines to the awaiting shore men. The lines were caught with complete accuracy and, heaving away, the large hawser ropes were hauled ashore and looped over the iron bollards. The winches on board started to whine as they took up the slack and pulled the ship gently into the protective timbers of the pier.

With everything made tight and secure, the side doors opened and the ramp lowered. We followed a flash, new MG sports car in our pale green and cream Bedford Dormobile. To our surprise, we were directed onto a large metal turn-table; the crewman held up his hand.

'Stop!' Then two burly chaps pushed the back of the van and we turned slowly around to face the side of the ship.

'Ok, all clear! Off you go!' shouted the crewman. Releasing the hand brake cautiously, I drove over the hump of the ramp, which by this time was rising and falling with the undulating waves.

This was it! We'd made it! It was nine years since we were last on this beautiful island; this island where we'd spent our honeymoon. The sky was a beautiful bright blue and there was not a cloud in sight. The air was warm and crystal clear.

I thought we had landed in paradise!

First stop was Cowes Secondary School. Surprisingly, this turned out to be just a couple of minutes drive from the ferry. Having located the caretaker in his bungalow, I was informed that Mr Goodson, the Headmaster, lived just around the corner opposite Northwood House.

I rang the door bell and Mr Goodson himself answered. So far, so good; he looked a nice sort of chap. I introduced Glenys and myself, and informed him that I had applied for the craft teacher's post.

'Oh, Come in! Come in! I am delighted to meet you,' he said.

I nearly fell over backwards as I walked into the lounge; there, over the fireplace, hung a large oil painting of Mont Blanc! I stood there flabbergasted and just pointed at the picture.

'That's Mont Blanc!' I eventually spluttered. He stepped back shocked.

'Er, yes it is. How did you know it was Mont Blanc? I've climbed it, you see.'

He went on to tell us the tale of how he had climbed it in his younger days. He was with a climbing group, who were sponsored by the Royal Geographical Society to film the ascent of Mont Blanc. He had been the chief cameraman and had total responsibility for producing the 16 mm movie film. He used reel after reel of film, and was quite excited over the fantastic climbing shots and dramatic avalanche footage he had managed to capture. Over the three days they were on the mountain, they used literally hundreds and hundreds of feet of film, in the production of what he was sure would be a masterpiece of cine photography. He had lugged the large movie camera, plus the heavy wooden and brass tripod, and a rucksack full of spare film, all the way to the top of this beautiful, yet dangerous, mountain.

Having returned back safe and sound to England, full of enthusiasm, he handed the equipment and films back to the Royal Geographical Society to be processed. The processing laboratory couldn't make it out. They went through reel after reel of film, and each one was completely blank; no scenery, no avalanche and no climbing! One of the technicians was then called in to check over the camera.

'Hey!' he exclaimed. 'There's nothing wrong with this camera. The lens cap has never been taken off; it's still got the original seal intact!'

With all the excitement of the climb and the difficult terrain, Mr Goodson had simply forgotten to take the lens cap off the camera; and, of course, on those cameras the viewfinder was separate from the lens, so whilst filming he had no indication of whether the cap had been on or not.

At this moment, his wife came in with a nice cup of tea.

'Oh, you're not telling them about your brilliant film making days, are you?' she said smiling.

He just nodded, and we all had a good laugh. I knew that if I got the job we would get on fine, as he was also a bit of a handy man. He and his son were building a six-foot high boundary wall at the back of the house, and they appreciated a couple of tips I gave them to make their block laying a little easier.

At the interview, held in Newport's County Hall the following day, I produced my portfolio along with my nice display case with a range of practical examples, and a collection of photographs of the larger projects we had completed. They spent ages passing them around. I was pleased to hear a lot of ooh's and ah's, and encouragingly favourable comments like, 'Now that's a really beautiful piece of work' and 'Oh, I do like that!' It was more like a market stall than an interview. I knew I had stiff competition as one of the other craft teachers awaiting the interview told me he was a head of department, but was prepared for a drop in salary just to live and work on the Island.

After all the interviews had taken place, I was called back in and offered the post; and not only that, they also asked Glenys to go in, and they offered her a teaching post at Northwood Primary School!

We were both hugely delighted and excited about the prospect of bringing our children up in these beautiful surroundings. Doesn't it just go to show, you have to be careful what you wish for, as it may just come true! (I am referring to the wish I made, sitting in the massive skeleton of a whale at Blackgang Chine, whilst we were on our honeymoon in 1951).

On our way to the interview, we had passed a lovely double-fronted house, standing majestically in its own grounds. It looked empty. We then spotted the 'Sir Francis Pittis & Son – For Sale' sign sticking out of the thick bay hedge. We both looked at each other.

'Did you see that?' I said to Glenys, 'Now that's something like a house!' But at that moment I thought it was way beyond our means. Let's just see how the interview goes…

We jumped down the steps outside County Hall two at a time, holding hands. We were so thrilled at the prospect of our new life on the Isle of Wight. Dashing up Newport High Street, we passed the Guild Hall and made a bee-line to Weeks Tea Rooms, for a well-deserved afternoon tea treat. All the waitresses were dressed in black with white pinafores and dainty doyley head bands. They couldn't do enough for us.

'Would you like another scone, Madam? More jam and cream, Sir? No problem!'

Do you know, at that time on the Island, there was only one set of traffic lights. They controlled the traffic flow over the swing bridge on the Yarmouth harbour road. The moment we landed on the Island, time stood still. Life seemed ten years behind the Mainland's hustle and bustle rat race.

Sir Francis Pittis & Son estate agents were situated just around the corner from Weeks Tea Rooms in a little old-fashioned street called Holyrood Street, which led down to the Railway Station. The middle-aged lady in the shop gave us a slip of A4 paper with the house details on.

> *FOR SALE –*
>
> *Freehold, with Vacant Possession.*
>
> *Detached Property, known as: 'The Briars' at 65 Horsebridge Hill, Newport, Isle of Wight*
>
> *Situation: Standing on high ground, the house commands splendid views of the surrounding countryside. Close to a bus stop with frequent buses to the shopping centres of Newport and Cowes. Fair size, half-an-acre garden of lawn, kitchen garden, fruit trees, and greenhouse.*
>
> *Rateable Value: £26 per annum*
>
> *Price: £2900*

She informed us that another party had been to see it and were trying to arrange a mortgage. I managed to acquire the keys for the house, casually saying, 'Just in case the other party drops out!'

This was something like a house, with its four bedrooms and wonderful views across the fields to the River Medina and beyond. The half-an-acre garden contained its own orchard of apple, pear and plum trees and, as stated, a nice big greenhouse stood to one side. We dashed from room to room.

'We'll knock this wall out here and open that area there. We'll put a nice big window in the side, here, to get the sun in all day! We can open up the kitchen and build a breakfast bar for the five of us…' The possibilities were simply endless.

We had fallen in love with it from first sight. I made a list of all the work required, like damp coursing, re-slating, etc. This was no trouble for me; I'd done it all before! I made a rough estimate for all the work that needed doing to bring it up to standard.

We shot back to Sir Francis Pittis & Son fired with enthusiasm.

'Yes! Yes!' we blurted out excitedly, 'We'll have it!'

'Oh, I'm sorry but the other party has confirmed that they are interested and can get a mortgage subject to a satisfactory survey report.'

I asked her if she could get hold of the farmer who owned The Briars. She phoned through and the farmer answered. I told him who I was and that I had surveyed the property and had found rising damp, penetration damp on the north wall, dry rot in the skirting boards, damp rot in the roof timbers, the roof was nail sick and would need re-slating, etc, etc. I listed every little job that needed doing. Then I offered him £2000 cash.

'Oh, no!' he said, 'The other party has offered me the full £2900 asking price!'

'Wait a minute, Sir,' I carried on. 'That is only subject to two things: one, that they can get a full mortgage offer and, two, the most important thing, will they get a survey done quickly and will the result of that survey be favourable?' I paused for a second, then said, 'I tell you what, I'm prepared to up my offer to £2150, and that's the maximum, as it's going to cost me over £1000 to bring it up to basic living standard.'

He hesitated, 'No. I think I'll still wait and see what this other chap can do.'

'Oh, did I mention I will not be requiring a mortgage or a survey report,' I continued regardless. 'I will be paying cash!'

'You're saying it's a cash sale?' said the farmer.

'Yep! Cash on the nail. Just think £2150 cash in your hand on completion. No messing about trying to get mortgages, or worrying about what will be brought up in the surveyors report. In fact, I'm even prepared, here and now, to hand over a 10% deposit cheque to your agent.'

Complete silence. Then he spoke, asking to be passed back to the estate agent. After a bit of discussion, she looked up.

'Seeing as it's a cash sale, he has instructed me to accept your offer.'

I was truly stunned! I had expected to haggle and finish up around the £2500 mark, which was really outside our financial capabilities, but I thought I would be able to raise the extra somehow, as no way was I going to miss this opportunity. It was just too good to be true.

Glenys and I were both physically shaking with excitement. Out came the cheque book; I looked at Glenys and she smiled and nodded. Two seconds later the deposit was paid. It had completely emptied our account, but who cares, we had got the house! The agent suggested we contact Newport solicitors, Jerome & Pethwick. The solicitor I spoke to was a nice chap and considerably helpful. I told him I needed time to get the money together but to get the paperwork done as soon as possible.

We'd done it! Two jobs and a home on the Isle of Wight, with not a penny left to our name!

(Much later, at a staff meeting, a teacher, Bill Hathaway, came up to me. 'Hey! Are you the Feldon who lives at The Briars?'

'Yes,' I replied.

'You pinched my house,' he continued. 'You and your money!'

I didn't feel too bad as he had ended up with a nice thatched cottage in the village of Shorwell. I knew he wouldn't have been able to tackle all the work we had done on the house; it would have cost him a fortune to get the builders in, and him on just a teacher's wage!!)

As soon as we arrived back home in Lancashire, we sat down at the table with a big sheet of paper in front of us. Right, this was it; we had to get the house sold, and quick! On the paper we wrote down every benefit this house could offer. From the attic where I had built-in the roof space to make a playroom for the kids to play in, to the extension we had built on the side, we put down every three pin plug socket in each room. This was going to be our advert in the next days Manchester Evening News. In those days a normal house advert cost around £1. When they worked out the cost of our lengthy description it came to £10! You would think we were selling a mansion instead of a small semi-detached house.

When the evening paper came out the advert was very impressive, although I say it myself! At six o'clock that evening the telephone rang. It was a lady from Salford, who had just sold her public house, and wanted to come and look at our home. She said she could make it by half past six, but I said she would have to make it a little later as we already had people who were interested and were viewing the house now. (I must admit, this was a little white lie – but it's surprising how a little competition helps to make up a person's mind!) In she came at quarter to seven on the dot; she had a good look round and was over the moon (just as we had been with The Briars). I told her we had two other people who wanted to buy it.

'Look,' she said, 'I can pay cash for it now! I'll give you a cheque for £1800 – here and now- as long as I can move in pretty soon.' Whoosh! That caught us both on the hop.

I looked at Glenys who said quickly, 'We'll take it! The house is yours.'

'Oh, thank you, thank you!' the lady said smiling broadly.

Then slight panic came over us. What do we do now? We couldn't move down to the Island until the summer holidays, we had three children and no where to live! The removal firm said they could shift our stuff whenever we were ready. Everybody, all our friends and family, said not to worry as we could stay with them. It finished up with Della and Vanda staying with Glenys's mum and dad, Tony living at a mate's, David, who was a couple of years older than him but they got on well, (then at Eric and Nora's house, who we had known for years), and Glenys and I had a room over Derrick and Mildred's grocers shop in Walkden.

The time had then come; all our furniture and belongings were loaded in the Summerfields removal van. The driver was about to close the rear doors, when I suddenly shouted.

'Hold it! We're not finished yet!'

'What?' he said, 'We can't get anymore in 'ere!'

'Just a couple more bits to fit in,' I said. Well, he nearly had a fit when he saw me bring the two extension ladders, two planks, ladder extension brackets, tools and a roll of lead from my workshop.

'No way will you get them in, mate!' Half an hour later, after juggling wardrobes and dressing tables around, we were ready to go.

It was agreed at the beginning, that if I was prepared to go with the van to the Isle of Wight, as an extra hand, he would knock me £20 off the estimate – done! We set off at 4 a.m. the following day and arrived at Yarmouth, after a very long and tiresome journey, at 4 p.m.

At The Briars, we unloaded the furniture as best we could in the various rooms. The front room was filled with ladders and planks, lead, and tools of all shapes and sizes; even the kid's swing had come with us. By this time we were absolutely shattered, but, as they say, there's no rest for the wicked. So back to Yarmouth we drove. The last ferry was just at the point of leaving when we arrived at the slipway.

'Sorry, mate,' said the chap in charge, 'You'll have to get your boarding tickets from the office.' I hopped out of the van and shot across to the office, and was handed the passes just in time to see the ferry leaving the slipway. Oh no! I couldn't believe it, we had been left stranded! "Welcome to the Isle of Wight", read the sign above the ticket office.

The van owner and his mate climbed down from the cab muttering and swearing.

To try and make the best of the situation, I said, 'Come on, let me take you for a pint. There's a pub across the road.' I asked the landlady if she had anything we could eat, and she produced three, stone cold, pork pies! We were absolutely starving; I wanted a hot drink and a hot meal.

'Excuse me,' I said, 'Do you think you could warm them up for us, please?' She raised her eyebrows, shrugged her shoulders and walked away.

'Here!' she said, as she plonked a pot of Coleman's mustard on the counter. 'That'll warm you up if you put enough on!' Then turned and walked off, winking at a couple of local fishermen who burst out laughing.

'Eh! You'll get no change out of our Ethel; she has an answer for everything and everybody! Ain't that right, Ethel?'

'You knows me, boys. I got an answer for everyfin'!' I thought she was joking, but no, it was mustard or nowt! So, mustard it was!

Mr Summerfield and I managed to find a bed and breakfast just round the corner. Matey stayed in the pub until closing time, then staggered back across the road, climbed in the back of the van and covered himself up with the furniture blankets and promptly fell fast asleep.

We drove on to the first ferry leaving the Island and were just outside Birmingham when the little window opened just behind the driver's seat. A head popped through.

'Where the hell are we?' asked a slightly hungover Matey. 'I could do with a spot of breakfast!' Fair enough. We pulled into a roadside transport café for a bit of dinner.

We continued on our way, finally arriving home at tea time. Well, not 'home' home, as the lady from Salford was now fully established in, what was, our home. I had to get the trolley bus to Walkden, then walk up the road to Derrick's shop – our new home until the summer holidays, when Glenys, myself and the three children would drive down once again to the Isle of Wight.

I didn't realise what was going to be in store for me in that old Victorian school room, at East Cowes.

11

We Could Hear The Pitiful Cry For Help

I left Winton School with mixed feelings, as the boys of the Adventure Club had pooled their money together and bought me a pair of real Austrian leather shorts, and young Evans had made a rather nice, black and white vase in pottery, especially for me. Reg and his wife told me not to worry as they would be coming down to the Island to see us; and they did, which really pleased me.

When I started my new post, to my surprise I found that I wouldn't be teaching in the main school in Cowes, but at the old technical college building, along Osborne Road in East Cowes. This was an old Victorian school. Fortunately for me, I had the largest room, with plenty of space to expand.

Of course, these old places have an atmosphere of their own, with ghosts and ghouls and weird knocking noises in the middle of the night. But this was broad daylight and the ghostly whispers were distinctly heard by me, all the boys, and by one of Her Majesty's Inspectors in that hushed and silent workshop. We all stood still and listened. Yes, there it was again; a muffled, squeaky sound. Then it came clearer.

'Let me out. Please let me out.' Cold shivers ran down our spines, we could hear the pitiful cry for help as it echoed around the room. Nobody dared to move, everybody seemed to be rooted to the very spot they were standing on. The uncanny, inhuman voice crying for help continued, and I found it difficult to pinpoint the source of the ghostly sound. One minute it seemed to come out of the old stone wall, next it reverberated around the room and faded into a far cry as it drifted up to the high lofty ceiling.

'Let me out. Please let – me – out.' The voice then seemed to come from under the very floor we were standing on. Suddenly loud bumps and banging echoed around the fabric of the ancient building. How long had this poor lost spirit been imprisoned in its tomb of despair?

I had only been at the school for a short while when we were informed that a general inspection, by Her Majesty's Education Inspectors, was scheduled for the following week. The craft inspector came down the two steps into my room.

'Ah! Mr Feldon. So we meet again!' Much to my surprise, he was the tutor on the course I had attended at Shoreditch College.

Tuesday morning was my GCE 'O' Level group; a smart and intelligent bunch of lads.

'Stop work, boys – and stand by your benches.' No problem! I introduced Mr Smith, the inspector, who was just about to say a few words when the eerie voice started its plea. We stopped, aghast, holding our breath. There, it could be heard again.

'Let me out. Please let me out.'

Nobody dared move, as we had all heard the rumours about how a young boy had fallen from the roof during construction of the school. The Victorian workmen knew they would be sacked if the accident came to light, so they picked up the broken remains of the dead little fellow and, it is said, placed him in a coffin hastily made from pine boarding, and laid him to rest under the floor. Others say he was put in a cavity in the brickwork. Some even suggest that he was thrown into the River Medina. His parents were told he had run away to join the navy which was not uncommon in those hard times, or so they say.

The cries then became much louder; 'Let me out. Please let me out.'

Mr Smith and I looked at each other, then the banging started all over again. The inspector walked over to the empty bench in the middle of the room and opened the storage cupboard below. Out tumbled Chiverton gasping for breath.

'Oh thank you, Sir. I thought I was going to suffocate in that dark hole!'

Well, the whole class was in an uproar, as everyone burst out laughing. It turned out that one of the boys had thrown Chevy's dovetail exercise to the far end of the cupboard. He had climbed in to retrieve it and "bang", the door had *accidentally* closed; the latch had even turned to lock itself!

When questioned the whole class agreed that, yes, it must have just locked itself. I thought to myself, oh my goodness, what is this going to look like on my report; and me in my first term at this new school! But I shouldn't have worried; within two minutes the keen lads had their shirt sleeves rolled up and were working like little beavers. The inspector actually congratulated me.

'What a lively, industrious group of lads you have here!' he said, and he thought it was great to see them all relaxed and having a good laugh in the workshop.

* * * * *

With the end of term summer holidays approaching, the 4 o'clock bell sounded, and the boys left with their latest project tucked safely under their arms. Peace and quiet at last; just another half an hour to transfer their marks to my record book then that was it, six weeks holidays.

Just as I was about to leave there was a knock at my door. Mr Taylor, the caretaker, popped his head round the door.

'Excuse me, Mr Feldon. You have a visitor.'

In stepped a red-faced tubby policeman, in full uniform, bobby's hat, whistle and silver chain, bicycle clips around the bottom of his trousers and the usual size 12, polished black boots.

'Sorry to disturb you, Sir, but you'll 'ave to come at once to the recreation ground in York Avenue. It's all out of control. I've got a riot on me 'ands and I can't stop it! Come on quickly. It's urgent, I need your 'elp!'

I dashed out and jumped into my car and drove off; followed by PC 49 puffing away on his bicycle.

When I got there I couldn't believe me eyes. I'm not kidding, the recreation ground was like a medieval battle field. The air was full of flying arrows. The two sides were battling it out and neither would retreat or give in. Around them a crowd had gathered; some were shouting and screaming at them to stop, but to no avail and the battle raged on.

On the command of 'Fire!' the archers released yet another volley of arrows from their crossbows. Those which missed their mark were gathered up quickly ready for the return fire. Scattered around the battlefield bodies laid dead or wounded, with gnarled, pained expressions. It was a gruesome sight. The men at the side were still shouting, and the women screaming in horror at the massacre taking place before their very eyes. But no one ventured into the path of the brave warriors determined to conquer their foe.

I pushed and shoved my way through the large crowd of spectators, which was getting bigger by the minute, as folk were just abandoning their cars on the main road to dash over and see what all the fuss was about. Eventually, I managed to get through the first row of the angry audience. Without a second to waste, I blew hard on my whistle.

'STOP!' I shouted as loud as I could. To everyone's surprise the troops stopped and froze on the spot. Then, very slowly, the dead and wounded got up, brushed themselves down, and looked across at me rather sheepishly.

I was then joined by the very red-faced policeman, still huffing and puffing, and pushing his bicycle.

'Ugh! You've done it, Sir! 'ow the 'eck did you manage that!'

'Authority!' I replied with a wink.

'Oh yes, Sir. Authority, that's it, Sir,' he said.

'Right then. Single file everyone,' I continued. 'Crossbows in a pile here, and arrows in a pile here,' I said pointing.

'Aw, but Sir. We 'aven't taken 'em 'ome yet. Our mums 'aven't seen 'em yet.'

Then a voice from the back of the crowd shouted, 'Oh yes we have! And you can put yours down with the rest of them!'

The battle was over and the victors were dragged home by their mums and dads, to the cries of 'Just look at yer blazer and look at the state of yer new trousers!', 'I'll never get them grass stains off yer shirt!' and 'Just wait 'til I get you 'ome!'

The policeman said, 'Come on, Sir. I'll give you a lift back to your car with these weapons of mass destruction.' He smiled and whispered, 'I wouldn't have minded but my lad was one of the ones laid out on the floor, and I dread to think what his ma will say when he gets 'ome in that state. What's more, I'm not too happy about what she'll 'ave to say to me either!'

Earlier in the year, I had come across plans for a crossbow. It was a nice exercise in cutting a mortice joint, grooving and intricate shaping of the stock. Now, I thought, that's just what I'd have liked when I was eleven years old; far more interesting than the usual teapot stand! And that was how it all began. Fortunately, I had been aware of the danger and had insisted that every arrow had a rubber sucker fixed firmly to the tip.

So, no real harm was done. Well, only to the pride of the

vanquished, and to my first year syllabus.

Back to the teapot stand, then? I don't think so! I had other ideas of what the boys of Cowes, the Mecca of sailing, should be taught. Unfortunately, they had their own ideas of recycling council property…

Now that's funny, I thought to myself, one afternoon before class, what the devil is going on here? The boys were all lined up outside my door and each one had a large paint tin under his arm. I never said a word as they marched into the workshop and stood beside their benches. I looked at them.

'Okay, you win!' I said, 'Go on then, tell me what the paint tins are all about.'

The spokesman cleared his throat, 'It's like this, Sir, we have a bit of a problem and we need your help.'

'Go on,' I prompted.

'Well, Sir, we need to take the bottom out of the paint tins, then we need to drill holes around the top edge.'

Now, I was always pleased when they used their imagination and initiative; that was my theme on teaching – Think around things and have a go; Don't take 'no' or 'it can't be done' for an answer.

'So, what do you think then, Sir?' questioned the boy.

'Well, first of all, what do you want them for?'

One lad piped up, 'Oh, they're just bait tins to catch fish.'

Well, I'm no fisherman, in fact, I've never fished in my life, so I assumed they were the experts, as I was soon to find out.

By four o'clock all the bottoms had been neatly cut out, and the top of each tin perforated with holes – and every boy was happy. A couple of the lads came over to me.

'Would you like us to show you how, and where, to fish, Sir?'

'Yes, okay then,' I replied, 'that would be great.'

'Right, then, see you tomorrow dinnertime. We'll bring the

rag worm bait and rods, and we'll show you how to catch a nice plaice for your tea.'

Sure enough, the next day, they were ready and waiting, and we headed off to the "blue bench" along East Cowes seafront. I was reliably informed that this was the spot where the fish came in to feed. After many attempts at casting out and trying to put the worm on the hook, I finally did it; the line and weight went hurtling out over the water and landed with a neat splash.

'Hurray! You've done it, Sir! Now reel it in slowly.' Suddenly the rod started to dip and flick about. 'Bring it in! Bring it in!' they shouted, 'You've caught something!' I couldn't believe my eyes as I slowly reeled in a nice 3lb plaice; I had caught my first fish!

On our way back, I asked them how they used the paint tin fish bait holders.

'Oh, don't worry about those, Sir. You're not ready for those just yet. They're for deep sea fishing.'

The following week I was presented with a couple of edible crabs, and a lobster.

'I caught these last night, Sir. I thought you might like them.' To be completely honest, I didn't really like the look of them, and they were still alive!

I gave them to the school cook who was highly delighted... unlike the clerk of the council, who telephoned me later that day, to say that all the brand new wire-net waste paper baskets, that had just been erected along Cowes seafront right through to Gurnard, had disappeared overnight; and could I shed any light on who might want to steal 20 baskets?

Uh oh! Warning bells started to ring in my head; 20 boys, 20 tin cans, 20 missing wire baskets! Now that was a bit of a funny coincidence. In trooped my class, the full twenty innocent-looking boys.

'Right, who's going to tell me what you've been up to,' I

asked calmly.

'Er, well, Sir,' said one brave lad, 'the lobster pots work a real treat. We've caught 27 lobsters and 32 crabs since we put them down. Even the Royal Yacht Squadron are giving us top price for them!' Teach them initiative and they'll use it!

Two weeks later new fibre-glass, square, solid waste paper bins appeared along the seafront, much to the disgust of my little fishermen.

Talking about fishermen, I must tell you about the two little boys who were staying in the holiday chalets. (The chalets actually consisted of old railway carriages, tumbled down sheds and the odd building which was in the process of being rebuilt). These were situated on the marsh adjoining Gurnard Creek.

The tide was nearly out and the creek was oozing with deep, slimy mud. Leaning over the bridge were the two budding fishermen; crab lines dangling down to the waters edge.

'Got one!' shouted the eldest, and started to haul up his prize. The crab was firmly attached to the rasher of bacon they were using as bait. The youngest one slid down the banking to fill his little bucket with water. Into the mud he stepped, and sank deeper and deeper, but wasn't the least bit concerned about his now black socks, and filthy shoes – if it's water he wants, it's water he's going to get!

Dragging himself up the slippery side he climbed back onto the bridge.

''Ave yer still got it?' he puffed.

'Yer, 'urry up, before it gets away.'

The bigger lad lowered the bacon slowly into the water, but no way was that crab going to let go of the tasty morsel. Lifting it back out of the bucket, the lad shook the line several times, but it was no use. So, grabbing the bacon, he slapped it hard on the top edge of the bucket. The crab finally relinquished its hold, but instead of falling into the water it ended up scurrying off along the road.

The little lad shouted, 'Quick, pick it up!'

'Nah!' was the reply. 'You pick it up, it might bite me!'

'It won't bite yer if yer hold its back.' The boy bent down bravely and grabbed the tiny, green crab and tossed it into the bucket, saying 'Got it! We'll 'ave that for our tea! Come on, let's catch another one.'

By this time, the bacon bait was looking a little worse for wear. It was black, slimy and chunks were missing out of it where the crab had enjoyed its tasty feast. This didn't put them off though, and over the side of the bridge the line was lowered once again into the murky depths of the creek, to await its next unsuspecting victim.

All was quiet and peaceful as the two little excited lads sat casually astride the old, stone bridge, with not a care in the world. When all of a sudden a voice shrieked out from the first chalet,

'Thomas, 'ave yer get the bloody bacon?'

'Er, yes, mum,' came the reply from one of the boys. 'We've caught yer a nice big crab for yer tea.'

Out came mum and flew across the road, narrowly missing a chap on a bicycle, who had to pull up sharp or he would have hit her square on. She grabbed the line and pulled up the slimy bacon, unhooked it and carried it down to the edge of the creek. She bent down and proceeded to "wash" the bacon back and forth in the muddy water, to remove the slime. Climbing back up she turned to the boys.

'Yer know, yer dad will go mad, if he don't 'ave his egg and bacon for breakfast!' And with that, she disappeared back inside the chalet.

Ten minutes later, the lovely smell of cooked bacon wafted across the creek!

12

Guaranteed To Make You Two Inches Taller!

You may be wondering what happened to my dad, when he moved to Altringham. As I said before, the chimney sweep business was now far too heavy for him. In the meantime, he met up with a nice lady called Judith Roberts, who, like him, was lonely and seeking companionship. They married in 1952 and I was the best man at their wedding. They then bought a café in Salford, and I helped to put in new fireplaces and sink units for them. Eventually they sold the business and moved down south to be near my sister Barbara.

Dad died with lung and heart disease in 1955, at the age of 60 years. I often wonder what new projects he may still be thinking up; I can just imagine St. Peter saying, 'Electric gates! That sounds like a good idea Charlie!'

Then my mam adding, 'But, Charlie, you haven't got an electric motor.'

Dad would then turn around and say, 'Ah! But I know an angel who has! You see, ma (as he always used to tell me) it's not what you know, it's who you know that counts!'

God bless them both.

Tom, my mate and climbing companion, married a lovely girl, Muriel, and they moved to Anglesey. (Sadly, he died just five months before I had finished my first book, 'The Spirit of Adventure'. This was a great shame; he had been a good pal, and we had shared all those wonderful boyhood adventures).

* * * * *

Whack! The brick flew out across the dining room floor. It was ten o'clock at night. That was the first brick of many to finish up on the floor during this summer holiday.

I'm a great believer in the old Chinese saying "It takes but one step to start a two thousand mile journey." Knock that first brick out, and you're committed! It's always the first step that most people are afraid to take. I urge you to take that step, or you'll never know what amazing adventures await you.

That summer, The Briars had a face lift; new patio doors, new kitchen/diner, new paths and a new driveway. At this stage, I must tell you about the school 4C concreting team I organised. It all started with John Gordon, the science teacher at Cowes, who wanted to know if I would lay a driveway for his car. As soon as this was mentioned, it was amazing how many other members of staff also wanted drives and paths around their houses. The 4C's – The Cowes Crazy Concreting Club – was therefore born, and believe me, it was a laugh a minute.

Everyone had to dig out their own footings for the pathways, drives or patios. Then along came 'Inspector Feldon', who would take a look and make an estimate for the quantity of ready-mix concrete required. If everything was in order, their name would go into the hat. We started off with some famous names in the team; John Gordon, Arthur Cleary, the metalwork teacher, Lew Cox, the P.E. teacher, Norman Barker, from the science department, and myself. We each had to supply our own wellies and spade. The wheelbarrows, however, were another tale.

Little garden wheelbarrows were not much use for this heavy-weight job. Luckily, I had two builders barrows and

Bill Dore, from down the road, gave me a whacking big barrow, which he used 'to shovel s**t out of the cow shed' in Wheeler's Farm, across the road from The Briars – and believe me, it was big! So, we had three barrows on the move all the time from the ready-mix wagon parked in the road, whilst the person having the job done would help me with raking and tamping the concrete down, to ensure it was nice and level. Everyone would shy away from the "big barrow", so it was usually a case of first there, first served.

Arthur was always the last to arrive, so he ended up being known as the "Big Barrow Boy." This name was a little ironic as he was actually the smallest in height. In fact, he once told us a tale, about when he was a young man living in the East End of London.

One night he went out with a group of mates and they met up with a few local girls. Arthur took a shine to Olive, but she was taller than him, and he didn't have the nerve to ask her out, in case she 'looked down on him'. Then a miracle happened; a half page advert in the local paper caught his eye, with the bold title "Guaranteed to make you two inches taller! – Send off a postal order for 30/- and we will guarantee you will gain an extra 2 inches in height."

Arthur hurriedly filled in his name and address, and first thing on Monday morning dashed down to the post office to buy his 30/- postal order. He popped it in an envelope, and posted it to the usual East End box number. He wondered if it would be a pair of shoes with concealed inner soles, or could it be a magic potion he had to drink? He'd try anything to gain a couple of inches in height!

Exactly three days later, there was a knock at the door; the postman had a brown paper parcel for Arthur. He removed the paper excitedly. Ah, ha! It contained a white cardboard shoe box. Carefully opening it he found a note with bold lettering, giving him instructions on how he could gain two inches in height immediately. Emptying the contents of the box onto his kitchen table, he looked and looked again at the two pieces of 3"x 2" timber blocks. Well, that's funny, he thought, they must have made a mistake. Unfolding the instructions fully, he found just three words, in bold, large print – '**STAND ON THESE**.' At that moment, his mother came in and burst out laughing, she could obviously see the funny side of it. Arthur however, wasn't so amused.

After tea Arthur and all the boys went down to the address shown on the paperwork to demand Arthur's money back under the guarantee. Rounding the corner, they found that No. 7, next to the chip shop, was an old house, with boarded windows and peeling paintwork. They knocked and knocked at the door, but there was no reply. Peeping through the letterbox, they could see a pile of, what looked like, complaint letters, all soggy from the rain that had seeped under the front door!

Dead on four thirty the concrete mixer arrived. Out came the chute and the ready-mixed concrete poured out, slopping into John's barrow. Fully loaded he shot off as Lew manoeuvred his barrow under the chute. The driver pulled his lever and again the concrete poured out, before moving off Lew whispered something to Steve, the driver. He nodded and gave Lew a knowing wink. Arthur trundled up with the monster barrow and placed it under the chute. Whoosh! The barrow was filled to the very top. Arthur just stood there flabbergasted, then, with a few choice words, attempted to lift the impossible load. How the driver kept a straight face, I'll never know; we all rolled over with concealed laughter. Steve looked at Arthur.

'Look mate, if you're not man enough to shift a barrowful of muck, then you shouldn't be on the job.' You can imagine Arthur's face on hearing this comment. Slowly, after a lot of huffing and puffing, Arthur lifted the huge load and gradually pushed it up the drive. With every step he seemed to be getting smaller and smaller as he literally sank into his wellies!

Arriving at the tip off point, his face was as red as a beetroot. I casually told him to simply lift the handles and tip the concrete in between the shuttering. He tried and tried but couldn't lift it any higher. In the end, Norman gave him a hand and after a great struggle they managed to tip it on its side, finally emptying it.

'Come on, Arthur. I'll be on overtime if you don't 'urry up and shape yerself!' shouted the driver.

'You did that on purpose, didn't you?' said Arthur.

We all pulled our most innocent faces – as if we would do anything like that!

Funnily enough, Arthur was the first one to arrive at our next job. Very keen, I thought!

I had dug a deep hole in the middle of my path to put a junction in my drain. Having laid the first half of the path and filled the hole with soft concrete, John was slowly tamping the path and working his way back and down. I somehow forgot to mention that there was a whopping big hole just behind him. Whoops! Too late; he suddenly found himself over his welly tops.

'Help!' he yelled, as he sank deeper and deeper into the quick setting concrete. In that split second, I had just walked round the corner to get the hosepipe. We yanked him out and hosed him down, telling him not to mess about so much, as we were all starving and wanted our tea.

No wonder we were called the 4C's – Crazy! You can say that again, but at least the job got done.

After we had finished off all my paths and driveway, Steve informed me that he still had about half a yard of concrete left. So, I decided to make a pond in the shape of the Isle of Wight in the front garden. The 4C gang unloaded the remaining concrete and just dumped it in a pile at the side of my newly laid drive. Next minute they were off! – leaving me with a mountain of concrete and a big hole. Tony, my lad, had the "fun" job of squirting a fine spray of water over the pile to slow down the setting process. I was still digging away furiously, and pinning wire-netting in the hole to act as reinforcing. By now it was dark, and we were very hungry, but I couldn't let the concrete go off before it was transferred into the pond. It was 9.30 p.m. before I had finished the last load.

I was very pleased with the pond, and the Isle of Wight shape certainly caused a lot of favourable comments, especially from passengers on the top deck of the bus, on their way to Cowes.

How could I know then, on that cold, dark, winter's night, that our pond would soon attract something more mysterious, more sinister, and even more mystifying...

13

'Banana Skin?' They All Repeated

Snow, snow, and more snow. The wind was howling around the house and the large snowflakes were settling on the already frozen ground. The wind whipped across the open land causing massive drifts against the hedges. It wasn't long before the roadway became totally blocked by the everlasting snowstorm.

It was New Year's Eve 1960 and this was the beginning of the 'deep freeze', when the Isle of Wight became the Isle of *White*. Nothing stirred and everywhere was silent as I fastened snow chains around the rear wheels of our Bedford Dormobile. Of course, we had seen it all before "up North" – but it never snows on this Island, or so we had been told!

We had been invited to the Robertson's, who lived just up the road in Northwood. Wrapped up nice and warm with hats, scarves, jerseys, gabardine macs and wellington boots, Della, Vanda and Tony climbed into the back of the van. Glenys and I got in the front. It was quite comfortable inside, as I had left the engine running whilst I had been attaching the snow chains. Off we started, it was a five minute ride at the most, or so I thought. By this time the snow was about six inches deep on the road. Approaching the open fields (where today they hold the Annual County Show), there were lights flashing everywhere, giving a ghostly scene as they reflected on the hedges and wall of snow in front of us.

I couldn't believe my eyes, a big, yellow JCB digger had dug out a single-line passageway through this tremendous snow drift. Along each side of the road cars had been trapped in the onslaught of the icy blizzard and abandoned, and eventually buried in the six foot layers of snow. Gently we eased our way, on the packed ice and snow, through this tunnel of glistening snow, knowing that we still had a return journey to make sometime after midnight, after we had celebrated the coming of the New Year.

That year was unbelievable; apart from the many cars buried in the snow drifts, the sea actually froze! On Cowes seafront there was a beautiful display of natural ice sculptures where the waves had hit the wall and rolled back, only to freeze in mid air! The River Medina, Wootton Creek and the harbours, were just a solid block of ice. Nothing could move in or out, and the Island came to a stand still for quite a while; in fact, walking along Gurnard seafront, at Easter, we could still see pockets of snow and ice being washed over by the sea. The Isle of *White* – you can say that again!

A few years later, we had a most unusual happening, after an overnight fall of snow. Eric and Nora Hewitt, and family, were staying with us for a short break. Drawing back the curtains in the morning we were met with a beautiful sight. There was a pure virgin snow blanket across the front lawn, and the trees were heavily laden with a white mantle, sparkling and reflecting in the bright sunlight.

The kids were already dressed and out at the back rolling a huge snowball around the garden, leaving an interwoven maze pathway where the snow had been picked up by, what was to become, the body of the snowman. The children were pushing and puffing away, their faces bright pink, noses running, but they were determined to keep it on the move. All this frantic activity at the back of the house, yet the front was calm and still, looking like a typical, peaceful, Christmas card scene.

Then I saw them; I looked again. Yes! There were two hoof-like prints in the snow, then another two, and yet another two. It was as if a two-legged creature had appeared from nowhere. They started about 6ft from the house, as if someone, or something, had just jumped off the roof, landed, then hopped towards the pond, and simply disappeared forever.

My mind drifted back to the tale Old Medon had told us about Giant's Hole and Satan's Hoof, and the High Priest, Lord of the Underworld. It all came flooding back to me. If you have read "The Spirit of Adventure" about my life as a young boy, you will recall that strange night we sat around the old pine table, the oil lamp swinging to and fro, the flickering candles giving off ghostly shadows, as a group of us listened to Old Medon's progressive tale of mystical goings-on on one moonlit night, from way back in the passage of time. Her left eye kept us transfixed whilst her right drifted and moved slowly around, as if in another world. She continued with her tale from long, long ago.

'Hurry! Hurry!' Satan's voice echoed, 'Before the Priest returns.' Out of the cavernous opening of Giant's Hole poured those two-legged creatures; a man's image for their upper body, whilst their lower half resembled some kind of beast with hooves in place of feet. Oh, yes! That was a night to remember. In the morning as the villagers emerged from their houses they were confronted with strange unidentifiable hoof-marks of some two-legged creature imprinted firmly in the blanket of snow which had fallen overnight. The prints were everywhere; they strode across the ground, over the roofs of houses and along the top of walls. The amazing thing though, about these prints, is that they all ended up in the stream that led into Peak Cavern. There were no returning tracks. The local folk were at a loss to suggest a natural explanation; if they were water animals, why did they have hooves, and yet, if they were land animals why did they head into the water, then disappear? These country folk were convinced that these were the devil's hoof-marks left in the snow...

Looking at the prints in our front garden, I thought to myself, it can't be one of Mr Wheeler's cows from the farm across the road. If so, it must have flown across, as there were no other signs of the snow being disturbed apart from the three sets of prints heading towards the edge of the pond. I shouted Eric over.

'Hey, what do you think of these then?' I asked, pointing through the window to the marks in the snow.

'That's most odd,' he replied, 'It looks as though something has just jumped off the roof and hopped over to the pond.'

Well, we nipped out smartish through the front door, had a good look around, and confirmed that there were definitely no other marks anywhere. I ventured further and looked up at the roof. There were no hoof prints, but it did look as though something had skidded down from the ridge to the gutter, then stopped.

Days later, when the snow had melted, sure enough in the soft lawn still clearly visible were, yes, you've guessed it, three pairs of hoof marks!

Another time, a strange thing appeared in our pond.

Glenys and I had just arrived home after a shopping trip to Newport. Whilst putting the shopping away something shiny and reflective in the garden caught my eye. Being the inquisitive type I wandered out to have a look, and there, much to my surprise and amazement, right in the middle of our Isle of Wight shaped pond was a very large, silvery fish, just starring up at me with those big round fishy eyes. In fact, it was a very large carp. Tony, our son, came dashing round the corner.

'Dad! Dad! I've caught a fish!'

So the tale goes, he was fishing in the large pond at the bottom of Stag Lane and caught this three and a half pound carp. He lashed it to his carrier on his bike, and with rod in one hand he rode like the clappers up the lane to get his prize fish home, as he wanted to make a glass display case to put it in, with his name engraved on a nice brass plate fixed to the outside.

Now, I was in a bit of a fix; I didn't think it would be too good an idea to place a dead carp in a glass case, (just imagine the pong!), but I didn't want to spoil his enthusiasm. So I came up with an idea. We laid the poor, now-dead, fish down on a piece of plywood and covered it with fibreglass gel-coat, and then proceeded to make a mould over the top. After it had set, Tony dug the fishy remains out and cleaned the mould thoroughly.

Do you know, when we made the final cast of the fish, it showed every scale, the eyes, the mouth, the fins, it was a perfect replica of the fish. We made a frame to go around it and fitted a strip light behind.

Wow! You should have seen Tony's face when we mounted it behind his bed. He was so proud of his very own fish.

Needless to say, when word got around, there was a great demand from my classes at school, to make one of these unique bedside lamps!

Talking about fishing, I took Tony on the River Medina once in one of the fibreglass dinghies that were in full production in my workshop at school.

'Dad! Dad! I've caught one!' he shouted as he jerked up his rod. The fish left the water like a missile from a submarine. Whoosh! Up in the air, and right over our heads to land about twenty feet behind the boat. Splash! And that was the last we saw of his own, personal, flying fish. Tony just looked at me, with tears running down his cheeks.

'I've lost it. It's just gone' he whispered.

But Vanda made up for it on another of our fishing trips...

Tony had a new rod for his birthday, and one warm sunny day we decided to go to Totland Bay and fish from the pier. We packed a picnic and set off early. Tony had dug a tin full of rag-worm bait. We arrived in thick sea mist, to find that the West Wight Fishing Competition was in progress on the pier. So, we found a space between two hardy fishermen, and settled in. Well, we sat there and sat there, with not a single bite; and neither had any of the other fishermen.

Suddenly Vanda shouted out.

'I've caught a fish, Dad!'

The other fishermen realising the excitement leapt up and dashed over to Vanda.

'What bait are you using?' they enquired. Taken aback by all the commotion, Vanda just stared at all the weather-beaten faces which had crowded around her. Taking her attention back to her catch, she proceeded to pull her crab line up. Firmly attached to the hook, was a nice-sized colourful wrass.

'Don't touch it, kid,' one of the fishermen said, 'Leave it to us, those spikes are poisonous!' They wrapped a cloth around it and removed the hook.

Out came a little pocket scale and they carefully weighed the fish, jotting down the details with great enthusiasm.

'Right now, little girl, what bait did you use?'

Vanda, still looking a little confused, said 'Do you mean, what did I put on the hook?'

'Yes! Yes! What did you put on the hook?' they asked leaning forwards eagerly.

'Oh, just a bit of banana skin,' she replied.

'Banana skin?' they all repeated, stunned.

'And, er, have you got any left?' one of them asked.

'Yes, a little. It's on the floor over there,' Vanda said, pointing.

Well, you should have seen the mad scramble to get a piece of that "wonder bait"!

It's interesting to note that the wrass was the only fish caught that day, and Vanda was the overall winner of all the classes; the largest, the heaviest and the "Most Unusual Fish" caught. She looked a little bewildered with all the attention, until they realised that she wasn't even entered into the competition! Ah, well. You win some, you lose some!

But that day, sitting on the pier, watching the sea mist just melt away in the blazing heat of the midday sun, I was confident and determined that I could win the large prize bottle of champagne.

14

Ole, O-Flippin-Le!

All work stopped; it was time for a cuppa. The lads, well really I should say men, perched on the stools around the large bench in my workshop. This was the first term of adult evening classes. This was the time for tales and yarns. The chaps from White's Shipyard would tell us about the near mishaps when launching some of the larger ships. The British Hovercraft gang would always have a joke or two, keeping us in fits of laughter. Then, of course, we had the real Isle of Wight farmers who always managed to top any tale that the others came out with.

I had just come back from Spain, and had been to my first bull fight. Half my class had never even ventured off the Island and were fascinated as I told them of the funny happenings in and around the bull ring. Then Old Bert interrupted.

'Ah, there's no need to go to foreign places to see a bull fight. If yer can afford the fare to Newport on market day tha'll see all the bull fights yer want! It's like this yer see, me and ta lad were after some sheep, and were leaning on railings, weighing up some bonny young lambs, when the large hammer on the side of the big, silver, outdoor telephone bell started to vibrate against the hard steel dome – Bring! Bring! The noise made me and lad jump, even tuther farm hands looked up in surprise.'

This was the Island's famous cattle market, held in the middle of Newport. (In actual fact, Morrison's supermarket now stands on this very site; quite appropriate really, if you've ever attempted to buy a weeks shopping on a Saturday afternoon!)

'The cattle truck at the far end of the stalls had its board down, and one of the dozy farm lads was gently coaxing a fine huge, well it was massive, white bull down the ramp, as the bell started to ring the startled bull reared its head up and, much to the horror of the young lad, suddenly lurched forward. The rope attached to the large ring in the bull's nose jerked forward and out of the young chap's hand. That was it, the freed white bull charged down between the aisles. By this time the bull was hurtling down right towards me and ta lad. Before you could say Jack Robinson, the lad leapt over the railings into one of the sheep pens. I'll tell you what, one look at that bull, and I soon made my mind up too. I was over the railings like some athlete in the Olympic Games, only to land, rather ungracefully, on my backside in a lump of hay. Well, the lad burst out laughing as I stood up, looking more like a scarecrow than his dad.' He continued.

'You should have seen the chaos that bull caused; there were people running in all directions. The bull, now totally out of control, came down the centre aisle, with its head weaving from side to side, and the horns clattering and grazing against the railings making a horrible din. There were folks hiding behind the safety of the railings, or peeping out dubiously from behind bales of hay stacked at each side. Nobody made an attempt to stand and face the onslaught of that bull in full flight. As it neared the entrance to the market, a gentleman farmer from middle of ta Island suddenly stepped out from one side. He was very well dressed, in his Saville Row tweed jacket, twill trousers, highly polished brown boots, and he had a Tyrolean-type trilby with a spray of tiny coloured feathers attached to the olive green band around the hat. His bright yellow tie stood out against the red tartan of his shirt. Proper posh he was. His red, stern, round, weather-beaten face, with thick bushy eyebrows and old-fashioned side whiskers, was, I thought, no match for this mad, frightened bull with its hooves pounding, slipping and sliding on the wet cobbles. This 'ere farmer then reached out and picked up the galvanised shiny lid of a nearby dustbin, and started to beat on it loudly with his walking stick. Bang! Bang! Bang! As the bull approached in its headlong dash, the farmer thrust the bin lid towards the animal. It stopped dead in its tracks, skidded and went down onto its front legs. It bent its head and touched the bin lid which was at floor level. Steam rose from the bull's back as the farmer, very slowly, bent down and picked up the rope which was still attached to the large, shiny, brass ring in the bull's nose. He carefully patted the bull, and then started to whisper in its ear. The bull shook its head and stood up quickly. The posh chap then rubbed the bull's nose gently and after a few moments turned and led the bull back up the lane towards the cattle truck. We all stood aghast, still hiding behind our barriers. Then a couple of farmers started to clap their hands. This was followed by another couple of farmers, and the noise increased as everyone else joined in too. That brave, gentleman farmer carried on his walk, as if he did that kind of thing every day; he neither looked to the left, nor the right, he just carried straight on ahead. How do I know it was a Saville Row jacket? Well, you can always tell, as they have four shiny buttons on each sleeve, or so I'm told! See what I mean, there's no need to go to a foreign land to see a bull fight; just catch yer bus to Newport on market day!'

Now let me take you to Barcelona, on a hot sunny Sunday afternoon. There were throngs of people heading for the bull ring, and cars, coaches and horse drawn carriages everywhere. It was totally chaotic, as General Franco's special police waved their truncheons in the air, and blew their whistles, in an attempt to control the traffic. They had the unenviable job of keeping the crowds and traffic moving around the huge bull ring.

A large, black car, with GB plates, pulled up right on the crossing. One of the policemen shot across and shouted, 'Move!' The driver's window wound down slowly.

'Keep yer 'air on mate! I'm just dropping me pals off; they're going to the bullfight.'

The policeman lifted his baton.

'Move!' he shouted once again.

This little dispute had managed to draw quite a crowd of spectators by now, including ourselves, and people moved in nearer to the old Brit car.

'Hey!' shouted the driver, 'Put that bloody thing down, and give us a chance to get out!'

With that, the policeman brought the truncheon down – wallop – right in the middle of the bonnet of the car. That was it, the little cockney driver, completely red-faced, jumped out of his car with his fists up in the air, like an old time prize fighter.

On seeing this, most of us were now reduced to fits of laughter; there he stood, all 4'-6" of manhood, in his string vest, wide baggy shorts held up with bright blue braces, knee-high black socks kept up with two elastic bands, and a pair of over-sized sandals which slopped about on his feet. The broad shouldered riot cop towered above him, like a huge giant. I thought the one and only word he knew in English was 'Move!' Then he surprised us all.

'Move! Now!' he shouted down at the little chap, as he raised his truncheon once again, and brought it down right on top of the car.

The little bloke now went completely berserk as he looked at the dent in his car.

'I'm going to report you to the British Consul. Yer can't do that, I'm a British Citizen!'

Up rose the truncheon once more. Briefly weighing up his, somewhat limited, options, the little chap speedily hopped back into his car, and banged his door shut. He drove off, bravely yelling through his window.

'You've not 'eard the last of this mate!' and he continued driving, on the wrong side of the road, weaving in and out of the oncoming traffic. The cop, staring after him, touched his helmet with one finger, and hunched his shoulders.

'Loco! Loco!' he muttered.

The crowd shouted 'Ole!', and slowly dispersed as they headed for the entrance of the bull ring.

On this beautiful, warm Sunday evening, Owen who came from Cardiff, Bert from Doncaster and me settled ourselves down on the cushions we had hired for 100 pesetas. I had no idea what to expect from the evening's entertainment. A lady, who was very smartly dressed, sat down next to me. She introduced us to her husband Juan, and said that her name was Maria.

'Is this your first time to the *Torear*?' she asked.

I, looking slightly surprised, replied, 'Ah, no comprehend.'

'Your first time to a bull fight?' she asked again.

'Ah, si! Si!' I said finally understanding.

'Would you like me to explain what it's all about?' she said. I nodded and Bert and Owen leant forward, all ears, as it was their first time in Spain.

We had all come with our wives, on a week's holiday to Malgrat on the Costa Brava, with a Northern travel agent, "Lords of Accrington"; their motto was 'Live like a Lord'. We were staying at a five star hotel with all mod cons. Flying from Luton to Perpignan in France in an ex-RAF, 30 seater

Dakota, we then had a long journey by coach to our hotel. I bet you'll never guess how much this full package tour cost? It was £17 per person per week!

'Well,' Maria continued, 'You see, Derek, it is not a *bull fight*, that is the English translation. It is not a sport; you must agree that you would have to be loco to, er…'.

'Sorry, to but in,' I said 'But what does *loco* mean? We heard the policeman outside say it as he described a little Englishman'.

'Sorry, my English is not very good. *Loco* means, er, mad, insane. Yes, that's the word. You would have to be insane to stand and fight a 1200 pound powerful, angry beast. The objective of the exercise is, in fact, just the opposite – to avoid a brutal confrontation by using the brain using your intelligence, grace and elegance. As you know, in sport, the main objective is to win. In bullfighting satisfaction is achieved by triumph of human cunning over brute force. The bullfight fans scream "*Ole*" not just because the matador has won, but because of the manner, form, grace, wit, and dexterity of the toreador performing a *veronica*, a *natural* or any other pass with the *capote* or *muleta*, by which the cape he holds in his hand is known. Do you understand what I am trying to say, Derek?'

'Yes, I'm with you so far!' I replied.

'The trophies awarded to the bullfighters are often nothing more than the spectators show of emotion. It is not unusual for a matador who only performed one artistic move, in the entire event, to be the true winner of the day – as it's the quality of that one move that makes the day for all of us. A famous matador once defined bullfighting as a type of dramatic ballet dance with death. As he would in dancing, the bullfighter must control his movements maintaining the rhythm, not of music, but of danger. On stage a 'faux-pas' means an interruption of artistic flow; in the bullfighting arena a faux-pas could mean the death of the bullfighter! You see, the relationship between the bullfighter and the bull is based on the distance between them. The matador must always be the creator and master of this relationship, instead of allowing the bull a chance to take command. The bull, by his very nature, attacks everything that moves. The man must always stand tall, exhibiting elegance and poise, whilst moving the cape in such a way that the bull will pursue it without ever catching it, and, at the same time should direct the attacking animal as close to his body as he dare; not so close that he has to make a jump or a quick side step to avoid being injured or killed, because that would ruin the flowing movements between the man and beast ballet. Anyone can bullfight if he knows the technique, and has the courage! The difficulty lies in being able to bullfight like Belmonte or Manolette, as if the bulls are made of glass and one was afraid to break them.'

The music blared out.

'Ah, hah. This is it, Derek.'

The gates opened and the grand parade entered the ring. Everybody involved in the fight presented themselves to the president and then to the public. As they left the ring, two '*alguacilillos*' on horseback, rode over to the president's box, looked up and symbolically asked for the keys to the '*Puerta de Los Toriles*' – the Gate of the Bulls. Behind that door the bulls were waiting.

When the door opened the first bull entered the ring. Everybody gasped; it was a massive, powerful, big, black bull, with wicked-looking curved horns. It pounded right across the arena, swerved around and then headed for the pink and yellow cape. The bullfighter made a few passes then casually sidled behind the protective escape barrier.

Maria informed us that the bullfight consists of three parts called '*tercios*' (thirds). In the first *tercio*, the bullfighter uses the '*capote*', a large pink and yellow cape. Then the two picadors enter on horseback, armed with a lance. The bull attacks them and they drive the lance into the back of the bull. This weakens the bull, not that I noticed any difference at this stage.

Then the bugle sounded for the second *tercio*; this is the *La Suerte de Banderillas*. Three *banderillos* must run towards the charging bull, leap up in the air and to one side at the last moment, and stick a pair of dart-like *banderillas* into the bull's back. Now, to me that move needed great courage and skill (…as I was personally to find out the following year).

In the third, and final, *Suerte Suprema* the bullfighter uses a small red cape draped on a stick held in his left hand. He then shows us his skill and courage as he masters and dominates the bull. With the bull's head down, touching the cape, and weaving back and forth in and around the bullfighter, we were hypnotised by this ballet between man and beast. Finally the ballet ends with the bullfighter facing the bull, the cape drops down, the bullfighter takes his sword, and leaning between the vicious looking horns of the bull, he drives his curved sword deep into the base of the bull's neck. There is deathly silence during this final act as everybody holds their breath. The bull slumps down dead and the bullfighter turns around and raises his hat towards the president. The crowds then go mad.

'Ole, ole, ole!' they shout, as they throw flowers and handkerchiefs into the arena. The brave bulls are pulled around to do a full circuit, by two horses, before being taken to the slaughter house where their meat is then distributed to the poor.

According to Maria, if the bullfighter puts up a poor show, then instead of flowers and handkerchiefs, he is bombarded with the hired cushions from the angry crowd!

Now I must tell you about the bullfight that took place the following year. We had all eaten our fill at the barbeque, and quenched our thirst with gallons of local Spanish wine, when the trumpets blasted out, denoting it was time for the bullfight. Well, it was really a 'mock' bullfight, as no bulls were actually killed. Glenys, myself, Della, Tony and Vanda followed the crowd to the entrance of the small bullring. On a stand outside were large green bottles of sparkling champagne – these were the prizes for any young budding bullfighter who was prepared, and who had the courage, to enter and fight the wild, deadly, young bulls awaiting beyond the gates of the arena.

I thought to myself, well I've seen how it's done at a real bullfight I reckon I could do that! Picking up a pair of *banderillas*, I fancied my chance of running at the oncoming charging bull, doing a quick leap sideward and at the same time place the darts in the back of the bull, as it hurtled past me like an express train.

The slightly tipsy matador, a big lad from Durham, stood with the pink and yellow cape awaiting the opening of the gates. The trumpets sounded and the crowd leaned forward in anticipation. The gates opened and a young lad dashed out pushing a bull's head on a trolley in front of him. The crowd roared with laughter and the bullfighter let out a great sigh of relief, as he went through a farcical comic routine of fighting the supposed ferocious bull.

'Ole, ole ole!' the drunken crowd hollered, as the bull departed.

The trumpets blared again. What now, we thought, here we go again!

But, much to our surprise and horror, what seemed to us a 'huge' young bull, with large curving horns, suddenly came belting into the arena. The bullfighter waved his cape about and the bull turned and charged him. It hit the very shocked bullfighter head on, and lifted him clean into the air. The bull then continued racing around the ring. The stunned bullfighter staggered out with blood flowing down his leg where the bull's horns had gorged him.

Funnily enough, instead of cheers and shouts from the audience, there was only silence. Then a voice could be heard.

'Tom. Tom. Are yer areet, lad?' Tom, the brave matador, looked up and smiled.

'I'm ok, Da. But, never again. Never again.'

The trumpets sounded once again, and I found myself pushed into the arena. Luckily, I was prepared, I was not going to be taken by surprise like poor, unsuspecting Tom. With my darts held high and at the ready I shouted to the bull. It turned, snorted, stamped its hooves on the ground, lowered its head and charged across the ring towards me. As it came near I could feel its hot breath snorting into my face. I will never forget the smell of that steaming, sweaty bull in my nostrils!

This was the moment of truth; I attempted to leap up into the air with my *banderillas* held high, but for a split second nothing happened. I remained rooted to the spot. What I didn't realise, was that the sand in the bull ring was soft and about 9" deep. As I pressed down to make my impressive, artistic leap, my feet just sank further down into the sand until I couldn't even lift them, never mind leap into the air!

Bang! The bull hit me square in the chest, and sent me and my *banderillas* flying across the soft sand.

And, there was something else I didn't know until later, this bull did this every day of the week, as the coaches brought new and unsuspecting wine-soaked budding bullfighters to show off their skill and daring in the blazing heat of the Spanish midday sun!

Well, yes, for my bravery and stupidity, I was awarded a large bottle of fizzy, warm so-called "Champagne" – which I found out later you could buy at a stall around the corner for the large amount of sixpence! Ole, o-flippin-le!

I am afraid that was the end of my career as a bullfighter. Nevertheless, I am always amazed and surprised at the resourcefulness of the true skilled matadors – along with the kids in my class...

15

How To Catch More Fish – In Comfort!

Having experienced the results of my bright idea in letting the lads make crossbows, I decided I would stick to something less offensive.

'Right, lads. Gather round the bench.'

You could see it in their faces; 'Oh, what's Sir going to make us do now?'

'Instead of making practice joints, which are usual at this stage, I've decided, as you are a really good class, that you can have a go at making one of these,' and I produced the famous camp stool, which had been so popular at Winton, my previous school. The stool consisted of two frames bolted together. It meant making eight "mortice and tenon" joints, shaping the legs and rounding the top edge, to allow the colourful canvas to stretch across the top to make the seat.

Silence! Then one boy spoke up, 'But, Sir, we don't want to make that, none of us go camping!'

Taking the stool I put it back on the floor behind my bench. Then with great gusto and with a flourish, I brought the stool back up and put it back on the bench and said with enthusiasm, 'How would you like to catch more fish – and in comfort, with this amazing folding fishing stool?!'

All hands shot up.

'Oh, yes! Can we try it out, Sir?' After, every boy in the

class had sat on it, they gave the stool their wholehearted approval!

'Fantastic, Sir!'

'Yer, I'll have one of them!'

I thought to myself, 'thank goodness for that', as I had already bought enough wood for the whole class. This is not teaching, I thought, this is psychology, this is capturing the imagination, this is about selling and marketing and gentle persuasion – and, boy, I've still a lot to learn!

Isn't it funny, you always get one; in a class full of boys there's always, without fail, going to be one who doesn't go fishing or camping. He stood there in front of me, a frail looking lad with NHS wire spectacles that kept slipping down his pale freckled nose. When he pushed them up with his forefinger they seemed to settle at a 45 degree angle, one lens on the eyebrow and the other down on his cheek. He had bright red, wavy hair, neatly creased trousers and a spotless white apron.

'Please, Sir, I don't want to make a fishing stool.'

A lad at the back of the workshop shouted, 'Take no notice of Spotty, Sir. Don't let him stop us making our fantastic fishing stools.'

Then Spotty's mate also ambled to the front, the usual round-faced tubby boy. They were a typical pair of harmless, nice lads; one small, pale and frail, whilst his mate was large, and rosy cheeked with bright blue eyes. (You also, of course, got the school bullies. They hung around in groups of three. One was the instigator and the other two his henchmen. It was amazing, but every year you used to see this pattern developing).

'So, you don't want to make the fishing stool, eh?' I asked.

'Er, no Sir,' said Tubby. 'Neither of us go fishing or camping.'

'Right, okay then. Not to worry.' You should have seen the relief on their faces. 'So, then, what do you do in your spare time?'

'Well,' ventured Tubby, 'we, er, watch telly and play games and things.'

'And, do you sit on the settee to watch TV?' I asked.

'Er, yes.'

'And do you put your feet up to watch TV?'

'Oh no, Sir,' Spotty said. 'My mum wouldn't allow that!'

With that I put the stool back behind my bench, and then brought it up again and placed it on the worktop.

'Now, how would you two like to make a television footstool? Just imagine yourselves sitting back comfortably on your settee, watching your favourite programme, with your feet up on your own television footstool!'

'Oh yes, Sir!' they said. 'Can we make one of these instead of that fishing stool? Please, Sir!'

'Well, I think we can manage that, although you'll alter my marking system!'

'Oh, thank you, Sir,' they said, and departed back to their benches wearing huge grins across their faces.

By the end of the term the two frames were made, varnished and bolted together. Of course, the two television footstools had also been stained and polished.

The best part was still to come. I brought in a full set of name stamps. This was the highlight of the session; actually stamping their own name permanently into the frame of the stool, no silly pencil marks for their masterpieces of craftsmanship!

Do you know, we didn't have one failure. Of course, there was always one who cut through his tenon by mistake or split the mortice joint. But two more pieces of wood would somehow miraculously appear, and they were given a second chance. No failures in this class.

'Now, next week, you are all to bring in a piece of canvas, 18 inches by 14 inches. I will supply the round-headed tacks to fix it to the stool. You two, making the television stools, will bring in a nice piece of material to match in with your settees.' They all marched out with a piece of paper tucked in their top pockets with the size of canvas required.

Thursday at half past one, the lads lined up outside the door. Not one lad had forgotten to bring a piece of brightly coloured striped canvas. They were at it like little beavers, helping each other to fix the canvas onto the stools. At break time I allowed them to stay in to finish them off. When I came back into the classroom they were all sitting on their stools in a huge circle facing each other, going through the motions of casting their fishing lines.

'Sir, they're fantastic!' they chorused as they saw me. After having them marked, they couldn't wait to get along to Cowes seafront with their fishing gear and stools.

I decided on my way home I would drive along the seafront to see how they were getting on, thinking to myself that at least it makes a change from dealing with irate parents at the battle of the Crossbow Warriors! Fishing stools must be the most harmless and creative woodwork project that one could imagine. But, oh no, it wasn't to be that easy...

There they were all the little fishermen sitting on their stools, fishing away quite happily. At the same time a group of holiday makers from North Yorkshire were wandering up and down the length of the seafront, in an attempt to find a comfortable deckchair to rest in, without the usual 18" x 14" hole in the middle of the canvas!

I overheard one of the Yorkshire chaps muttering and swearing, complaining that 'These Isle of Wight deckchairs are useless and look more like commodes, than flaming deckchairs!'

At that moment Smithy shouted out.

'I've caught one!'

Cedric, the big Yorkshire fellow, dashed over, as Smithy reeled in a nice 4lb plaice. I backed away as the onlooker pointed to the "magic stool". Cedric tapped Smithy on the shoulder, and realising the source of the canvas, pointed to the deckchair as he burst out laughing. Cedric's wife ran over with a plastic bag and the boy dropped the wriggling fish into it. Cedric was highly delighted at the thought of the lovely fresh fish they were going to enjoy for their tea. Smithy pocketed the money that Cedric handed him, and sat back on his stool with a huge grin on his face. He re-baited the hook and cast it out once more.

I turned around and made a hasty retreat before anyone saw me. Everyone was happy – but I couldn't speak for the deckchair attendant, could I?!

Thousands now own their very own fantastic fishing stool who never thought they could or would.

STOP THE PRESS! – STOP THE PRESS! – STOP THE PRESS! – March 2005

How about this? I've just watched Adam Hart-Davies presenting the Open University programme 'What the ancients did for us', exploring the legacy of the Ancient Egyptians, whose inventiveness included boat building and dam construction. Among the tombs they found beautiful furniture. Included in the collection was a fine example of a 'folding stool'! He states that these were very popular, especially when the Egyptians were on the move. Now, wait for it, on the walls of the tombs were pictures depicting the folding stool being used as a fishing stool, along the banks of the Nile, over 5000 years ago!!! I wonder what the Ancient Egyptian deckchair man had to say about that!

16

First Come First Served!

'How much? You must be joking! Well, how much for two? Yes. Can I meet you on site in half an hour?' and with that, I put the phone down.

The old army camp adjoining St Mary's Hospital was desolate and deserted. The rain dripping off the broken asbestos gutters formed green mouldy puddles along each side of the long timber huts.

I spotted Jim, the demolition contractor, sheltering in the old guard hut at the far end of the camp. As I approached he waved and pointed to the two huts next to the main road. I went over to the first one; on the corner, down at floor level, I noticed a bit of wet rot on the ship-lap boarding. I gave it my usual back-kick and the board crumpled up and fell off onto the pavement.

'Oh, dear me. Jim, how much did you say you wanted for this firewood?'

He looked down at the rotten wood and said '£30 each'.

'Thirty Pounds!' I gasped.

'Well, that's what I got for all the others,' he said.

'You must be kidding,' I continued, 'if you expect anyone to pay thirty pounds each for these two! I'll tell you what, I'll give you forty five pounds for both of them.'

'Na, I can't let 'em go for that. But, seeing as you want two,

I'll let you have 'em for fifty five pounds the pair.'

By this time we were both wet through; he only had a pair of bib and brace overalls on over his short sleeve shirt and I could see he wanted to get rid of the last two huts, and me, so he could get home for his tea! I looked him straight in the eyes.

'Well, Jim, I can see you are a fair and reasonable businessman, so let's make a deal. I'll come up £5 and you come down £5, and we'll shake on fifty pounds, cash in hand, to get rid of them.'

He stood there with the water running off the back of his cap and dripping straight down the inside of his shirt. Then taking one hand out of his pocket, he spat on it and held it out. I spat on my hand too, and we shook hands; with that, the deal was clinched. (The old wizard had taught me well!)

Twenty five pounds each for a 60 foot hut – not a bad day's work.

'Well, where's the cash, then?' asked Jim.

'Oh, I don't carry that sort of money with me, but if you can come on site on Saturday at 12 p.m. I'll be here waiting for you with your money.'

To be quite honest I didn't even have £25 cash. So, with fingers crossed, I put an advert in the Isle of Wight County Press, "Asbestos, heavy duty, roofing sheets for sale. 6 ft long, 10 shillings each. 8 ft long, 15 shillings each. Call on site (address) 9 a.m. Saturday morning. First come, first served!"

How it all came about was that I needed some heavy timber to build an extension and balcony at the back of our house. Also Gurnard Scouts and Guides needed a new hut. So, when I spotted the advert for the ex-army huts, I thought to myself, I could kill two birds with one stone if I shape myself. I then phoned Eric and Dot Chivers, friends of ours, who like us, also had a son in Scouts. Our Tony was in the Scouts, Della in the Guides and Vanda in the Brownies. I put my idea to Eric, and straight away he said, 'Go for it! I'll give you a lift to dismantle them.'

That Saturday morning I arrived on the site at 9 a.m. to find a long queue assembled comprising of tractors with trailers, two builders lorries, and vans of all descriptions, not realising they were all waiting for me! Within ten minutes I was up on the roof with my crowbar and a flat iron plate. One chap said he would have all the ridge tiles. I said he could have the lot for £15, if he took them all off himself. No problem, he was up my ladder like a flash, and the fifteen quid went into my back pocket.

At 12 o'clock sharp Jim turned up, just as the last tractor was leaving. The roof was completely stripped and I had £52 in my pocket. I slid down the ladder, paid Jim the £50 I owed him. I still had £2 profit – plus, all the timber off the first hut, weather boarding from the outside and beautiful pine cladding from the inside, thousands of 1" thick floor boards, dozens of 20 ft lengths of 6"x 2" floor joists, what seemed to be 'hundreds' of 5" x 1.5" framing and roof timbers.

Then to cap it all, I also had roof trusses, which I ended up selling for £80 to a farmer that same Saturday and another chap took all the window frames to use as cold frames on his allotment, and paid me the £25 cash in hand! From the first hut I had made a grand total of £327!

With the help of family and friends, within a fortnight I had completed my extension at home.

Peter and Tony were busy knocking all the nails out of the timber. Thirteen year old Peter Hewitt came down to stay with us for a holiday, from Lancashire. Some holiday; he worked like the clappers, and soon became a complete DIY expert.

Della and Vanda had the job of collecting all the nails up out of the grass. The garden looked like a timber yard. All through the orchard were stacks and neat piles of wood – the girls were in charge of that department too. Any wood they couldn't move was soon shifted by Peter and Tony, as they kegged it onto the right pile.

Glenys was mixing mortar whilst I built the stone-walling around the garden patio.

When Glenys and I sat down for a cup of tea, the rest of the gang, who still had so much energy, took the time-out to swing like monkeys from the trapeze ropes hanging down from the old mature fruit trees in the orchard.

I must admit I couldn't have got through all the alterations we did on the house and garden without the help and support from all our family and friends; it was real teamwork and everyone was so enthusiastic and interested in what we were doing. It was quite funny really, we had lots of our friends from the North coming down to stay with us that year, but by some queer coincidence they all seemed to finish up with either a hammer or a shovel in their hands!

Of course, it wasn't all work. At the end of the day we would pack up a picnic and end up boating, canoeing or fishing down at Gurnard Creek, until well after the sun had set. We would all stand watching, spellbound and in complete silence, as the blazing red summer sun sank ever so slowly into the inky blue sea; down, down, until just a thin gold light shone on the surface of the water. Then with a sigh it was gone and the sky would become a blaze of red, pink and gold as it reflected on the small puffy clouds gently drifting across the Solent. It was amazing. Nobody spoke a word during this daily ritual. I am still enthralled by the splendour of the sunsets that we have had the privilege to enjoy in the company of family and good friends.

A while later, Les Scott, a friend from up the road, helped me to build a large double garage for his boss at Cowes using the leftover materials – another £80, split between us. And, do you know, that garage still stands today and is in everyday use. You can't get solid seasoned wood like that these days. (By the way, the only rotten piece of wood I found was the one that received my famous back-kick!).

Oh, and I mustn't forget the final deal, I sold an apple-barrel full of bent nails to an old chap for 2/6, who spent a good part of a week sitting in our garden straightening them out. I think it cost Glenys more than 2/6 in cups of tea to keep him going. Anyway, he was a very happy chappy, especially when I offered to give him, and his barrel full of nails, a lift home in the back of my car at the end of the week!

At school I had started a building course which included plumbing, electrical, carpentry and bricklaying. The brickwork was done outside in the yard adjoining my workshop. It became so popular that the dads enrolled for my evening classes, as they wanted to do the same course as their sons. Naturally, the evening courses were only run during the winter months, when rain meant no bricklaying! Problem? No problem! I supplied enough timber to build a huge covered-in area. The boys built it as part of the carpentry course and, lo and behold, were out in all kinds of weather practising their bricklaying skills under the powerful flood lights supplied by the British Hovercraft Corporation.

Goodness knows how far and wide the timber from my ex-army hut went. Some of the timber was cut and planed to use in the construction of the camp/fishing/television stools and I do know that some of the asbestos roofing sheets went towards building a workshop in Ventnor, and the roof trusses ending up as a tractor shed in Freshwater... but I've often wondered what became of all those nails in the apple-barrel!

The second hut was dismantled in sections, and Bill, another friend down our road, borrowed a tractor and trailer to cart the hut up to Gurnard. Now, Bill had an interesting job – he was a barber at the hospital. One day, he untied his canvas case and showed me the tools of his trade. I was expecting to see combs and scissors, but to my surprise he produced three wicked-looking cut-throat razors, a small one, a medium size one and a large one, all with beautifully engraved ivory handles. Then he produced a shaving mug, soap and a brush.

'Well, where's your comb and scissors, then?' I naively asked.

'Oh' he replied, 'I'm not that sort of barber – I don't give haircuts! My job is to shave the patients, men and women, in readiness for their operation. I can tell you a tale, or two, about the so-called blondes who have had the pleasure of meeting my razor. Yer know what I mean, a different colour top and bottom...'

'Okay' I butted in, 'Yes, I know what you mean!' and he started laughing his head off.

'Aye, there's many a lass who turns and blushes when they see me coming towards them carrying me little box of tricks!'

Bill could turn his hand to anything. In his back garden, in the poultry shed, stood a massive petrol driven circular saw with a three foot diameter saw blade. I gave him a lift to slice down solid oak railway sleepers. The saw cut right through them as if they were made of balsa wood. And, boy, did the sparks fly when the blade met an unsuspected piece of gravel chipping. It was one of those sparks that managed to set light to the sawdust lying around the base of the huge saw. Then the petrol caught fire and, whoosh, the whole shed went up in flames. There were sparks and chickens flying in all directions. That was a night to remember!

Talking about a night to remember, I bet a few lads from school will never ever forget that night they spent alone on a desolate, dark, isolated Welsh mountainside...

17

'When The Saints Go Marching In'

As we drove the dormobiles around the bend there was an almighty gasp from behind. The view in front was absolutely stunning. There, Snowdon, in all its glory, seemed to appear from nowhere. The back cloth of vivid blue sky enhanced the white mantle of the snow-capped mountain range.

'Crikey! We don't have to climb that do we, Sir?' one of the boys whispered.

I just nodded my head.

'Will we need oxygen, Sir?' another lad piped up.

This was the first time the majority of the group had seen a real mountain.

I had arranged with the Headmaster that I would take a group of boys climbing and mountaineering in North Wales this coming Easter. I put the word out and before I knew it I had sixteen names, with parent's permission, on my list. I'd had a chat with Lew Cox, the head of the P.E. department, and no way was he going to miss out on a trip like this! He organised the transportation and the hiring of the two dormobiles from a firm in Southampton and planned the route and journey to our camp site at Gwern Gof Isaf farm lying at the foot of my favourite mountain, Tryfan, in the Ogwen Valley.

I was responsible for all the climbing and camping gear we would require, together with route planning on the rock climbs and mountains. I had over twenty years experience among the peaks of North Wales, and during seven of those years Tommy and I had assisted in Mountain Rescue based at Ogwen Cottage. This was my stomping ground where I felt comfortable and at home in all weather conditions including sun, rain, mist, snow and ice; and this is where I wanted to share my experience with the young lads in our charge.

Before any of the lads were accepted they had to learn the theory of mountain craft, reading a compass, tying knots and finally abseiling down the school's 85 foot water tower. It may not have been the Eiger, but to pupils of Cowes Secondary School there were plenty of thrills to be had. This spectacular way of descending down a vertical wall caused quite a stir, with pictures appearing in the local paper, and we even had a mention on the television news that night! All the boys passed the test with flying colours.

Our first stop on the journey was at Lower Swindley Farm in Chippenham. Mr and Mrs Chalk allowed us to sleep in an old barn at the rear of the farm. They gave us a good hearty breakfast before we waved goodbye and continued our journey.

We had a break at the famous Swallow Falls where I had stopped and met old Gwedden on my cycle trip when I was just seventeen years old. The café was still there, but unfortunately it was closed. It brought back memories of stuffing myself with scones, butter, jam and cream, whilst listening to the story of the "Ugly House" and the wonderful tales of the red and white dragons.

There was snow on the mountains as we pitched camp in the failing light. During the night we had a howling gale and I don't think many of the lads had much sleep that first night. Of course, you always get the ones who fall asleep as soon as they zip up their sleeping bags. Zonk! They were out like a light.

Morning was spent cooking breakfast on the primus stoves and drying out all the sleeping bags.

We climbed Tryfan by the Heather Terrace route.

It was quite a struggle battling against the snow and strong winds, but eventually the lads conquered their first ever mountain, and one or two even managed to jump from Adam to Eve, the two large ten foot high monoliths standing on the summit of Tryfan. It is traditional to leap across from one rock to the other. On a fine, dry day it takes a bit of nerve but in these conditions you needed nerves of steel to leap out into space and land firmly on a 4 foot square pinnacle!

With the thought of that lovely roaring log fire in Mrs William's farm house and the scrumptious evening meal that would be waiting and ready for us, believe me, the lads didn't need much persuading to leave Adam and Eve where they belonged and make a hasty retreat, climbing and clambouring over and down the large boulders to the Heather Terrace, then the final scree run to the lower slopes of the mountain.

It's funny how quiet a bunch of starving hungry lads can be as they tuck into a large plate (and when I say large, I mean large, those plates were more like dustbin lids) overflowing with chunks of prime Welsh lamb, roasted potatoes, carrots, cauliflower and sprouts with lashings of rich brown gravy, and not forgetting the white jug of home-made mint sauce. It didn't take long for them to empty that jug, they each thought it was their birthday. Mrs Williams came out of the kitchen with a second huge plate of thick slices of roast lamb which she placed in the centre of the table.

'Help yourselves! There's plenty more where that came from,' she beamed.

By the time the last of the steamed puddings and custard had been demolished, the lads were full to overflowing and slumped back in their chairs. Together with the heat from the flames leaping up the old stove chimney, they soon started to close their eyes and one or two even started to nod off. It took Lew all his time to get the lads to redress in warm clothing to face the cold bleak wind blowing down from the snow-covered mountainside.

In the meantime, back at camp, I had the dixie with my special brew on the boil. The boys dashed into their tents, grabbed their tin mugs, and with comments such as, 'Come on, Sir. It's freezing out here!' they lined up for a ladleful of my hot coffee laced with a special ingredient (a real climbers drink) to warm the very cockles of their hearts.

Within a quarter of an hour all the torches had been turned off in the tents and the lads were fast asleep. All tents, that is, apart from one – Chiverton's! We stood outside whilst they chatted away,

'Hey, did you hear the one about the Englishman, the Irishman, the Welshman and the Scotsman…?' I gave them a warning to shut up and go to sleep. All went quiet.

Then a voice whispered, 'I think they've gone now, carry on with your joke…' They must have been under the illusion that the thin canvas of the tent was soundproof, or that everyone else was deaf!

Ah, well, there was nothing else for it, Lew looked at me and nodded.

'Right, out you come, you lot!' I shouted. There was panic.

'Quick pass me that map,' one of the lads shouted, and grabbing at it he shoved it down the back of his trousers. The other lads looked at him confused.

'This is it,' the lad was heard to say, 'Sir's brought Sammy with him!'

'Oh, no not Sammy,' the other two moaned.

Who is Sammy, you may be asking? Well, when I first

arrived at the school I laid down strict, and I mean strict, safety rules in the workshop. On the first page of their technology notebooks were written a set of safety rules. Anybody breaking or disobeying these rules had a whack from "Sammy the Slipper". It all started when I was teaching in Lancashire. Reg, my head of department, like myself, didn't believe in or like the idea of caning a boy. So he explained the psychology of the slipper. First warn the boy. Then move away, giving him time to put a notebook down his pants. Bring him out to the front of the class, and get him to bend over. You can see the bum-protector sticking out of the top of his trousers, but just ignore it. Whilst the lad touches his toes, you slowly, very slowly, walk over to get the slipper. By this time the lad has blood running into his head and is getting flustered. Slowly coming back, as all the rest of the class stare in anticipation, give the lad a nice sharp tap with the slipper. The noise, as it strikes the notebook, is horrific! Okay, it will sting for a minute or two, but no real harm is done, only to his pride. It works every time, sometimes they even have tears in their eyes before the slipper even lands, but it's okay as long as there's no lasting effect.

It was surprising, but the reputation of Sammy the Slipper was increased and enhanced as it was passed down year after year, especially to the new kids coming into the school. Funnily enough, I never had any discipline problems in my class!

Sammy hung on a nail at the side of the blackboard, and had one day somehow acquired a nice smiling face and a cheeky winking eye. The work was very artistic, I must admit. When it was done I'll never know, but I have my suspicions that my fifth form O'level class whisked it away one break time to return it as "Smiling Sammy". I never said anything about it, and neither did any of the lads. Over the years it became a cult symbol; every time a boy passed it, he would stop, look and wink. Some say it even brought them good luck!

There was a great ceremony one year when our workshops were transferred up to the main school. Two lads made a beautiful miniature coffin out of solid oak, complete with shiny brass handles. Inscribed on the brass plate, by an ex-pupil who by then worked at British Hovercraft, were the words "Keep smiling Sammy. It's your turn next". Sammy was finally laid to rest underneath one of the flagstones in the playground on a warm sunny day in July. R.I.P. Sammy!

Out of the tent the lads tumbled, including the one with a square bulge sticking out at the back of his trousers. Well, it took me all my time to keep my face straight. Lew put on one of his stern looks and ordered them to get into the van. We took the three noisy lads a couple of miles up the road and set them down on the Old Roman Road to walk back to camp. We kept our eyes on them – from a distance! They were shattered and dragged themselves along, moaning and groaning.

'Come on, let's show them we're tough!' we heard one of them say, and with that they burst into song, singing Southampton Football Clubs rally 'When the Saints go marching in' at the top of their voices, as they staggered back into camp. Believe me, there was no more talking after lights out from that moment on.

Excerpts from the school magazine report:

...owing to the effects of Mr Feldon's special brew (coffee) we were thrown out of our tents to walk a distance of two miles for making a lot of noise.

On Wednesday, under the tutelage of Mr Feldon and Mr Cox, one teacher taking two boys up at a time, we got down to the serious business of rock climbing. While two boys were climbing the rest of us practised abseiling with a karabiner, which means that, aided by a rope and standing at 90 degrees to the rock face, the student climber walks down.

The Milestone Buttress was the hardest climbing that we did, and here we found in places a sheer drop. From here the climber looking down below gets a wonderful view of Llyn Ogwen and the mountain and sees the boys down below walking about like ants.

The next day I took a couple of keen boys back to the Milestone Buttress to climb my famous "Soap Gut" (which is classed as Hard Severe). This pushed them to their limit. One came off and fell a couple of feet. I held him firm and two minutes later he was back on and climbed up to my stance. I asked him if he wanted to call it a day.

'No way, Sir!' he said firmly, 'I'm going to master this b****y climb if it kills me!'

(Many years later I met up with the lads, who were by then working on the mainland. They had both been back to Wales, camped below Tryfan and had tackled many of the climbs around the area! They couldn't thank me enough for taking them to their beloved mountain and introducing them to the pleasure and excitement of rock climbing).

Lew took the rest of the lads to Bethesda, a village five miles down the Nant Franchon Pass. Chiverton was, as usual, stuffing himself with chocolate, crisps, sweets and pop. Feeling somewhat 'ill' he laid out on the steps of the old War Memorial in the village square.

'Oh no! Oh no! As if I ever will,' he moaned out loud. Lew went over to him.

'What on Earth's the matter now?' The lad pointed his finger at the message carved in the stone monument from the First World War, "Lest We Forget"!

Excerpts:

...we walked five miles to Bethesda. At Bethesda Chiverton was unable to continue as he was so ill, so he went back on the bus. Others walked back. Woolford was sick just outside Bethseda but bravely continued until given a lift at Llyn Ogwen and the rest of the party were given a lift to Helig, our camp site.

That night a huge brush fire was sweeping down the valley and might threaten the camp and we had to take it in turns all through the night to watch it, but by morning it had burned out. The next night the three groups each had a map reference to find. Mr Feldon's 8 year old son, Tony, joined our group. In the reference we were to find a shepherd's hut but did not succeed and pitched our tents on the side of a mountain.

I was absolutely amazed to see Tony, my eight year old son, coping with the harsh conditions, with the older lads who were doing their Silver Duke of Edinburgh Award on that cold deserted mountainside. He took the Milestone Buttress in his stride although he had to balance on some very fine holds to reach the same height as some of the taller lads. Over the garden wall he came and, much to my surprise, he had to climb down to the small ledge which led to the cave, then scrambling up the chimney at the back of the cave he appeared, puffed out but with a huge grin on his face.

'I've done it, dad! I've done it!'

And he had done it – in great style! He'll never know how proud I was to see his happy smiling face pop up and over that difficult rock face.

The following year Glenys and I took our three children to Butlins Holiday Camp at Pwllheli, North Wales. Unbeknown to them I had put all my climbing gear in the back of our dormobile. Tryfan came into view and Tony shouted out.

'Hey, Tryfan! I've climbed that!' Della looked at him.

'You lucky beggar! It's not fair. Dad, why can't we climb it?'

Vanda agreed as Tryfan had been the name of our house in Lancashire. I never said a word; I just pulled up on the road opposite the Milestone Buttress, and much to their delight, unloaded the climbing gear – and that was it. They all climbed the Buttress, over the garden wall and up the chimney, and with a bit of a struggle but with great determination, they made it. Then up the Heather Terrace we clamboured until we were finally standing on the summit of our beautiful mountain!

Back to the lads, and one of them had jammed his knee into a crack to keep his balance. When he finally removed it there was a nice tear right down the leg of his trousers. When he arrived at the top he panicked a bit when he saw the state his trousers were in.

'Sir, have you got a sewing kit with you?' I looked at him with disgust.

'What do you think this is – a girl's needlework class?' Then out came my famous "First Aid Kit". 'Come here. Let's have a look at you.'Taking my tube of Magic Liquid Stitches (otherwise known as a tube of Copydex glue), I proceeded to smear a generous helping along the length of the tear. 'Press down, and hold it for a minute,' I instructed the boy. All the other lads had gathered around and were watching intently.

'Wow! That's fantastic, Sir! You can't even tell where the tear was,' exclaimed one of the budding mountaineers.

Later that night, screams of, 'Ooh! Ah! No! No! Cor!!' could be heard from one of the tents, as the lad attempted to take his trousers off. With each tug more hairs were being torn from the young chap's leg. The Copydex had made a jolly good job of repairing the trousers, but at the same time it had reinforced the tear with a mixture of hair and skin! The other lads standing by watching the dance macabre were highly amused at the unusual acrobatic routine in performing the simple task of dismantling a pair of trousers!

Funnily enough, after that, every time I mentioned my Magic Liquid Stitching the boys were off like a shot down the mountainside.

At 7.30 a.m. the following morning we all met up in Capel Curig ready for our mountaineering trip to conquer the snow-capped Snowdon.

One boy muttered, 'Cold raw bacon and beans sandwiches, that's what I had for my breakfast!'

'Why didn't you cook it? You had your Primus stove with you' I said.

'He forgot to ask for the blooming matches, didn't he!' his mate piped up.

Another boy said, 'Well, you ought to try beans, grass and sheep droppings for breakfast, mate!' Their group had forgotten to bring a tin opener. They had held the tin of beans on the gate post and slammed the five-bar gate too hard. Bang! Whoosh! The beans shot out like a rocket spraying everything within a ten yard range! Starving and cold, they scraped up all the congealed orangey beans and put them in their mess tins and cooked the lot. Oh yes, when you are so hungry after a night on that cold, deserted, desolate mountainside you'll eat anything!

It was really hard going battling with the wind, snow and occasional icy patches, but nothing deterred the brave young warriors; 'onward, ever upward' was the battle cry! Of course, I gave them plenty of encouragement, as I explained to them about the café on the summit of Snowdon, where pretty girls served steaming hot mugs of cocoa, and lashings of toast just oozing with butter. There was just one thing I forgot to mention, and that was it didn't open until the 'high season' starting in June! Well, they'd only have to wait three months at the most!

Against the odds they made it to the top – I'm afraid my name was mud though. They threatened to send me to Coventry and not speak to me ever again, but unfortunately for them, I was the only one who knew the safest and quickest way down again. I had been going on about the 'lashings of toast just oozing with butter' for so long that even Lew was dribbling at the mouth; I think that he too thought there might be a chance of a café on the top. (Of course, on the following year's expedition he was as bad as me with the 'encouragement' of pretty girls and lashings of toast just oozing with butter, to keep the lads going!)

It was a cold clear night when I took the five boys on a survival expedition up Penyr-Ole-Wen. No sleeping bags tonight, just a survival bag made from a single bed plastic mattress cover. We settled down on an outcrop of rock to protect us from the biting wind.

'Get everything inside your plastic bags, lads. Your boots, emergency rations, the lot. Then use your rucksacks for a pillow and keep the plastic over your heads in case it rains.'

Well, of course, you get the tidy one; you know the sort, everything has a place and there's a place for everything. He settled himself down in his plastic bag. Down each side, within arms reach, he had neatly placed his chocolate, flask, whistle and torch. Oh yes, he was highly organised.

I wasn't too happy about the cloud building up over the mountain ridge and I set my alarm to go off every hour on the hour so that I could keep a check on the weather, and the lads. One, two, three and four o'clock and all was well. The sky by now had clouded over and looked snow laden. I thought to myself, I wouldn't be surprised in the least if we didn't have snow showers later in the day. The five o'clock alarm rang out and everything was pitch black. I was comfortable and warm but, as expected, wet with condensation. Sitting up with a start I saw that everywhere was white! Virgin snow, and not a lad in sight.

My first thought was that the little blighters had packed up and gone back to camp when they realised it was snowing leaving me to sort myself out. I hastily got all my gear packed in my rucksack, fastened my boots, had a swig of drink from my flask and shoved a piece of chocolate in my mouth. I started the long trek down.

I hadn't taken two paces when, 'What? What?' and up sat one of the lads. 'What time is it, Sir?'

With that I started laughing with relief, the noise echoed around the mountains. I then had the job of kicking the small mounds of curled up bodies which were completely covered in snow. They weren't the happiest of folk being awakened at that time in the morning, but we survived, and afterwards they said it was the most exciting sleep they had ever had in their lives.

'When can we do it again, Sir?!' they asked.

Excerpts:

When we left on Saturday we had our last look at Tryfan and Adam and Eve, standing like two lonely climbers on the summit, and at Snowdon looming in the distance over the mountain range. By this time most of the boys, and teachers too, were physical wrecks, having hiked over 80 miles and climbed Snowdon.

I shall not forget Mr Feldon waking us in the morning with shouts of 'It's a lovely day, today!' whether the sun was shining or the rain falling. If we turned over to sleep again, we were pulled out of the tent and emptied out of the sleeping bag.

It was a very happy and exciting holiday.
GORDON CHIVERTON
PAUL WOOLFORD
ANTHONY WHEELER
DAVID BARRY

With everything packed up, tents, climbing gear, food and drink, it was time to leave our base camp and head for home. One of the boys borrowed Mr William's wheelbarrow to clear the site and replace the rocks we had used to hold the tents down during the gales. We drove down the path and over the old stone bridge, waving and shouting.

'See you next year, and don't forget to put the kettle on!'

'You're all welcome anytime!' Mr Williams said as he laughed and waved back.

* * * * *

Talking about wheelbarrows, I like the tale Derrick, our friend, told me. As a young man he worked at a large engineering firm in Bolton, Lancashire. The annual stocktaking had just been completed and it was now time to go home, when the phone rang in the accountant's office....

18

Stocktaking?!

It was late afternoon when the telephone bell on Rupert's desk rang – Brrr. Brrr. Brrr. Oh dear me, thought Rupert, whatever now. He was just putting the annual financial reports back in their folders. Picking up the receiver a soft silky voice answered.

'Ah, Rupert, my dear chap. Would you be kind enough to come up to the Board Room immediately. And I say, old chap, can you bring the latest stocktaking sheets with you?' There was a sharp click and the phone went dead.

That's funny, Rupert thought to himself, I've checked and double-checked all the ledgers to make sure everything is in order before today's annual audit.

Rupert was the firm's Senior Accountant and was very meticulous when it came to running the finance department of this large engineering works. He just hated stocktaking; he was more of a desk man and therefore the dirty, messy job of stocktaking was left to Norman who was his deputy, and was quite happy to fraternize with the common tradesmen and storekeepers in the various departments.

The bespectacled Senior Accountant checked himself in the mirror before leaving the office; straightening his bow tie and adjusting his starched white collar, a quick flip of the hair, a double-check of the immaculate creases in his pin-stripped trousers and finally he fastened the middle button of his newly acquired charcoal grey Burtons jacket. Puffing and panting his way slowly up all the steep stone steps, every now and then he would stop to mop his brow with his handkerchief. His ample stomach wasn't built for this type of athletics, especially at the end of a gruesome day.

Poor Rupert never felt at ease in the magnificent boardroom. With the large table running the whole length of the room, a dozen chairs were carefully spaced evenly around the table, and desk mats sat tidily in front of each chair. The huge oil paintings were overpowering with past chairmen looking down over the proceedings. The far wall had large paintings depicting their earlier engineering achievements, such as railway locomotives, large guns in action on the battle fronts of the First World War, tanks pounding over desert landscapes with their guns blazing away. Oh yes! This Bolton company was proud of its past achievements and had every intention of keeping the good work up.

The little group of Senior Management were helping themselves to gin and tonics from the antique drinks cabinet in the corner when – knock, knock – the tall Senior Financial Officer turned slowly around still laughing at the joke Old Bertie had told him about the 'blonde in the bath'.

'Ah! Come in, old boy!' he said. 'I say, Rupert, there seems to be a little discrepancy with the stock sheets. While you were away with that dratted hay fever of yours, Charles, here, did a spot check on the stores and found certain items missing.'

Rupert could feel his face reddening; he hated being caught out like this, especially in front of the chairman. He did one of his silly coughs.

'Just leave it with me, Sir, I'll sort it all out. It won't happen again.' And with that he stumbled backwards and disappeared through the still open door.

Arriving back in his office he slumped down in his chair, a real bag of nerves. Then he banged down on his desk and shouted out.

'Norman! Norman, come in here at once!' There was no reply, then a young office girl popped her head round the door.

'Sorry Sir, Mr Norman has gone home. The Wanderers are playing Manchester City today and he wouldn't miss a game like that for the world!'

'That's it. That's it! I'll just have to do it myself, then' shouted Rupert. Picking up the list he found that some of the "missing items" were quite large. Now, how the heck did they get them out of here, he wondered to himself. Standing up he pushed and pulled at his substantial desk until it was immediately under the window, where he could keep a personal eye on the yard down below.

During the next month he made spot checks on all the equipment and tools. The word got around that 'The Hawk' was on the trail and bit by bit the rate of loss decreased. The store man was delighted to announce that all tools were correct and accounted for, as was all equipment. However, Rupert noted that there were huge chunks of brass fittings and scrap metal still disappearing and finding their way to the local scrap metal merchant up the road. Now, Rupert knew that they couldn't carry them out in their knapsacks; this stuff was too big and heavy for that. So just how did they get it out?

It was late afternoon when Rupert happened to glance out of the window.

'So, that's it!' he muttered excitedly, 'I've got yer now!'

Heading across the yard was one of the "Flat Cap Joe's", a member of the labouring gang, pushing a wheelbarrow full of straw straight through the gate and passed security. The foreman labourer told Rupert that all components coming into the factory were delivered in crates and were packed tightly with straw to avoid any damage. The straw was then taken outside later onto the waste ground and burned.

'Why? What's the problem?' asked the foreman.

'Problem? No Problem!' said Rupert, as he walked away with a sly smile on his face.

The very next day at 4 p.m. Rupert was missing from his desk. There he crouched, lurking in the shadows of the old warehouse, watching and waiting, but not in vain. After just a few minutes along came Flat Cap Joe, faithfully pushing his wheelbarrow full of straw. Rupert pounced out, right in front of Flat Cap Joe who nearly jumped out of his skin.

'Cor, mate! Yer frightened the bleeding daylight out a me, er, Sir!' Rupert puffed himself up to his full 5' 4" height and stood directly in front of the barrow.

'Now, now, what have we got here?' he asked pointing to the straw.

The Flat Cap, somewhat bewildered, lifted his cap, scratched his head and said 'Ay?'

With that Rupert said 'Are you deaf or daft? I'll ask you once again,' and raising his shrill voice asked 'What have you got in the barrow?'

Old Flat Cap shuffled about a bit, bent over towards Rupert.

'Ay! Can't you see man, I've got a barrow full of 'ay!' he whispered.

'Ah, ha, but what have you got underneath the 'ay? I mean, hay' continued the red-faced Rupert.

By this time one or two of Flat Cap's mates had gathered in the yard to see what all the fuss was about.

'I've got nowt under ta 'ay! See fer thar self!' and with that he tipped the whole barrowful of hay onto the floor. That did it, Rupert started to sneeze, his face went even redder and his eyes started to water, and he started with one of his coughing fits. He turned and ran for the sanctuary of his office clutching his handkerchief over his streaming nose.

The following day Rupert was off work with one of his worst bouts of hay fever.

On returning to work he continued his spot checks, and at last had it under control; no tools missing, no components missing and no metal fittings missing! Success at last!

The month end came and the office telephone rang – Brrr. Brrr. Brrr. Picking up the receiver a soft silky voice answered.

'Ah, Rupert, my dear chap. Would you be kind enough to come up to the Board Room immediately. And I say, old chap, can you bring the latest stocktaking sheets with you?' There was a sharp click and the line went dead.

Rupert smiled, as he checked himself in the mirror. He felt full of confidence; up the stairs he bounded, I might even get a nice bonus in my pay packet this month, he thought smugly. Knock, knock.

'Come in old boy!' answered the familiar voice of the Senior Financial Officer. 'Splendid, splendid! Now, Rupert, I have just checked out the stock sheets, and I must say, what a wonderful improvement there has been; no tools missing, no components missing, no materials missing, Marvellous, marvellous, old boy! How do you do it?'

Rupert felt 10 foot tall, he puffed out his chest with pride.

'It's all to do with taking control, and letting them know who's in charge!'

'Excellent, excellent!' continued the Senior Financial Officer. 'But there's just one thing we can't understand. How do you account for the 5 WHEELBARROWS that are missing?'

Poor Rupert hurried back to his office as he started to sneeze, his face turned a shade of beetroot and his eyes started to water, as he looked down into the yard below only to see Flat Cap Joe pushing his wheelbarrow full of 'ay' out through the main gate!!

* * * * *

Now, I don't know about you, but one thing I really enjoy is a jolly good challenge. What's more exciting, is getting youngsters to take up a challenge and see the look on their faces when they succeed.

19

The Sleeping Giant

The air was electrified. Everyone waited with baited breath; would the giant come awake today or would it be another day of frustration and disappointment for the doctors in charge. It was a sorry sight to see such a wonderful mass of muscle just lying there not making the slightest effort to get up and move. I had to admire the determination of the team, no way were they going to give up on this lifeless soul.

Ted leaned over once more in a determined effort to bring life into this, their creation. Leaning over he continued with the kiss of life, with no avail. Dave passed more magic liquid over. With great patience and understanding Ted poured a few more drops of the precious life-giving liquid down the giant's throat.

Cough! Cough! Cough! The giant gave a huge sneeze. All the onlookers scattered as the giant took a deep breath and raised himself with a noisy, angry roar. Poor Ted was taken completely by surprise and was lifted bodily up into the air. Dave panicked and grabbed onto the giant in an attempt to hold him down.

Now, Dave was a farmer's boy and had dealt with sheep, horses and cows, as well as the odd bull or two, but this was a real challenge; he had never fought with a giant before. He always had a good tale to tell, like the one about the sheep who ate long grass and blew up to twice its normal size. Dave would then have to take a long hollow needle and thrust it straight into the sheep's belly and the gas would escape with the force of an express train. He used to say that you could light the methane gas, which lit up like the chimneys at Fawley Oil Refinery, but you had to be careful, because, if by any chance you had a 'blow-back' then the sheep would just explode into thousands of pieces, with barbequed legs flying through the air and cooked lamb chops hurtling across the field, like a McDonald's take-away.

'Oh, you've got to be careful, Sir, if you don't know what you're doing!' he would say.

With Ted still floating in mid air, Dave shouted out.

'Clive! Clive! Get round the other side and hold him down!'

Other brave kids rushed in. They surrounded the giant and grabbed hold of his skirt around his waist and at last everything was under control. Still swaying from side to side the giant seemed to be calmer now and Teddy managed to stand up on the giant's chest and with a big grin on his face he looked over to me.

'Sir, Sir! We've got lift off!'

This was the moment our hovercraft was born!

Now, I don't know about you, but I thought that Christopher Cockerell invented the hovercraft. During the background research of the project, the lads discovered that Christopher was indeed credited with the invention of the hovercraft and took out a patent in 1955, but, wait for it, also in the 1950's an American, Doctor William Bartelson, invented and built an "air car" so that he could visit patients who lived out in bog land, a swamp like area which was part of his practice. He had intended to patent his already-working machine but was beaten to it by no other than Christopher Cockerell, an Englishman.

So who created the original idea of the air-cushion craft? Well, in 1916 an Austrian called Dagobert Muller built a torpedo boat which floated on a cushion of air, but the First World War put an end to that. Of course, 45 years before that in 1870, John Thornycroft designed a boat which floated on a film of air trapped underneath the hull. Unfortunately the steam pumps couldn't produce enough air for the job. So is that it then? Oh no! Because 150 years before that in 1716 a certain Emmanuel Swedenberg dreamed up the idea of reducing friction on a boat, thereby increasing the speed, but unfortunately the oarsmen couldn't produce the power to lift the boat on a cushion of air and at the same time propel the vehicle along. So, as far as we know the air-cushion vehicle was first thought about 235 years ago!!

So there we were, highly delighted and excited that we had produced a working hovercraft, capable of carrying two people. Well, in actual fact the cockpit was designed for two people but the three Volkswagen engines were so powerful we had to put two bags of sand in the forward end as ballast!

At that moment it didn't matter who had come up with the original idea, and it didn't matter who was first to patent the idea; what really mattered was the interest and enthusiasm created by these budding hovercraft engineers and pilots. When it was completed our hovercraft was a real showstopper, and we were encouraged to put it into the ESSO Technology Competition. Believe it or not, it took first place and we were awarded the £100 prize money! Not bad for a non-examination, non-achedemic group of 5T boys! And the lads were thrilled to bits when they were invited to display the craft at Bembridge Air Show.

Of course, the hovercraft wasn't the only project going on in the workshop. Two of the lads were fast completing a portable, lightweight electric concrete mixer. This appeared on the domestic market eighteen months later as the "Barrow Mixer"; it is now common place to see them in everyday use. A couple of the fibreglass canoes were also having their final trims fitted and the tenth fibreglass dinghy was being released from its mould. This was Applied Technology in action! For those of you in ignorance, Applied Technology is the 'science of materials put to a practical use'. There was always great excitement in my workshops, as boys and girls discovered new uses for materials in their design and technology projects.

I had found the plans of an electronic metal detector in a magazine called Wireless World. Now, in one of my groups I had a bit of a whiz-kid in radio, which reminded me of my youth when I was producing four valve radios. This East Cowes lad was being harassed by the police for having a pirate radio broadcasting station in the shed at the bottom of his garden. Fancying himself as a bit of a D.J. he was producing his own music programmes with the help of half-a-dozen other lads. It was a great success, but the authorities weren't so keen!

Well, our local D.J. took up the challenge to make this metal detector, which consisted of a broom handle, six feet of plastic curtain rail, a coil of copper wire, and certain electronic items, like the new transistors that had just come out. The coil was about two feet in diameter and on the first test run it managed to detect all the nails in the workshop floor boards. I took it home to try in the garden and found over twenty nails and one horseshoe, but the most exciting find had yet to come.

Glenys shouted from the kitchen that tea was ready, so I started to drift back down the garden, when 'Ping!' A dear, sweet sound echoed through the headphones. All the nails had given off a dull, clucking noise, a bit like the sound a hen might make – Cluck! Cluck! This beautiful, clear 'Ping!'

was completely new. Taking my trowel I knelt on the soil and dug down a couple of inches, and there before my eyes was a silver coin! It looked as if it was covered in dark lead, but where I had touched it with the trowel it shone like polished silver. Gently extracting it from the ground, to my amazement and delight I found that it was a 1811 Silver Newport Shilling – Yes, Newport, Isle of Wight!

Well, that was it, the bug had truly bitten, and from that moment on I was completely hooked on finding buried treasure. Of course, I had to pay the five shillings to purchase a Pipe Finders Licence at the local police station. You needed this licence if you were using any kind of metal detector in those early days.

It wasn't long before I managed to buy a new (second hand) C-SCOPE TR7 Metal Detector. Now, a metal detector is only as good as the person using it, you have to 'tune in' to the various sounds and notes and learn what each one means. Some time later, I heard a very gentle 'ping' in the headphones whilst searching the fine, sandy beach at Ryde and I actually found a 3 inch length of very fine fuse wire. Now, that's some going! You may be thinking, that's not treasure, but it was to me, as it was a real confidence booster, and I knew I could rely on the machine and myself to find anything within the depth capability of the detector.

One thing always leads to another, and I soon found I could dowse with a pendulum over maps, and with two bent rods in the fields. Of course, a lot of people think you can only dowse for water, but in fact you can dowse for anything – water, wood, metal, oil, and even for answers to any question, as long as you phrase them to reply with a 'yes' or 'no' from your pendulum or rods. I went into a nearby field holding a copper coin in my hand. I focused my mind on this coin and within one hour I had located and dug up thirteen copper coins, the latest of which dated back to 1821!

I then thought I'd try dowsing using a Y-shaped branch off a tree. Holding it firmly I focused on a shilling which I held in my palm. I turned around slowly to find the correct direction, and 'whoosh!' it shot upright! It really frightened me, at the time, as I wasn't expecting a reaction as positive as that. Up it went, pointing straight towards the sky. I realised that my hands were burning, and when I looked at them I noticed that all the skin on my palms was blistered and red raw.

My first lesson taught me to relax and let go, and not to expect results, just let it happen, and believe me, it will! Once you start on this road of discovery you find that you start to tune into all sorts of weird and wonderful things... just like the time I met the White Lady drifting silently in and out of the mist on that late summer's evening!

20

Not A Soul In Sight!

It was a warm, balmy evening and everything seemed to be at peace. Nothing stirred; there was an eerie stillness in the air. My consciousness was totally in tune with the slight buzzing sound of my C-SCOPE metal detector. I listened very carefully to any variations of tone in my headphones, straining for even the slightest change of note. Up to now I had only found the odd nail or two. Then everything seemed to change. I had the strangest feeling that somebody was standing behind me watching me; I could feel eyes looking right through me. With a slight turn of my head I glanced behind me, but nothing!

Quite often when you are metal detecting, you get the odd inquisitive person, taking the dog for a walk, who will come across to see what amazing treasures you have found. But this time there was no one in sight, and yet I still had the feeling of being watched. Then it happened, a band of mist descended slowly around me. It was cold and damp and I could feel goose pimples on my arms and legs. The hair on the back of my neck started to bristle and stand up. I had the feeling that something uncanny was about to happen as cold shivers ran up and down my spine. This is an unusual story of the weird and unexplainable thing that was about to take place, as the wailing ghostly organ music seemed to reach out through the cold, dank mist...

Sometime earlier, leaning against the old church tower by the sea without a care in the world, I was idly watching the frantic activity of the bait diggers. I nearly jumped out of my skin as I felt a tap on my shoulder. The old, salty fisherman pointed to my metal detector.

'Does that contraption of yours ever find anything? 'Cause it won't be the first time that me and the lads have found ancient pirates pieces of eight, when we pulled out a nice fat juicy rag worm.' I looked at him.

'What? Real pieces of eight treasure!'

Before he answered he looked sharply round.

'There 'e goes again. Did you see 'im?'

'See who?' I enquired, though I thought I had seen a shadow drift by.

'Well, 'im, Little John. He just walked right past us. Oh, aye! He frightens the life out of poor souls who meet 'im on a moonlit night. He's 'armless enough, never says owt just goes into ta church ta do 'is duties. It's a real shame about the lass though.'

'What lass?' I almost spluttered.

'Well, it goes back a long way, or so my old Grandpa tells me. In fact, it goes back to about 1640. Yes 1643, so I recall.' And then he started his story. 'At that time, there lived, in one of them small stone fishermen's cottages next to this 'ere old church, all gone now, a small funny little man by the name of John Wolfry and his beautiful nineteen year old sister, Mary, or so my Grandpa says. Now John was the church warden of the old dilapidated church. They say he was a god-fearing man and took 'is duties very seriously. Often, late at night, you would find this lonely man, dressed in 'is frock coat, tight leather shorts, long stockings and laced-up boots, repairing one of the old windows or putting another screw into the rusty iron hinges on the old oak door. Of course, he was fighting a losing battle, as the wind and the sea were slowly, but surely, taking their toll on this battered old church.

On these lonely evenings, Mary would go into the church and sit at the organ practising the music she had discovered in a small wooden box at the back of the vestry. It was at that time she fell in love with Tim, a handsome, young, fair-haired smuggler who lived with his Grandfather on the shores of Brading Haven. Of course, in those days most folk on the Island were in someway connected with the rather lucrative trade of smuggling; oh aye, and some still are!' he laughed. 'The problem was, how to dodge the armed Custom and Excise men who used to hide in the bushes at the side of the path leading up from the beach, ready to pounce on any brandy runners delivering their kegs of French brandy to the innkeeper up at the village. Now, unbeknown to the Custom and Excise men, this old churchyard by the sea was an ideal spot to hide contraband on a dark night. It is a known fact that some of the large slabs of stone on top of the tombs in the graveyard were loose, and after a bit of gentle persuasion from the smugglers, would swivel round easily on the sharp sand that had been inserted between the large slabs, allowing kegs of brandy, or other smuggled goods, to be hastily stuffed inside to await collection when the coast was clear. Now, a ruse, to put the fear of the devil into any stranger when a delivery was about to be made, was to disguise a young man in a white sheet wearing a gruesome skeleton skull mask. He would sit on one of the tombstones playing a slow beat on a drum. This would terrify any country bumpkin and gave rise to the legend of the dead drummer in churchyards that gave people a horror of passing such places at night!

Now, Mary had an arrangement to warn her lover whenever the Custom and Excise men were on patrol. Into the church she would go and play a prearranged piece of music over and over again. It 'as been said that on a still night the sound of the organ music could be heard drifting out over the water as far out to sea as what is now known as Nab Tower.' The old fisherman pointed out to sea towards the distant Tower. 'They tell me that even the excise men wouldn't go anywhere near the church, afraid that the uncanny music of the dead would haunt their very souls. Night after night over those dark, bitterly cold winter months she would go to the church, wrapped only in a thin shawl, to warn her lover of any danger.

It was on such a night that the owner of the old Priory Manor Farm, up the hill, returned from a night drinking with his cronies at the local watering hole, and he heard the ethereal sound of the phantom organ music drifting up from the direction of the sea. Now, this was nigh on one o'clock in the morning, or thereabouts. He said the sound wasn't real and sent shivers up and down his spine, and not only that, his Labrador dog started to howl mournfully. The only way he could explain this uncanny sound of the dead was that he had drunk too much mead, seeing as it was New Year's Eve – but no, he was by this time stone cold sober and would swear in a court of law that he had never heard music like that before, or since, on a cold, dark winter's night.

It was one of those wet nights, when the rain splattered down on the ancient church tower. Shafts of moonlight broke through the cloud in places, giving an eerie light to the ancient churchyard. The smugglers carried the contraband brandy kegs on their shoulders across this very beach just below the church. The music playing was the "all clear" tune, so there were no excise men in the vicinity. Tim arrived at the churchyard, turned the huge slab of stone, and stacked the smuggled kegs of brandy in the tomb for collection at a later date. The other smugglers bid Tim a farewell as he lifted the latch and opened the creaking, old oak church door to meet his girlfriend Mary. But what awaited him, still sitting at the organ, was a transparent, ethereal figure of his beloved Mary, dressed in her best white dress which flowed down her slim body to her ankles. "Oh, no! Please, God, no!" he shouted, but in his heart he knew she was dead. Or was she, was it just a trick of the candlelight that produced that ghostly figure? I was told that the keys of the organ were still moving in a mysterious way, producing that eerie sound of ghostly music.

Tim dashed out of the church in fright and ran straight to her little cottage by the sea. Mary was laid out and at peace. She had died some hours earlier in her bed, with that dreaded illness pneumonia, and was unable to keep her date at the church.

Very soon, Mary was buried in the old churchyard attended by her brother John, and a score of local smugglers that she had protected over the past few years. It is said, that just before the coffin was closed, Tim placed a hand-worked, filigree shawl fastener into her hands, to remember him by. The coffin was lowered into the ground and a calm fell over that churchyard scene on that cold January morning.

John Wolfry, the little church warden, with his frock coat, tight leather shorts and long stockings could often be seen replacing loose stones or knocking a nail in here or there, but to no long-term avail, and it wasn't long before this old church fell into a state of complete ruin and was beyond repair. Indeed, local legend has it that a major collapse came during the great storm on 20th November 1703, when Winstanley and his lighthouse were washed away from the Eddystone Rock, and bit by bit, stone by stone the old church fell into the sea.

It took another fourteen years before the new church at the top of the 'ill was at last started. Yes, in 1717, the first stone was laid and in June 1719 the dedication ceremony took place. The bell tower was a wooden structure in those days, as the funds were getting rather low, but they had to have a bell tower as they had rescued the bell from the old church; it was inscribed with the date of 1610, and do you know that the same bell is in use today!'

The fisherman cleared his throat and altered his stance, then continued, 'They tell me the incumbent at the time was the Reverend Francis Deacon. Many of the old memorial stones, tombs and even skeletons were being exposed by the vicious pounding of the sea around this old church. The old gravestones were carried up to the new site in the local farm cart and some were used in the making of the floor in the new church. The skeletons and bones were wrapped in sail cloth and carried up the old footpath across the fields and finally reburied in the newly dedicated graveyard. This was done in the hours of darkness so as not to frighten or distress the local folk. One tombstone in particular is to be remembered, the one bearing the surname Wolfry. But now this strange story unfolds, as you can see even today a portion of that old headstone bearing the name of Mary. Yes, Mary Wolfry resides in the porch of the parish church of St Helens. But, wait for it, the story doesn't even end there, you see, in the year of 1727 it is reported and written down, that weird and unexplainable things began to happen at the new church of St Helens.

Many people reported organ music coming from the empty church at night. Then a strange thing 'appened as the vicar Reverend Francis Deacon was preparing to welcome his parishioners for the midnight service on New Year's Eve. He was alone, when suddenly the candles began to flicker sending ghostly shadows flitting across the ceiling. He reported that there was an odd, unhealthy, cold, dank feeling pervading the church. Then he was taken completely by surprise, as the sound of 'aunting organ music filled the church. On turning around he claims that he saw an unearthly figure of a young girl dressed in white sitting at the organ. The music then faded and the poor girl just melted away in front of his very eyes. Then there was nothing but silence. After that uncanny incident, the ghost of the "White Lady" as she was called, was seen many times and her appearance has been recorded down to the present time, and she has even been seen by persons unaware that St Helens church even had a ghost. Now what do you think of all that then?' he asked.

Before I could reply he continued, 'Do you know, over the years many of the organists have sensed an invisible presence sitting beside them on the stool and felt the fingers gently touching the keys. It makes you shudder, doesn't it! In the Roadside Inn, tales are told of motorists driving around the corner by the village church, only to see a ghostly white figure drifting across the road right in front of them. Now, listen to this, young Ted was returning from a village darts match with his pal, Ken. He was driving 'is dad's van around the bend when suddenly 'is headlights picked up a lady dressed in white standing in the middle of the road. He jammed 'is brakes on but no way could he miss that poor soul. Both Ted and Ken awaited the impact, but there was nothing. They went straight through her. As the car stopped, they both jumped out shaking with fear at what they might find. They searched and searched but couldn't find a body anywhere. In a bit of a panic they drove trembling straight to Ryde Police Station to report the incident. Well, PC Harry Coffins just laughed – mind you, I think I would too with a name like that!' said the fisherman with a hearty chuckle. 'The policeman told the lads that they get quite a few reports from people who swear that they 'ave just knocked down a lady dressed in white. The policeman told them to run along and not worry about it saying that they 'ad just knocked down the ghost of St Helens! I reckon that was poor Mary they keep seeing.'

With that he bent down and lifted the wet newspaper off the top of his mud stained bucket. I looked inside. Ugh! Crawling all over each other were the most horrible disgusting creatures I've ever seen; the rag worm were long and fat just like big black giant maggots.

'Well, I think I'd better be getting these little beauties 'ome and in the fridge before me missus sees 'em!' He covered them up gently, then stood up as if to go. Then he pointed his old briar pipe at me, 'I bet you wouldn't be leaning against this old tower if you knew who was inside!'

I jumped up.

'What do you mean? Who's inside?'

'Tha' wants to ask yon fellas about that night when they saw a strange dark figure gliding along that wall. It came straight to this tower and, whoosh, it vanished, just like that. Well, they put their fishing gear down and came down 'ere but the place was deserted. Not a soul was in sight, if you see what I mean! Ah, ha! Ah, ha! Not a soul in sight! Course they'd seen Little John, Mary's brother. Oh yes, I've seen 'im many a time, he's 'armless.

Of course, my owd granddad used to say that back in 1784, or thereabouts, they sent masons to repair this tower, and when they got on the top, they found a little chap. Now listen to this, he was dressed in tight leather short trousers, and knee-length woolly stockings. Well, this little fella was very cross at being disturbed and cursed the masons for interfering with 'is church. After the repairs had been done they painted the wall facing the sea white, as instructed by their employers at Portsmouth. They didn't take much notice of the curse, which said that they would suffer the same fate as the original masons who built the tower; they all lost their lives in a storm at sea. The job was well and truly finished and the little fella never appeared again. So the workmen set their sails and headed out to sea, – but they never arrived at Portsmouth, and what's more, their bodies were never washed up on these shores!'

With that, he re-lit his pipe, picked up his mud-covered bucket with his "little treasures" crawling all over each other beneath the wet County Press, and turned to go.

Touching his forehead with his pipe he whispered to me.

'Does that contraption of yours detect ghosts? – Cause I wouldn't hang around here when the sun goes down, as yer might find more than yer bargained for! Well, I've enjoyed our little chat but I must be off now, and I bid you good day, young fella!'

I thought to myself, a good chat? I couldn't get a word in edgeways! But, by heck, he was a mine of information, and I must admit, I was completely enthralled by the potted history lesson I had just received. The last I saw of him was dipping his oars and rowing out to sea.

Well, getting back to the story, I still had this uncanny feeling of being watched. Those unseen eyes were peering at me through this cold dank veil of mist that had gathered all around me. By this time I had lost all concentration and just stood there staring into space with my metal detector touching the ground. Then I heard it again; it was as if my headphones were plugged into a CD, but the music coming through them was out of this world – it was soft, strange, ghostly music. For a minute or two, I thought I had picked up a radio station signal. The mist was now swirling, as if to the rhythm of the phantom organ music and for no reason whatsoever the hairs on the back of my hands pricked and stood up. A shiver ran down my spine. Then it happened, and slowly, very slowly, a ghostly white figure appeared out of the mist from nowhere.

Suddenly she turned, and this almost transparent white apparition was walking straight towards me. I wanted to run, but I couldn't move a muscle, I was rooted to the spot. The figure seemed to be of a young woman dressed in a shroud-like dress. There was no sound and the music had faded away. A sad silence seemed to descend all around me. She beckoned me to follow her, and turned. I felt a magnetic-like pull as I found myself slowly following her, step by step, to a point in the field where she pointed down to the earth, then moved back out of the way.

Warily I allowed the detector to scan over the spot, and it immediately emitted a loud signal through my headphones. Bending down with excitement, I dug a small hole – lying there was a pretty filigree fastener with two jade stones embedded into the delicate jewellery. It was slightly misshapen and the chemicals in the ground had taken all the gilt from the brooch but to my eyes it was the most precious thing I had ever found. I held it out to her. The white figure nodded and took a step back, then turned and glided back soundlessly towards the church.

The mist cleared, as if by magic. It seemed to take hours before I could move, although I'm sure it was really only a matter of minutes. Then I had the funny feeling that I had been dreaming, until I looked down into my slightly dirty hand and realised I was still holding the beloved fastener.

Hurrying to the gate and back onto the road, I just caught sight of the white lady entering the church. Then, the faint sound of ghostly organ music drifted across the deserted graveyard...

* * * * *

Do you believe in ghosts? Well, it makes you think, doesn't it; me, in a state of high awareness with the uncanny tale of the old fisherman whirling around and around in my mind. Did I really see the ghost of the White Lady, or could there be a simple logical explanation?

Come to think of it, I've heard many a tale of mountaineers seeing a ghostly apparition known as the "Brocken

Spectre". This is an unusual weather phenomenon formed by your own shadow cast on a cloud or mist. This three-dimensional image of your shadow is always surrounded by an unworldly rainbow coloured halo. The Brocken Spectre is named after the mountain peak in Germany where the occurrence was first recorded.

Back in the graveyard, there's no arguing about it, I definitely saw that ghostly figure appear out of the mist, but was my mind simply working overtime and did I just assume it was the White Lady, because at that moment I really did expect to see her!

Now, the question that springs to mind is 'Do you see what you believe, or do you believe what you see?' Well, my friends, I'll leave you to be the judge of that!

But, you may ask, what about the figure you saw entering the church? I certainly saw a lady dressed in white enter the church, but naturally I didn't hang about when the organ music started up. Anyway, I'd had enough of these 'ere' mystical happenings for one day, and I quickly scarpered home to show my family my latest metal detecting find.

There was, however, a time when Colin, a good friend, and myself came face to face with an old monk dressed in a brown habit – and he was smiling! Ah, but that is another spooky tale just waiting to be told!

21

Sir! You've Got A Boat!

Bass took me down to the side entrance of the East Cowes sailing Club. There on the slipway, adjoining the River Medina, rested the 18 foot open clinker-built fishing boat with the 8 horse-power in-board engine. It looked massive to me, but Bass assured me it would be easy to handle once in the water.

'Right, the first thing to check for is rot', said Bass.

He climbed into the boat and lifted the loose floorboards up. Out of his pocket he produced a screwdriver, and started poking it into the clinker timber and the keel on the inside. After about ten minutes he climbed over the side and started the same process on the outside; again starting at the stem and working his way back to the stern. 'Well, Sir. It looks solid enough to me. I can't find any rot or worm damage. It's nicely painted up and that always makes me think there's summit to hide, but it's been well maintained. Course I can't say 'owt about the engine until we get it in the water. The propeller and bearings are in good nick and the packing gland is nice and waterproof.'

It was at that moment three other pupils came round the corner.

'Hi ya Bass! Oh, hello, Sir!'

'Well, what do you think, Bass?' I asked.

'Looks okay – let's get it in the water and see how she goes.' With that they all lifted the stern and passed a couple of rollers, which looked like scaffolding poles, to me.

Well, I stood there, a bit out of my depth, if you know what I mean! Within two minutes the boat was in the water.

'Hey, wait a minute,' I shouted. 'What about the owner?'

'Oh, old Charlie won't mind. I go deep sea fishing with him, at weekends in his big boat. That's why he's getting rid of this old girl.'

I quickly removed my shoes and socks and rolled up my trousers, and hopped smartly into the boat. Now, I must admit, I wasn't very happy about it as the owner was nowhere in sight. Everything had just happened so quickly. Here I was, a well-respected school teacher sailing up the river with four thirteen year old boys dressed in their best school uniforms; black blazers, trousers, white shirts and red and white striped ties.

'Give it a crank up, Lug!' shouted Bass, who was holding the tiller. The old engine rattled into life. Clank! Clank! Clank! And we were off! Crab sidled up to me.

'I reckon that old motor 'as got twenty years of life in 'er yet!'

Cod pulled the oars aboard and stored them neatly under the seat. It was at that moment that I realised they all had fishy nicknames! Bass, Cod, Crab, but what about Lug? I quizzed Crab as to how Lug got his name.

'Oh, that's easy, Sir! He digs the biggest and best lugworms around these 'ere shores!'

I thought we had better turn around before the owner finds his boat missing, but no, they were giving it a fair trial.

'We're going to sail as far as the old cement works at the bottom of Stag Lane, then you can see if she's shipping any water.'

I was quite enjoying my first trip up the River Medina

and thought that it was really too late to worry now! I could just imagine it in next week's County Press: "Teacher steals boat – aided and abetted by four thirteen year old pupils of Cowes Secondary School."

Crab lifted the floor boards up.

'As dry as a bone, Sir. And she's 'ad a good run. You'll be alright with this old girl, Sir. She won't let you down.'

As we turned, we could just make out the silhouette of Charlie, standing on the jetty, looking up and down the river, shielding his eyes from the blazing sun.

'Hi ya, Charlie!' they all shouted as we approached the slip. Charlie nodded but never said a word.

I was ready to take the blame and had all sorts of excuses prepared in my head. We gently floated up to the slip with the engine switched off. The lads jumped out of the boat and put the rollers under the keel. Charlie steadied the boat as the youngsters heaved it up onto the dry land; I was still sitting in the boat, holding on to my socks and shoes like a real land lubber! I climbed out clumsily and Charlie came over to me.

'Well, Sir, tha'll find nowt wrong with the old girl. She's as solid as the day she was built!'

'Yes, yes,' I said, 'but how much do you want for her?' (Have you noticed how nautical I was getting; 'her' this and 'she' that, instead of just 'it'!)

'Now, 'ere is my grandson, and he says I've got to look after you or he'll be after me!' And with that, he gave me a knowing wink, then his wrinkled and weather-beaten face broke into a huge grin as he turned to Bass. 'Well, what do you reckon fifty quid?' Bass stepped back in horror.

'Charlie, that's daylight robbery! I wouldn't give you more than thirty quid for this old piece of rubbish! You know you only want to get rid of it, and my dad said that you'll only spend the money on beer.' Charlie looked at me and nodded his head again.

''E's a little bugger, when it comes to money! Well, alright, 'ow about forty five quid?'

Wow, I was more than happy to pay forty five quid, as I'd already made my mind up I was going to have this little beauty, whatever the price!

'Oh, come on, Grandpap, Mr Feldon's a good teacher and he's letting me make a fibre glass dingy as a tender for your new boat.'

'Ah! Now you've got me in a corner, 'aven't you!'

At that moment I thought about Levi, the old wizard, who taught me to bargain first. Here was young Bass bargaining away on my behalf against his old granddad, and I didn't even come into the discussion!

'Well,' said Charlie reluctantly, 'forty quid and that's final.'

Bass thrust his hands into his pockets and stamped his foot, and looking at me he said 'Do you know, Sir, he can be really stubborn at times. Can you afford forty quid, Sir?'

'Well, yes,' I said 'but how do we get it up to my house in Newport?'

'Just leave that to me, Sir,' he replied.

Turning back to his Granddad, he said 'Okay, we'll make a deal at forty quid, but that includes the oars, rollocks and the anchor – oh, and a full tank of petrol.' His Granddad burst out laughing.

'Yer little bugger! Whose side are you on?'

With that both Bass and Grandpop spat on their hands and headed towards each other ready to shake on the deal, when Bass casually dropped the bombshell

'Of course, that's delivered to Sir's house as well.' Bass quickly grabbed his Grandpop's hand and shook it vigorously. 'That's it, Sir, you've got a boat, delivered!'

Bass told me later that people always ask for more than they expect to get when they sell anything, and his Grandpop

Charlie had told him to always negotiate a good deal before you buy. I said to Bass that I suppose his Granddad wasn't very pleased when he knocked the price down for him.

'Oh yes, Sir. He said I did a good job for him and he gave me a couple of quid for myself.' I passed Bass another couple of quid as a thank you gesture, and for the brilliant way he negotiated the sale of the boat.

Della, Tony and Vanda all helped in cutting up sheets of Mahogany Marine Plywood as we built a very nice cabin, complete with seats and a lockable door, so that we would be able to leave our lifejackets and gear on board. Lifejackets? – well, they were actually called "life-preservers" and consisted of two large pockets of kapok, one at the back and one at the front. In fact, I bought them through Exchange and Mart magazine. You could buy anything from a rubber duck to an ex-army tank – a bit like purchasing items on e-bay today! Anyway, these lifejackets were originally from an old oil tanker which had been scrapped.

Another thing we saw advertised in Exchange and Mart were Fishing Knives, which were guaranteed not to sink if dropped overboard – they simply floated away!

Well, the big day came; all was complete and everything was shipshape. Bill, from down the road borrowed the farm tractor and trailer, and Lew came up and gave us a lift to get the boat on to the trailer. Then off we went, in convoy. Lew was in front and I was behind to keep my eye on it. I must admit I felt rather pleased with the transformation we had achieved as a family team.

We arrived down at Gurnard Creek just as the tide had gone out. Not deterred, Glenys got the Babycham out and we christened our boat "Playmate". By teatime the tide had come back in and we finally slid the old girl into the water. Ron Snook suggested I put a couple of long mooring poles in so that the boat would rise and fall with the tide.

Another lovely evening Glenys and I decided we would take a flask of coffee and have a little trip along the coast in Playmate. Well, you should have seen it! When we arrived at the Creek and looked out to sea we could see the waves rolling in and the white horses were prancing about like nobody's business! Wow! It was absolutely terrific. Safely aboard, I started the engine and we headed slowly out of the Creek. As soon as we cleared the sandbank and foreland the wind and the waves caught us and we were off. Climbing slowly up one huge wave, balancing on the top of the crest for a moment with the engine racing as the propeller came out of the water, then we hurtled down into the foaming trough below us. Talk about a white knuckle ride! It was a cross between a roller coaster ride and shooting the rapids. The spray was being driven into our faces as we hung on to the top of the cabin. I was thankful I had rigged up a steering wheel on the panel at the side of the cabin door, no way did I fancy sitting at the back hanging on to the tiller in these conditions.

We certainly enjoyed the adrenaline rush; it was great fun, even though we were soaked to the skin. I'm afraid our idea of sitting in the cabin casually drinking coffee whilst watching the sun go down, didn't quite come off! It took us all our time just to hang on for dear life in these lively conditions. We eventually decided to turn back and I managed to swing the boat around to face the shore, when a huge wave hit us broadside. This brought it home to us that it would be virtually impossible to motor back, battling against the wind and the mountainous seas. Turning the boat we headed at forty five degrees towards the shore and managed to land on a sandy patch. I leapt on to the beach and pulled the boat up enough for Glenys to disembark safely.

Then the fun started. I don't know if you have seen the film African Queen, where Humphrey Bogart, waist deep in the river, pulls the old tug boat along with the rope over his shoulder – well, this could have been a repeat performance. I held the rope over my shoulder as I struggled along the shoreline pulling the old girl along. Every few yards I would climb the shingle piled up against the heavy timber breakwater, only to drop down waist-deep in water over the other side. Breakwater after breakwater we struggled on. Glenys held on to a rope attached to the back of the boat. I suppose we were making quite good progress considering the weather conditions and the huge rollers bashing against the shoreline.

Then it happened; I climbed up a steep bank of shingle, and, as before, dropped down the other side of the breakwater into the sea – but, plop! The next thing I knew was the unpleasant sensation of finding myself out of my depth and looking upwards from the seabed to see the hull of Playmate floating directly above my head. Pushing myself up from the seabed I burst through the surf like a flying fish.

'Ugh!' I shouted, as I struggled to get inshore and back to terra-firma. Glenys just stood there laughing her head off.

'Come on,' she said, 'stop messing about. Let's get back to the Creek and out of this lousy weather.'

After another half an hour we eventually re-entered the sheltered waters of Gurnard Creek. I climbed on board and started up the engine then motored the boat the last few yards to our mooring posts. Glenys walked around the tennis courts and over the old stone bridge to meet up with me. She came aboard and we both started laughing as we swallowed the hot coffee, laced with a well-needed tot of rum.

Ron Snook came out of his cottage, dressed in yellow oilskins, a souwester and gum boots, carrying a lantern. Of course, by this time it was pitch black with menacing clouds racing across the darkened sky. As he approached I said he looked like the shouting sailor in the cod liver oil advert. In the next second he put his hands round his mouth and started shouting – well, that just about finished us off, as we fell about in fits of giggles.

The wind had really got up now and it was difficult to hear what Ron was shouting.

"What the devil do you think you're doing, going out in a Force 8 gale?" I'm afraid nautical jargon, like 'Force 8', still didn't mean much to us. I shouted back, "Yes, it was a bit choppy so we didn't get very far, but it was great fun while it lasted."

After a bit of a reprimand from Ron I promised to have a word with him first, if I intended going out again in rough weather. I wasn't too concerned though as we had our ex-oil tanker kapok life-preservers on and, of course, I carried my trustworthy fishing knife, guaranteed not to sink, just to float away, if dropped overboard!

Not like young Tony, who, when I dropped him in the water, just....

22

He Shot Out Like A Rocket!

Boxes, boxes, everywhere! Big ones, small ones, you couldn't get in to the shop for boxes!

'Norman, it's no good, you'll have to move them before somebody gets hurt.'

'I know' replied Norman, as he looked around. His wife was right; whatever happens, those boxes will have to be moved right away.

I stood in the doorway of Transatlantic Plastics, in Ventnor. All I wanted was two small pieces of Perspex. Most of the boxes were large and made of cardboard, with white labels attached denoting the contents. One of the smaller boxes nearest the door had printed on one side, in large black letters, "Pump and Filter Unit". Now, being a plumber, I thought that maybe I could make use of that in the pond I had made in my front garden. Looking across at the owner, I casually enquired what the pump could be used for.

'Oh, it's part of this bloomin' lot,' said Norman, pointing to the rest of boxes. 'It's all very well these people ordering three of them, then only collecting two – leaving me to shift the third one! All I can say is, thank goodness they paid for them before I placed the order!' With that, he began struggling to drag one of the larger cardboard containers to one side.

'Hang on a minute,' I said, taking off my jacket and hanging it on a hook next to the door. 'I'll give you a hand.'

I was surprised at how big and heavy the first box was; this was labelled "Bottom Rails. Then we shifted "Top Rails", followed by "Vertical Uprights". By this time I couldn't hold back my curiosity. My first thought was that the boxes contained some sort of storage shelving. That was until we came to a very huge, very heavy box labelled "Handle with Care – 75ft of Corrugated Pool Side".

'Pool Side?' I gasped, eyeing the lovely coloured picture, stuck on the top of the box, depicting a large circular swimming pool with a couple of smiling people throwing a beach ball to each other, whilst a couple of children leapt excitedly off some decking into the glistening blue water. Wow! My mind boggled – a swimming pool, now that was something beyond my wildest dreams!

'Hold it! Hold it!' I said to Norman. 'What are you going to do with this lot?'

'Oh, I don't know. I suppose I'll advertise it and see if I can sell it off cheap!'

I took a deep breathe, to calm my nerves and rising excitement, and casually muttered, 'Well, I'll take it off your hands, right here and now, if we can come to some sort of satisfactory arrangement.' Norman looked up.

'What? You mean you'll move it out of my way today?'

'Well, I don't have much money, but if you want to get rid of it, I'll be glad to take it off your hands.'

Two minutes later, and I was the proud owner of a 24ft circular swimming pool, complete with pump and filter unit, for just £35! I loaded it into the back of the dormobile and ten minutes later we were driving off. Oh heck! I turned the van around and headed back to the shop; with all the excitement I had forgotten the two pieces of Perspex I had come to get in the first place!

I later found out that the other two pools had been erected at the Pop Festival site over at Freshwater, and were used as water storage tanks.

Within three days, Tony and I had levelled the site in our garden and had the pool filled. Of course, our Tony, then had the privilege of christening the pool, fully clothed, as he was hurtled into the fresh, icy cold water! He landed in, and whoosh, he shot out like a rocket!

'Cor, it's freezing, dad!' he shouted.

It then became a ritual that we cleaned out the pool and had it working by the 13th of May, Tony's birthday, every year. And every year it was a ritual that he would race round the garden shouting, 'You can't catch me, you can't catch me, for a penny cup of tea!' and when I finally caught him I would drop him in the water amidst screams of laughter. Down he would go, and somehow, he shot out like a rocket, every time! I don't know how he did it.

Just in case you were wondering, the two pieces of Perspex were fitted onto Playmate, our boat. Now, there was a bit of excitement one year, as Derrick Langhorn and I, decided we would head out on the Solent and film the annual Cowes Power Boat Race. Phosphorescent coloured bubbles popped up to the surface as the propeller slowly rotated. It was a calm, moonless night when we sailed slowly out of Gurnard Creek; drifting behind, was the heavy, solid teak dingy that Bill Capps, the woodwork teacher, had made for us to use in the sheltered waters of Newtown Creek Nature Reserve.

The only other tender we had to Playmate was the original canvas canoe I had made a few years earlier. Well, that was alright but it was quite hairy stepping out and climbing aboard if it happened to be choppy or rough out at sea.

On and on, we chugged our way out into the Solent waters. Over on the starboard side (very nautical, eh!), we could see the light flashing on Egypt Point. Derrick suggested this would be a safe place to drop anchor, as we didn't want to be too close to the Power Boats which would be racing by at 10 o'clock the next morning. With that, I switched the engine off and Derrick manoeuvred his way to the front of the boat.

'Anchor, aweigh!' came the shout through the darkness.

'Don't forget to fasten it on firmly,' I shouted back quickly.

'Already done, Captain!' was the reply, and the next minute the First Mate clamboured back down into the cockpit.

Out came the flask of coffee, heavily laced with rum, and we just sat there in silence. It was so peaceful gently rising and falling with the lapping of the waves, with not a care in the world, just a couple of sea dogs enjoying the fruits of their labour!

'This is the life!' Derrick muttered, as he took another swig of the rum-laden coffee. Isn't it funny, being out at sea with the gentle rocking of the boat, the fresh salty air (and the hot soothing coffee), our eyelids seemed to get heavier and heavier! As we were both nodding off, we decided it would be a good time to have a little doze...

Bang! Bang! Bang! We both jumped up with a start.

'What the heck is that?' Derrick shouted. Another Bang! Then to our surprise we found our heavy tender boat trying to knock the hell out of the side of our own boat. It floated away, then in it came again, Bang! At this point I managed to grab it. Keeping a firm hold, we decided to abandon ship and head for shore. Clambouring over the side, into the dingy, we left Playmate bobbing up and down in rhythm with the calm sea.

Up early, the girls had made us a fantastic cooked breakfast with eggs, bacon, beans and lashings of toast. I made a flask of onboard coffee in high spirits. Back down at the Creek, Derrick and I pushed the dingy out and I started to row out towards Playmate. It looked a long way out, but it wasn't a problem, as we still had an hour before the first race began.

I had just made it to the headland of the Creek and I had this feeling that I wasn't getting anywhere. I was rowing for all I was worth, and I just wasn't gaining an inch. We might as well have been anchored, the moment I stopped rowing, we drifted backwards. Playmate was still a long way off. Glenys and Mildred started waving and shouting from shore.

'Come in! Come in!'

Well, no way were we going to go in, so Derrick climbed next to me and took one of the oars and we both started to pull with all our strength. But still to no avail, we just remained stationary. For a moment or two I thought we had got stuck on the sandbank, but the minute we eased up, back we would drift. By this time we were both red in the face and had quite a sweat on. I realised that it was no use in carrying on and I eased off. But Derrick wouldn't give up and he was puffing away and rowing like a lunatic. Then it finally dawned on him that we were going round and round like a spinning top.

'Come on' he yelled. 'We're not going back in.'

The girls were still shouting and waving frantically from the shore. It's funny, I thought, I wonder if they can see something that we can't. So reluctantly we decided to head back. Two minutes later we were in calm waters. As we came in nearer, we could tell what that the girls were shouting.

'Go down towards the tennis courts, then go out to sea. You were in the middle of a tidal whirlpool.' And do you know, within quarter of an hour, we were boarding Playmate, absolutely whacked out! Tying the dingy to the back of our boat, we both collapsed on the seats, but after a little mug of special coffee, we were ready for anything!

Now, at this time, I had just bought a smashing little 8mm standard movie camera. It was a wind up clockwork job, no batteries to go flat in those days. Of course, it wasn't sophisticated with zoom lens or telescopic lens, so I had the bright idea of holding the binoculars close up to the lens of the camera, and, Hey Presto!, we had a close up lens.

'Wow, look out, they're here!' Derrick suddenly shouted.

The noise became deafening as the almighty roar of twenty power boats going at full throttle came nearer, leaping out of the water like dolphins. What a sight! I was concentrating on catching this wonderful event on movie film, whilst Derrick shouted out comments like, 'Did you see that? It nearly did a back flip!'

To be honest, I didn't see much at all, looking through the little eye piece of the camera, but I wasn't bothered as I would have the pleasure of watching it all on the cine screen later.

As soon as the boats had all hurtled past, I looked for Derrick. He'd disappeared, just vanished. Then he re-appeared, from out of the cabin with one of our ex-oil tanker kapok life jackets half pulled over his head.

'What's all this about, then?' I asked. He pointed out to sea, still struggling with the jacket. Speeding towards us was one of the biggest waves I have ever seen. Derrick managed to get the large life-saver over his head and fought to tie the tapes around his waist.

'I can't swim, I can't swim!' he shouted.

Well, I knew that if this wave hit us broadside we would both be in the sea. There was no time to crank the engine up so I grabbed an oar and started rowing like mad to bring the boat round to face the oncoming rolling waves. There was one snag, the dingy fastened to the stern of Playmate wasn't the least bit worried about the plight we found ourselves in, and acted like a huge drift anchor, pulling us broadside into the wave. I can tell you, I was in a bit of a panic too by now, and was paddling like mad over the stern. Slowly the old girl gave in and swung around, just as the massive wave hit us head on. Bang! Up went the stern like a young stallion taking flight. The boat stood upright for a moment and Derrick flew down towards the back of the boat, legs and arms everywhere. How I managed to stay in the boat, I'll never know. The next minute, we were both sitting on the deck bobbing up and down, as if nothing had happened – at least Playmate lived up to her name. Naturally this called for a generous swig of coffee, whilst we checked everything was in tact. We hauled the anchor up, started the engine and headed back to shore.

Yes, the film came out alright. Apart from the black screen with a light circle in the centre (courtesy of the binocular technology) where the small tiny powerboats shot across one after the other, leaving behind the unforgettable foaming white wash behind them, which started to build up into that vast wave which headed straight towards us. Then the film stopped – the camera had needed winding up again!

We were very lucky to have a boat that stayed afloat...not like one of my pupils who suddenly found himself hanging on for dear life, in a boat that was completely airborne!

23

Opening The Door, He Stopped And Gasped!

'Help! Help! Help!' The pitiful, young cries echoed across the waters of the River Medina.

Everybody was fully occupied in the Cowes shipyard of J. Samuel White. Moored along side was a foreign Naval Frigate in the process of being re-fitted out. It was an amazing sight as washing was hung up on lines tied between every vertical structure. It looked more like a Chinese laundry than a fighting ship. There were second-hand bicycles, washing machines, and dozens of other "previously owned" objects scattered about the deck. The sailors had just received their monthly pay and they were dashing around Cowes buying up all the second-hand goods. They couldn't get around fast enough. It was bedlam in the high street; sailors were everywhere struggling with all sorts of large electrical appliances.

A sailor was in the process of tying a spin dryer to one of the bollards on deck when he heard the childish cry for help. There in the middle of the river he saw a black rowing boat, half submerged, with a young lad, wearing a school blazer, on board. The boy was rowing like the clappers in an attempt to reach the opposite bank of the river. The sailor swiftly grabbed a life belt and threw it overboard, soon realising the futility of his action. He then dashed to the shore side of his ship and shouted down to one of the workmen. The workman couldn't understand a word he was saying.

'Look, Look!' the sailor shouted again, as he pointed to the sinking boat.

When the workman eventually realised the situation the nipper was in, he dashed over to the foreman in charge of the huge crane. Within a couple of minutes, he had swung the crane out over the river and the large hook with a wire sling was hastily lowered to the young lad in distress.

I think the idea was for the boy to put the loop around his waist and they would bring him ashore, but no way was the lad going to leave his precious craft to the fate of the river. When the sling came down, he grabbed it and threaded it through the mooring ring on the stem of his boat. He waved frantically to the crane operator to lift. Well, what else could he do? So the foreman gently eased the hook upwards. The forward end of the boat slowly rose but the young lad was more concerned with rescuing his oars. Up and up went the boat until it stood on end like a sentry box, the lad was standing upright on the transom lying back on the seating still clutching his oars. Now totally out of the water, the boat was spinning round and round. The crane driver manoeuvred the completely airborne vertical craft, towards the shore.

All the sailors held their breath as they stood in a line watching this amazing rescue take place. As the boat was lowered gently on to the quayside, the lad hopped out and the boat bumped down and collapsed into a heap of scrap wood. The lad grabbed his oars, looked up at the smiling crane operator.

'Thanks mate!' Then he walked past the frigate.

The sailors shouted and cheered. The lad, with a little tear running down his cheek, put his thumb up and jauntily headed for the Floating Bridge to join his mates on their way to, "just another day, at school"!

The first I knew of the incident was when young Paul

entered my classroom still carrying the pair of oars. His main ambition was to possess a boat of his own. He had spotted the old dilapidated boat on Shepherds Wharf. After worrying the life out of the workmen, they gave him permission to work on it. He had read that in the olden days they used to waterproof their boats with pitch (tar). After a little persuasion, he managed to acquire a tin of cold tar from one of the contractors working on the roads. One evening, after school, he gave the outside of his boat a nice thick coat of black spirit-based tar. It's a good job he took his school blazer off, but I'm afraid his white shirt was a bit worse for wear – goodness knows what his mum said behind closed doors!

The following morning, a ten gallon drum of resin plus a roll of fibre glass, was delivered to my workshop with the compliments of the British Hovercraft Cooperation, to allow the "brave young nipper" to build his very own fibre glass dingy. Later in the afternoon, a lorry from the shipyard dropped off some mahogany planking and strips to fit out his boat. I couldn't get over it; talk about the Island bush telegraph system, it was certainly buzzing that day!

The lad was highly delighted and called around to the factories to thank them for their kind generosity. They were touched when they saw the size of the youngster standing there in his new shirt and short trousers. Exactly one month later, with the help of his pals, he was seen up the River Medina in his brand new blue fibre glass dinghy.

I believe 90% of education is interest and encouragement, but this can back-fire in the most unusual way, like the time the caretaker met me at the door holding a large empty cardboard box.

Two lads came in on a cold and frosty morning.

'Sir, do you know anything about stained glass windows?'

'Well, as a matter of fact I do,' I replied.

When I had my plumbing firm we also had a glazing

section. Oh yes, we replaced many a shop window that had been broken. I was a bit of a dab hand at cutting all shapes and sizes of glass. In fact, I had even once repaired and produced a stained glass window on a church.

'Okay, lads' I continued. 'What have you done?'

'Well, Sir' they started, 'It's like this. We were playing cricket in the street, with a stone instead of a ball, and stupid, here, belted it and it went straight through this lady's stained glass front door. She said she would report it to the police and tell our parents if we didn't pay to get it repaired.'Stupid" then butted in.

'The problem is nobody does that sort of work around here, and, we haven't got any money. So we thought we'd ask you to see if you could help us out.'

Well, what an opportunity to teach them how to cut glass and make a stained glass window, or at least repair the lady's door. I went to see her and she was delighted. She even offered to pay for the glass, if we could repair it for her! Out came the old glass and we put a temporary plywood panel in its place. And that was the start of another lesson.

I bought half-a-dozen glass cutters and strips of "H" section lead from Alderslades in Newport. They were very generous when I explained what we were doing and gave me a free box of coloured glass off-cuts.

The boys started by designing some beautiful stained glass panels. One boy came up with the idea of making a picture frame with a stained glass picture of the hovercraft we were making. When he had completed it, he fitted a strip light behind to show it off; it was fantastic. I was so pleased with the enthusiasm the lads showed in this new technique. And yes, they made a wonderful job of repairing the lady's door. She rewarded them with tea, biscuits and five shillings each as a thank you. After that they would call round to see if she wanted any shopping doing, and they became great friends.

One lad came and asked me how to cut a circle out of an existing window, as his father had bought an X-pelair fan for the bathroom and needed a hole cutting in the window to fit it. I had an adapter which consisted of a centre piece and an adjustable arm with a cramp to fit the glasscutter at any distance along the arm. I must give the boy credit, he worked at this technique over and over again on some waste glass. He cut the circle then made a series of cut marks to an inner circle forming small glass segments which could be tapped out. It's a tricky job and, time and time again, the glass would crack on the outside of his circle. But not to be put off, he persevered and eventually mastered cutting a perfect hole in the glass.

Off he went with his mates to cut the hole in his bathroom window. His dad was very pleased when he came home to find a neat hole exactly the right size for his fan.

Well, the next morning the caretaker turned the large key in the mortice lock, then took the padlocks off the door to the tuck shop. Nobody, but nobody, could break into that tuck shop; it was like Fort Knox. Opening the door, he stepped inside and gasped; all the sweets and chocolate had disappeared from the shelves. On the floor was a pile of empty crisp boxes. The cheek of it – the culprits had even munched their way through a couple of packets and left the rubbish on the shelf!

The caretaker, stood there scratching his head. Who the devil had managed to pinch his keys and then had the audacity to lock it all up again when he left? As he glanced around he noticed that all the window latches were down and secure, but, then he spotted it – a fine neat round hole, cut out of the first window, just big enough for a small hand to reach through to lift up the window latch! At assembly, one of the pupils (a boy, of course) had a nice white bandage wrapped firmly around his wrist.

Funnily enough, nobody turned up to purchase the somewhat 'rundown' stock at the tuck shop at playtime. Now, this was the first time in the history of the school that no sales were made. But, there was quite a queue building up just behind the row of outside toilets, and the youngsters were walking away looking very pleased with themselves – as they had just bought packets of crisps, at less than half price!

Young "bandaged-arm" was dragged off by the caretaker to see Mr Nicholson, the Master in Charge at that time, who was also his form tutor. Old Nic stood there with his cane at the ready.

'Bend over boy, and touch your toes.'

Whack! Whack! Whack!

'Now get back to your classroom.' The young boy stood up and walked away smiling, jangling his pockets which were full of loose change – I think they call it free enterprise!

Now, that brings me to the lad who came into my workshop and wanted to make a two-wheeled trolley.

'Okay,' I said. 'You design it and show me your working drawings with all the measurements, and list of materials, and I will consider if it is a worthwhile project.'

I think he must have been up all night, as he appeared the next morning with a scale drawing showing the plan, and two elevations, with a pictorial view plus a material list, right down to the last nut and bolt. With enthusiasm like that there was no holding him back; every spare minute, playtime and after school, he would be beavering away cutting tubes and filing them, ready for welding.

Eventually it was ready to assemble. I stayed behind to help him with my newly-acquired welder – of course, I had been welding since I was fourteen, and held a City and Guilds Certificate in both gas and electric welding. The wheels slid smoothly onto the greased axle. The washers and split pins were fitted and finally two coats of Royal Blue paint were applied to the framework, which contrasted nicely with the bright red wheels.

By the end of the week, I had four more lads entering my lesson, each carrying some tubing and a pair of wheels.

'Hey! What's this?' I asked.

'Can we make a luggage truck, the same as Spiv's?' And so they did!

I later found out that all the lads used to meet the passengers from the Red Funnel Ferry at West Cowes terminal.

'Carry your bags for you, Sir?' they would shout. 'Anywhere in Cowes, for a shilling!' Well, as you can imagine, by the end of the day their arms were aching like anything.

Then Spiv arrived with his luggage truck and he was doing twice as much business, with twice the income and less effort!

Now, talk about enterprise; he offered to supply all the tubing and wheels free to the lads if they built their trolleys exactly to his plans and specifications. They couldn't wait to get started. But there was just a small catch – Spiv insisted that he dealt with the customers and their money, and would hand out the deliveries in strict order so there was no fighting, pushing or shoving to get to the customers. Well, that sounded fair; he supplied the trucks which were now on loan to them and he paid them half of the takings. On a Saturday they could make ten shillings or more!

Of course, nobody worked out that Spiv was making five times that amount, by just organising and distributing the work! During the summer he had increased his fleet to ten trolleys, and by now they all had a nicely stencilled sign attached to them, reading "Cowes Luggage Transport – Registered Carrier"; yes, he actually registered them! Boys were fighting to get on his waiting list as he now had the full monopoly on a very lucrative business.

It was after this summer that we had a new, dynamic headmaster, Mr Winder, and I became Master in Charge of the East Cowes School; my new Applied Technology Department was about to become a reality.

24

I Can't Feel My Legs

Mr Nicholson retired and I was appointed Master in Charge of the Osborne Road School in East Cowes. Betty Robinson continued as school secretary and did a fantastic job. I had the responsibility of keeping the school running smoothly and efficiently. There were half a dozen teaching staff, four kitchen staff and Mr Harrison the caretaker; I don't know about caretaker, he was a jack of all trades and helped me enormously with setting up the bricklaying course.

I had a group of non-examination pupils who wanted to stay on at school to better their chances at getting a good job. Now I recognised that they were all willing and eager to learn and, with this in mind, I set up a fifth form course allowing the pupils to stay on an extra year to develop their potential and introduce them to industrial experience. With the help and support of Bill Winder the headmaster, and co-operation from the parents, the fifth form Technology Course was born, and was to become known as '5 Tech'.

At one meeting a parent came up to me, 'I would like my son to stay on at school, so he can get more brains.' Well, I couldn't argue with that, could I?! The boy in question did stay on, and matured very quickly, and "got the brains" which landed him a full apprenticeship with Plessey Radar after competing with lads from other Island schools. Of course, he had the advantage of twelve month's industrial experience in various industries and understood the requirements of the employer.

After months and months of discussions with industrial leaders, unions, education authorities, parents and insurance companies, I eventually managed to persuade them to accept my plans for the new concept of work experience. The first pupils to try out this very successful experiment were my own 5T form. You may not be aware, but from that very seed of an idea the whole National Work Experience scheme was founded which is still up and running today.

I am proud to say that every boy on the scheme was offered a job or apprenticeship in a variety of firms throughout the Island. You may well ask, 'What is Applied Technology?' Well, moving away from the old woodwork and metalwork image, I decided that all materials should be investigated. We had just entered the new age of 'plastics'. (So, *Technology* being the science of materials, and *Applied* meaning 'put to a practical use'). This was a very exciting time. My new purpose-built Design and Technology unit was completed at the main school. This consisted of a design and drawing centre, woodwork, engineering, foundry, metalwork, plastic development and boatbuilding workshops, with boat storage and sailing facilities at the National Sailing Centre on the River Medina.

It was a great day down at the NSC as Tony Wyeth and the school sailing club proudly displayed the seven mirror dinghies and the powerful RIB rescue boat that they had worked very hard to have completed for this special launch day. Oh yes, it was special. As well as the top folk from County Hall and the headmaster with the board of governors, we had a well known and unique guest of honour, who was known throughout the sailing world as he often raced with Prince

Philip; yes, it was none other than Uffa Fox himself, who had the privilege to launch our first fleet of sailing dinghies!

Well, the pre-drinks reception went down very well, and we all assembled outside in the beautiful sunshine; it was a day to remember. Uffa Fox came outside with all the dignitaries. Bill Winder, the headmaster, said a few words, as Uffa took hold of the large bottle of champagne. He flicked the cork off and whoosh! Champagne shot into the air, as everybody cheered and the ceremony started in real earnest. Uffa walked (well, staggered) over to the first dinghy, singing a rather naughty sea shanty. With a flourish, he bent down and looked at the name on the boat.

'I name this ship Dopey', he slurred, and poured a drop of champagne into the dingy to christen it. With that done he took a large swig out of the bottle for himself, as he staggered over to the next boat. 'I name this ship Grumpy', a spot of bubbly on the boat and another substantial swig for himself! As you have probably gathered, all the dinghies were named after the seven dwarfs. And so the ceremony progressed. Lastly, Uffa came to the rescue boat. 'I name this ship Snow White and God bless all who sail in her,' he announced as he poured a good dose on to the boat. With the job finished, he tipped back his head and poured the rest of the champagne down his throat. We all thought this was very funny and clapped our hands. With all eight boats in the water, gently swaying in the breeze, Uffa (swaying quite a bit himself) turned to the dignitaries and smiled, 'Well, what are we waiting for? Let's get down to some serious drinking!' And he headed off to the bar and promptly ordered himself a double whisky!

* * * * *

Talking of alcoholic drinks, the strong 'Chesters' beer brewed in Manchester was no match for Ted Cummins home brew....

On the last day of term, everybody was more than ready for the six week's summer holiday. The kids were let out an hour earlier than usual and all the staff were invited for a drink at Ted Cummins' house. He lived on the corner of Park Road and Victoria Road in Cowes, just a short walk from the school.

It was another beautiful, hot, summer's day with a clear blue sky and golden sunshine. Ted's wife, Audrey, had set out tables and chairs on the lawn, with colourful umbrellas over each table. Ted, who had managed to get away a little earlier, had set his stall out with a whacking great big barrel of homemade beer, together with bottles and bottles of red and white homemade wine.

As you can imagine, after a very strenuous examination term, parent's meetings and final preparations for the new intake in September, on this last day we were all just about dropping. It didn't take long for us all to relax after a glass or two of wine or beer, and soon everyone was feeling almost human again.

Audrey, much to our surprise, brought out a lovely selection of pies and fancy cakes. It was turning out to be quite a garden party. As some folks left, others popped in, to enjoy the free beer and wine. Like all good things, the party eventually came to an end (however, this wasn't because the drinks had run out – Ted informed us that there was a further twenty gallons of beer still lying in wait in his cellar!).

Now, Bill Shelmedine, head of science, being a Lancashire lad, like myself, was brought up on the famous extra strong Chesters beer. Manchester folk reckoned that, 'If you could drink Chesters, then you could drink owt.' – But they hadn't reckoned on Ted Cummin's home brew! By now, Bill had had a belly-full of Ted's brew. He suddenly stood up and informed everybody, 'Got to go now folks, me tea will be ready.' Then very slowly his knees gave way and he gently slid down the edge of the table. Looking up in amazement, he whispered 'I can't feel me legs!' then sat down on the lawn, giggling away. Well, we all looked down at him and burst out laughing.

A couple of staff from Gurnard said they would see him safely home. The two teachers, who were half kaylied themselves, staggered off holding the unfortunate Bill between them. When they reached his house, they sat him down on the front porch steps, rang the doorbell and falling over themselves, staggered back down the path and out through the front gate before Mrs Shelmedine opened the door and spotted them.

At first the poor woman couldn't make out what her husband was doing sitting on the step – but then she smelt the beer! He was as drunk as a newt at a wedding. Funnily enough I don't think Bill ever went to one of Ted's 'little drinkies on the lawn' again.

Esso Petroleum Company sponsored the annual Technology for Schools Competition. It's funny, but the tradition of Cowes High School winning the competition year after year became an accepted norm. We were years ahead of the other traditional craft departments, and the other schools soon realised the benefits. I was inundated with Head of Departments coming over to the Island to see our set up and discuss how they could make a start along the same lines. Keith Simmons, my deputy, entered some of his pupils in the Young Engineers award. Again we were successful, as one of his pupils had designed and made a folding bicycle (nowadays, of course, these are common place, but back then they hadn't even been thought of). The boy won the coveted award of "Young Engineer of the Year" and, imagine this, Prince Charles actually rode the bicycle!

I was on the development board for the Open University and was the chief advisor for the new Design and Technology course to be introduced as a university examination. It was also about this time that I was approached by the Home Office to become a member on the Board of Governors at the three Island prisons: Parkhurst, Camp Hill and Albany. This I accepted and was soon invited to serve on Her Majesty's Parole Board for these prisons. I found it very interesting and had many interviews with some very notorious prisoners for parole. But of course, any names or outcomes can never be revealed, as I had signed the Official Secrets Act – so enough said about that!

One of our combined efforts in integrating all crafts was the design and production of a full activity adventure playground for the handicapped children at Watergate School in Newport. Ted Lock came up with the idea and Keith followed it up by taking a group of pupils from our department to spend time with the children and to assess their needs. It was great fun and very exciting to see all the staff and pupils working very hard as an integrated team.

The playground equipment consisted of a huge elephant-shaped climbing frame, fibre-glass slides, boxes, tunnels and tubes also made out of fibre-glass and plastic for the youngsters to climb through. We also designed some mobile transporters which were basically triangular-shaped wooden bases with three wheels attached – youngsters with physical disabilities who couldn't walk would crawl onto the transporters and, without any effort or fear, would propel themselves at great speed across the play area. In the end they also used them in the school to get from classroom to classroom. They became totally mobile and free to go anywhere they wanted, without assistance from the staff or carers. It was super to see their faces as they, quite literally, hurtled down the corridors to their next lessons!

Eric, our technician, and Peggy, our store lady, definitely had their hands full trying to keep up with the pupils and their constant enthusiasm. Many of the local firms supplied us with free materials for various projects. Pupils would often take their drawings of a new project, show it to the folk in charge of the firm and come away with all the materials they needed to complete the task. BHC (British Hovercraft Corporation) who were based in East Cowes at that time, supplied us with two large industrial lathes, a milling machine, a couple of pillar drills, and a huge punch which was capable of punching one inch diameter holes out of thick sheet steel.

I must tell you about the disruption that was once caused in all the local cafes in Cowes High Street. It all started when Eric started punching holes in a piece of sheet metal. At the end of the day, a couple of pupils inquired if they could have the scrap metal discs for fishing weights. 'Help yourself!' said Eric, 'Take as many as you want.' And with that, they loaded their pockets and set off for home.

A couple of days later, Pete, an ex-pupil and irate café owner, came up to school dragging with him two unfortunate pupils by their blazer collars. 'In yer get!' he said as he shoved them through the door and into my office. He stepped towards me and poured out a pocketful of familiar metal discs onto my desk. I looked at him in surprise and asked what this was all about. He pointed to the discs. 'Did you know these are exactly the same size and weight as a two-bob piece? And these two nippers 'ave just about emptied my cigarette machine!' 'Right! Leave it to me. I'll deal with them personally,' I said, glaring at the boys. 'Oh, I don't want them to be punished' Pete said, 'I just want to make sure that the other nippers don't get their hands on any of them discs. You can't blame 'em, I would have done exactly the same at that age!'He also said that he wished he was back at school, with all the opportunities that are available to these 'lucky lads' now. The boys thanked him and said how sorry they were, but Pete hadn't finished. 'Now listen, you two ragamuffins!

You can come down to Greasy Pete's Café at exactly four o'clock after school and give it a good clean out. Then we'll call it quits! Of course, when you've finished I'll make you both a nice mug of tea, and if you're lucky, you may even get a bacon butty!' They both burst out laughing. 'Don't worry, we'll be there!' (The next day they informed me that Pete had been so pleased with their cleaning skills that he had given them both a regular part-time job!)

My dream had come true and my new department was born. But this was nothing compared to what was soon to become a reality as I felt a tap on my shoulder.

'Come on, Mr Feldon. It's time!'....

25

The Door Opened Silently, 'It's Time!'

Dawn; the prison walls were bathed in warm, golden light as the sun began to rise. I took a deep breath; all was still and at peace. It had been a long, long night. From my elevated position, I could see the odd light going out around the prison. I left, feeling sorry for the inmates, as the only blue sky they ever saw was square-shaped and bordered by the high prison walls. I felt a gentle tap on my shoulder.

'Come on Mr Feldon, it's time!' The nurse held a green overall out. I put my arms into the sleeves and turned around, allowing her to fasten the gown at the back. I followed her meekly back into the hospital – which was situated directly across the road from Albany Prison.

The automatic doors of St Mary's Maternity Unit opened silently and I entered into a different world, a world of activity. Everybody knew exactly what they were doing. Apart from me, that is!

Of course, I'd been "a dad" before, but somehow the babies just appeared. Della was tucked up, peacefully asleep in the cot at the foot of the bed, while Vanda was wrapped up in a snug pure white blanket, like a little parcel, held out by the nurse as if it were a loaf of bread, for me to see for the very first time. Of course, she was wide awake, with that little mischievous smile and a twinkle in her eyes, as if to say,

'I'm going to lead you a right dance, my daddy!' (And she was right. It wasn't long before we were on the dance festival circuits on the mainland as well as the Island. From the moment she was born, she knew exactly what she wanted to do, and eventually she was accepted for the London College of Dance and Drama, where she attained her full teaching qualification).

In those days, on your first visit after the birth, it was 'Congratulations. Here's your baby,' and you were suddenly a dad!

This time, however, it would be very different. There was a nurse sitting by Glenys's side.

'Take a deep breath. That's it, now push. Push! Push! Well done, you're doing fine!' Then she wiped the sweat off Glenys's forehead, as she pulled away the gas and air.

I walked into the room in a bit of a daze and headed for the top of the bed to sit with Glenys, but a hand steered me to the end of the bed, where all the action was taking place. Then I saw it; a tiny head covered in a mass of dark hair. Well, I nearly passed out!

'Come on, now, Mr Feldon. This is your baby. Come and hold its head' said the Midwife. 'Don't' worry, it won't fall off!' And with that, she took hold of my hands and placed them firmly under the baby's head. Two minutes later and the baby popped out, like a cork out of a bottle.

'It's a beautiful baby girl!' I heard someone say. By this time, I had tears of emotion running down my cheeks.

The nurse quickly cleaned our little girl up, then handed her over to me; there was no slapping of bottoms, or anything like that. That little girl was wide awake. She was so beautiful. Then she gave out a little cry, and I nearly dropped her in fright. I think she was just letting me know that she had arrived. By this time I wasn't too sure what was going on around me, I was just fascinated with this little bundle of joy. Somewhere in the background I heard a voice speaking to me.

'Well, aren't you going to talk to your new baby?'

'Oh, er, yes' I replied, finding it difficult to speak as I was still so overcome with the emotions of happiness, relief, joy and wonderment. In a hoarse whisper, I said 'Hiya, baby. I'm your dad!'

For a second or two she seemed to focus and made eye contact, and gave me the most wonderful little smile, as if to say, 'You silly old fool, I know you're my daddy – who else would be looking at me like that?!' A few minutes later she met the most amazing person in her life; her mother.

I held Glenys's hand, and we both shed a few tears of relief and happiness – Mother and baby doing well!

I was so thankful for everything I had; three loving, supporting, fantastic children, and now a beautiful newborn baby girl, and a wonderful wife and mother for my children. What more could I ask for?

* * * * *

'A dad's love gives strength to his sons, guidance to his daughters and protection to the home. He is the most important teacher in their lives, because, in him, his children see the qualities they will look for in other men'.

26

'No, Thank You. I've Just Had A Cup Of Tea.'

When Glenys and I went up to see Vanda at college, we were both shocked and appalled at the condition of the buildings. It was like being in a time warp, as we hurried up a narrow, old, cobbled side street. A sign announcing "The London College of Dance & Drama" in cracked, faded gilt lettering, hung crookedly over the door, swinging precariously on rusty wrought-iron brackets.

On entering the building we were immediately transported back to the era of Dickens. Old, twisted, bare wooden stairs went up to the dance studios. The hand rail felt loose and I was afraid it would come off in my hand. Isn't it funny how thoughts flash though your mind; now, I wondered, if it comes off do I try and wedge it back up, or should I just lie it carefully down on the stairs as if nothing has happened?! To save me from having to make a decision, the door on the landing creaked open, and Vanda came out smiling, thrilled to bits to see us.

'Come in and meet the girls and my tutor' she said excitedly.

All the decayed, plastered walls were covered with huge gilt mirrors. The old girl at the piano was banging away, whilst the girls dressed in black leotards and hanging on to the bars in front of the mirrors, were standing up on one toe whilst at the same time lifting their other leg high into the air, way above their heads. I cringed at the sight, and thought to myself, they really ought to be very careful, as they could do themselves a nasty injury!

'No! No! No!' the small petite dance mistress called out loudly. 'The music! The music! Listen carefully, and keep in time!'

A few years later, as I was up in London, I thought it would be nice to take Vanda and her pal, Joyce, out for a slap-up meal at a posh restaurant. We were escorted to the table by the restaurant manager and he held the chairs back for the girls whilst they sat down. They both looked at one another and burst out giggling. The manager looked at me and smiled, then clicked his fingers and a waiter came across and presented us with the menus, which were nearly as big as a double-decker bus! We spent a lot of time studying the beautiful engraved lettering. The girls looked at me and shrugged their shoulders.

'We know it's French, but what does it all mean?'

Following discussion, we all decided to have the same; soup for starters followed by an interesting-sounding meat dish. The waiter recommended a bottle of wine, and we all settled down until the soup arrived. I must admit, it was delicious. We tucked into the soup and rolls, as if there was no tomorrow – I had the feeling that Vanda and Joyce has existed on beans on toast for the last three years, as they shared digs together and had to manage on their students allowance.

Then Clang! Clang! Clang! The bell rang out.

'Everybody out!' someone shouted. 'This is an IRA bomb alert.' All the diners looked at each other, startled; they must be joking, we thought. But no! We were all ushered outside, grabbing at our buns and taking one last dip in the delicious soup before our rather hurried departure.

It was absolutely freezing standing outside on the pavement. The police swiftly cordoned off the street and we watched as the army bomb disposal unit arrived, whilst nibbling on our soup-soaked bread rolls.

The only consolation was that we all had benefited from a 'free' half-bowl of tasty soup and a soggy roll, as we bade each other goodbye!

* * * * *

I must tell you about a funny incident whilst I was in London studying for my Diploma in Safety Management. Bill, John, Cecil and I were having a drink in the lounge of the Piccadilly Hotel.

Bill was an ex-Metropolitan Police Vice Squad Officer. After retiring he was offered the post of Head of Safety and Security at a large electronic manufacturing company in the Midlands. He took us round all the sleazy nightclubs in Soho; boy, we were like little kids as we wandered up and down back alleyway. All the dubious characters and bouncers on the door would acknowledge Big Bill with a nod of their head or a handshake. It was an amazing experience meeting all those criminals on their home ground. It was certainly a different kettle of fish when I met them in prison, in controlled surroundings.

John was a nice quiet chap, who was there, like myself, to study, swat and get that very important Diploma, which gave membership to the exclusive International Institute of Safety Managers; the passport to the world of industrial opportunities.

Cecil was the most mild, unassuming and gentle person you could ever meet. He stood about five foot two in his stocking feet. He was very lightly built with a balding head and thick black bifocal glasses perched on the end of his nose, which somehow seemed unattached to his small, round face. When we were doing the rounds through Soho with Big

Bill, Cecil actually hung on to the sleeve of my jacket. I think he may have even held my hand given the chance! He was scared stiff and kept muttering, 'I don't know what my wife would say.'

One evening Cecil decided to make his way to his room on the third floor, as he needed his beauty sleep, and the toilet, after consuming two cups of tea in a row. So with that, he bid us goodnight and departed towards the lift. Two minutes later he came running down the stairs and across the foyer towards the lounge. His face was bright red, he was puffing and panting, and shaking like a leaf.

'Derek, Derek. Get me a brandy, quick, before I pass out!'

'Whoa! Hold it!' I said. 'What's the matter, Cec, old boy?'

'Brandy! Brandy!' he demanded as he collapsed into the chair opposite. After a couple of sips from the glass, he seemed to calm down a bit, and then he started to stutter and gabble on.

'Stop! Hold it right there,' said Bill. 'Now tell us what's happened. Have you been mugged?'

'No! No!' he replied. 'Oh, what will my wife say?!'

After a long deep breath, it all came out.

'When I said goodnight to you, I strolled across to the lift and pressed the button and waited. The door of the lift slid open and two young, black ladies were standing at the back of the lift, so I stood to one side and said, "After you, ladies." "Oh, no, Big Fella!" they said, "we're going up." "Oh, that's alright then" I said and stepped into the lift. I asked them what floor they were after and they asked me which floor I wanted. "I'm on floor three," I said. "Same for us, then," they both chorused. I smiled and realised that the big lady, and I mean 'big', was smiling back at me. The smaller lady then winked at me, so I nodded and thought to myself how friendly they both were. At the third floor we all got out and I politely wished them a goodnight. "Oh, yes," said the shorter lady, "we can assure you of that!" Anyway, I headed towards my door, put the key in the lock, and turned round to find they were both standing there behind me. Then the big lady put her arm around me and said, "Well, Big Fella, how would you like two hot chocolates for a night cap!" I was scared stiff, so I just grabbed my key and ran, saying "No, thank you. I've just had a cup of tea." As I tore along the corridor I could hear them laughing, even when I got down to the first floor. Oh, dear me. Oh, what would my wife say?'

As you can imagine, we all just roared out laughing.

Anyway, after that, he always waited until we all went up to our rooms, and even insisted that Big Bill open the door to his room and checked it out, before he went in.

By the last night, his confidence had returned and all nerves were forgotten. We all said goodnight and Cecil entered his room by himself. The three of us dashed down the corridor and hid round the corner near the staircase. We waited for some kind of reaction from Cecil, but there was nothing.

We were just about to give up, when Cecil's bedroom door flew open, and he shot into the corridor holding his blue-striped pyjama bottoms up with one hand, frantically waving his other hand up and down, as if he had just disturbed a nest of wasps.

'Help! Help!' he croaked.

He suddenly realised that other guests were walking towards him, so turned and re-entered his room somewhat sheepishly, closing the door behind him.

Then his door opened again, and he stepped into the corridor. He glanced up and down, and spotted us peeping from behind the corner.

'You b-ggers! he said, waving a sheet of the hotel's notepaper in the air. 'I'll get you for this,' he muttered, as he stormed back into his room.

He looked at the two glasses of steaming hot chocolate sitting on his bedside cabinet, then burst out laughing when he read the little note grasped in his hand – '*Hi, Cecil! Pleasant dreams! We won't tell your wife, if you don't! Sleep well, Big Fella! Bill, Derek & John.*'

27

Bon Appetite! Bon Appetite!

Sun, sea, sand and brilliant blue skies heralded the arrival of Edelgard and Andrea from Germany. Della and Vanda had been writing to them as pen pals, and it had been arranged that they would come to us for a holiday and then we would take them back in our motor caravan. The idea being that Della and Vanda would then stay with them in Germany, whilst Glenys and I continued on to Switzerland and France before picking them up for the journey home.

Well, we'd all had a whale of a time, with a visit to Blackgang Chine, coloured-sand collecting at Alum Bay, and swimming, picnicking and sailing down at Gurnard. It was at this time that we launched my newly designed two-seater fibreglass speedboat, which motored along with the aid of a two-horsepower engine. Our good friends, Les and Yvonne Scott were the first to own the prototype model. This little boat soon became a firm favourite with the pupils at school, as most of them already owned a 2HP outboard. Up and down the Medina we sailed and then off to East Cowes to watch the newly extended cross-channel hovercraft SRN4-004, 'Princess Margaret', being launched. It was a very exciting time, and little did we know that we would soon be on this car-carrying hovercraft, sailing from Dover to Calais.

The Island holiday came to an end and it was time to start

our journey to the Continent. Barry Price checked our van over and fitted a brand new exhaust system, so we felt confident that we would have a safe, comfortable journey. I had fitted the original van out as a motor caravan. One Saturday morning in the school workshop, Glenys and I had moulded the new van roof out of fibreglass, and I designed an easy lifting device which raised the roof to give ample headroom when we were camping. Oh yes, we had all mod cons – a cooker, sink, wardrobe and even a toilet, together with full sleeping accommodation! It was fantastic!

We were motoring excitedly along the duel carriageway just outside Lewes when there was a loud bang, followed by 'Clatter! Clatter! Clatter!' I pulled over and jumped out to see what on earth was going on, only to find the exhaust dragging along the ground. So, out came the wire, and I spent the next half hour laid on my back underneath the van, doing a temporary repair job. In the meantime, Glenys naturally put the kettle on and made us all a nice cup of tea! I flagged down a chap and asked if there was a garage nearby.

'Sure, mate,' he said as he pointed down the road. 'Take the first right, go down for quarter of a mile, or so, and on the left you'll find Jack's Place. You may have to bang hard on the door, as they're closed on Saturdays, but Jack lives in the flat above.'

I thanked him and we set off once again.

A big sign over the garage door read 'Motor Engineers'. I tried the door, but, as expected, it was locked, so I gave it my usual back-kick just to make sure. A voice from the other side of the door shouted at me.

'Sorry, we're closed!'

'Please help me, it's an emergency!' I shouted back.

With that, the door opened and out came Jack. He was a middle-aged chap with grey hair sticking out from under a black greasy cap. He had large bushy eyebrows and large blue eyes which sparkled in the sunlight. His navy Bib and Brace overalls were clean and well pressed, and you could almost see your face in his highly polished ex-army boots.

'Now then, fella. What's this all about then?'

I explained we were off to the continent and had to take the four girls to Germany. I then pointed at the exhaust and told him that it had just fallen off.

'Ah! Well, yer better bring her in then, and put her over the pit.'

So over the hole in the floor I parked the van, and Jack immediately climbed down an oil-stained ladder and disappeared underneath her. A few moments later and he popped his head up.

'Well, they made a good job of the exhaust; it's the bracket on the van that has rusted away.' With that, he jumped out of the hole and went over to his workbench. Out came a piece of angle iron, and he drilled a series of holes along its length, and finished up by welding hanging brackets onto the angle iron. Then back under the old girl he disappeared. The sound of the electric drill echoed through the workshop as he drilled the fixing holes in the runners along the base of the vehicle.

'Pass me that box of nuts and bolts off the bench' he yelled. I grabbed it quickly and passed them down to him. Ten minutes later out he climbed. 'That'll do the job, you'll have no more trouble with her. She won't let you down.'

'Thank you, thank you, thank you,' I gushed, 'and sorry for getting you out on your day off.'

'Don't worry about that, son. It got me out of the missis hair for an hour.' He winked, 'Of course, I'll have to stay down here for a while now, to do a bit of tidying up!' He winked again, as he picked up a bottle from under his bench, 'And that's real thirsty work, you know!'

As we backed out, he went into his little office, sat down and put his feet up on the old battered waste paper bin, took a swig of beer and nodded his head,

'Now that's what I call a good Saturday afternoons work! Have a safe journey' he called, as he pulled his cap over his eyes and began to settle himself down for a nice little snooze.

I knocked on the door of the four-storey guest house – no reply. Well, we'll just have to try another one. This didn't seem to be much of a problem as the street was full of guest houses and small hotels. I then spotted the large brass bell pull, just below the brightly coloured stained-glass window. Here goes, I grabbed the brass knob and pulled. Somewhere at the back of the house I could hear the bell ringing away – dong, dong, dong! It sounded like a solemn church bell, ringing out single notes as if a funeral party had just arrived. The door was flung open and a flustered landlady appeared, with sleeves rolled up, hands bright red and wet through. She was puffing away completely out of breath.

'Sorry, about that! I was in the back yard hanging the washing out. Now then, what can I do for you?'

'Have you a vacancy for tonight?' I asked.

'Yes, I have a single room.'

'Ah! There are six of us altogether, and I think six in a single bed might just be a bit of a squeeze!'

She burst out laughing. 'Oh you are one! A proper little teaser, you are. Let me see, yes, I think I can fix you all up. Would you be wanting tea tonight and breakfast in the morning too?'

'That would be great, but we have to be off pretty early in the morning though, as we're booked on the first hovercraft, and we have to be there half an hour before sailing.'

'That's no problem. With six of you in one booking, I'll stay up all night if I have to!'

On the top floor we looked straight out over the white cliffs of Dover, or so we thought. Then we realised we were actually looking out over rooftops, covered in years and years of accurately deposited seagull droppings. It was quite a sight. Did we sleep? No way! I've never heard so much squealing and screeching in all my life! For a wonderful second or two, it would go deathly silent. We'd all breathe a deep sigh of relief and close our eyes – Then, it would start up all over again! The birds sounded as if they were squabbling, it was an awful din. What a night. It's funny, whenever we mentioned Dover to the girls, their first reaction was, 'Oh, those blooming seagulls!'

After a good hearty full English breakfast, we said our goodbyes. I casually asked the landlady how she managed to sleep every night with all the racket from the gulls.

'Noise?' she answered. 'I just put my head down and I'm off in dreamland within two minutes sharp. Seagulls? I don't hear no seagulls at night.'

Ten minutes later we were being ushered into a queue ready to board the hovercraft. It was like being in a huge aircraft hanger, as we were guided to a parking lot inside the new hovercraft. Chains were wrapped around our wheels to anchor our van to the car deck. Climbing the steep stairs we made ourselves comfortable in the luxury aircraft-type seats. We seemed to tower above the sea. The engines roared into life, and we had lift off, gently easing our way down the slipway and out of the harbour. Soon after, the thrust engines opened up and we hurtled across the English Channel, landing in France, before we even knew it!

With passports checked and handed back, we knew we were now properly on our way. As we approached the Belgium border we spotted a nice little roadside café, with tables and chairs scattered along the pavement. The older gentlemen were all wearing berets, as they sipped their thick black coffee whilst studying their local newspaper. It seemed to be quite popular with the locals; there were bicycles everywhere most with large baskets fitted to the handlebars full of the days shopping. I thought to myself, well, if it's good enough for the locals then it's good enough for us.

I put it to the vote, 'Anybody hungry?'

'We're starving!' came back the chorus of replies.

I parked in a little side street nearby and we made our way to the empty table at the side of the road. Drink orders were taken by a dapper waiter dressed in a smart black waistcoat and bowtie, with his hair plastered down and shiny with some overpowering hair cream, who presented us with the menu. He then proceeded to rattle off the special of the day. Of course, I couldn't understand a word, but the girls who were learning French at school managed to come up with 'a sort of beef stew, with a special sauce'. At the next table a couple who had also ordered the special were eagerly pouring tomato sauce all over their beef – by heck, it looked good! I thought to myself, that I would have some of that. The others must have all been thinking the same, so an order for six specials, with mouth-watering tomato sauce, was promptly placed.

The waiter soon reappeared, waltzing between the pavement tables carrying on high a large silver tray stacked with dishes and a large silver tureen complete with a very ornate lid. I was baffled as to how it all stayed on the tray; the pots slid gently from side to side as he gracefully made his way to our table. The table was set in a jiffy with dishes, spoons and napkins. Then with great ceremony he raised the lid of the tureen, lent over it and inhaled deeply into the steaming aroma. Raising his eyebrows, he exhaled with a loud satisfied 'Ahhhh!'

I started smiling, it was just like a 1920's farce, or if not that, then the 'Bisto Kids' advert! With great gusto he proceeded to fill all our dishes to the brim. And, it did indeed smell absolutely delicious. With another flourish the waiter then placed the silver jug full of tomato sauce in the centre of our table. Standing back, he looked at the girls, stuck his tongue out and touched his tongue with his fingers, pointed to the sauce and then back at his tongue. The girls burst out laughing. He laughed with them then bowed and departed back to the kitchen, muttering 'Bon Appetite! Bon Appetite!'

We started on the stew which had a beautiful, rich flavour. We were told that the meat had been marinated in the local red wine, which looked and tasted more like sweet, sherry.

Andrea grabbed at the jug and started to pour masses of the tomato sauce on to her plate; she just loved Heinz tomato ketchup! We noticed that Andrea's antics had gained interest from the diners at the tables surrounding ours. They were all gawping with amazement. One chap nearby, pointed at the sauce and waved his forefinger backwards and forwards.

'Non, non, non! Ce n'est pas tomate!' he warned.

'Hang on, Andrea,' I said, finally realising what the problem was. 'I don't think it is tomato sauce.'

So, I took a small spoonful and tasted it. Whoosh! My hair stood up on end and my eyes nearly popped out of my head, my ears seemed to explode as my poor tongue took the full force of the full strength Rouille (a traditional French sauce whose name translates literally as "rust." Chillies, garlic, bread crumbs and olive oil are pounded into a spicy, rust-coloured paste and then lightened with fish stock).

After three glasses of ice cold water I was just about able to speak again. The audience were in tucks of laughter.

'That's hot! Really, really, hot!' I managed to mutter.

After finishing our meal, minus the sauce, everybody waved us goodbye and wished us 'Bon Voyage', as we slowly drove back past the café.

We carried on our journey, passing through Belgium heading straight for the German border town of Aachen. It was getting quite dark and foggy as we drove on to the autobahn, towards Cologne. There wasn't another car in sight. It was a really weird sensation driving along this huge, wide deserted roadway. All of a sudden Andrea shouted.

'You should have turned off at that last junction. We need to head towards that big, floodlit sign, "Bayer Pharmaceuticals", that's quite near our home.'

Well, there I was speeding along in the opposite direction from where we should be going. I checked my mirror, and the road ahead, there was not a soul in sight. I quickly made a decision and moved into the outside lane. All was still clear in both directions, so I made a quick U-turn onto the opposite lane and we were once again on track, heading towards Leverkusen. Five minutes later we were off the autobahn and heading for Oppeladon, where the family Schultz lived.

'This is it!' the German girls shouted in excitement.

I pulled up at the side of the curb and got out. I climbed the steps to the front door and rang the bell. A lady soon appeared.

'Hi, Marga! I'm Derek.'

You should have seen her face. She stared at me in disbelief; there I stood in my open neck shirt, shorts, sandals at two o'clock in the morning. I shouted to the girls and they came dashing around the corner.

'Mama! This is Derek.'

I couldn't make out all the confusion, until later when we were having supper, she explained that she expected me to be wearing a black pin-striped suit, black bowler hat, and be carrying a rolled up black umbrella. Well, we all had a good laugh. Marga explained that at school, when she was learning English, all the text books showed pictures of the Englishmen dressed in a black city suit standing in front of Big Ben usually waiting for the approaching red double-decker bus. And, as far as she knew, all Englishmen dressed like that!

That night both Glenys and I were sick and had diarrhoea,

and by the morning had terrible pains in our stomachs. We laid there absolutely exhausted. Marga took one look at us and shot round the corner to fetch the doctor. She appeared with two very large suppositories.

'You must take these' she said, and bent over to demonstrate where to put them!

Trying hard not to laugh, as it hurt so much, I took the glass of water from the bedside cabinet and pretended to put the suppository in my mouth, and then swallowed, making a bit of a show as if it was too big to go down. Eyebrows raised, she jumped over and grabbed the glass.

'No, no, no! Not there. Down here' she yelled, pointing to her rear. With that, I opened my hand, and showed her the suppository.

Up until then, the Germans had been a little cautious in what they said, but that certainly broke the ice. We all laughed (some of us gently), as they realised we were just as daft as they were! Do you know, after taking the suppository we were completely free from discomfort and pain within four hours, and were fully recovered.

Ernst, Marga's husband, had been in the army, fighting on the Russian front. He had a huge hole in his stomach where he had been hit by a shell. He survived by being determined to get home to his lovely wife and family.

Another thing we noticed whilst walking around the town, was that eight out of ten men were either on crutches or used walking sticks, or had some other disability that they had suffered during the war. I suddenly realised that these were ordinary, normal folk, who had simply got caught up in a war, where people were just numbers, and here they were happy and friendly, trying to piece their family lives back together again, and earn a basic living.

Whilst Ernst was away, Marga's mother helped in bringing up the children. She was a lovely person, but kept mostly out of the way, whilst we were there. We had a really nice time with the whole family before it was time for Glenys and I to move off. We were heading for Zermatt in Switzerland to see the Matterhorn. Then we went on to Chamonix in France to show Glenys Mont Blanc, before we returned back to Germany to pick up Della and Vanda from the Schultz family home. They had four daughters altogether; Edelgard, Andrea, Dietling and Petra. (Yes, we named our youngest daughter after Petra, we thought it was such a lovely and unusual name).

Down the Rhine Valley we motored, passing the picturesque castles perched precariously on top of the cliffs, and wandered through mediaeval villages. There was a continuous stream of boats sailing up and down the river. We camped in the Black Forest overnight then continued down to Basle, where we motored around Lake Luzern and arriving in the Swiss Town of Altdorf. We sat in a little coffee shop in the square where the famous statue of William Tell, the national hero of Switzerland, stands.

There is a legend of William Tell, who became the national hero, and it tells about the beginning of Switzerland. Gessler, official or "governor" delegated at that time by the Emperor to the area, did not fail to notice that the people were generally unhappy. In order to test the loyalty of the citizens of Uri, he had a pole planted with a hat in Austrian colours in the square of Altdorf. Everyone passing had to bow to the hat in order to show their respect. The hat was guarded by soldiers who made sure that the governor's orders were carried out. One day, an inhabitant of Bürglen, William Tell, passed the square, accompanied by his son, without saluting the hat. Immediately he was arrested and brought before the governor. 'I know', said the governor, 'you are an accomplished marksman. As a punishment for your disobedience of my order, you shall shoot an apple put on your son's head'.

Tell tried to convince Gessler to carry out a different punishment but with no success. Gessler insisted and even threatened to have Tell and his son killed if he did not follow his orders. Tell was brought back to the square of Altdorf. Gessler followed with his soldiers and servants. An indignant crowd surrounded them. Tell's son was placed against a tree, an apple on his head; 50 steps were counted. Tell put an arrow on his crossbow, aimed slowly and pulled. The arrow pierced the apple without touching the boy. The crowd applauded the skills of the courageous archer. Tell, however, had hidden a second arrow under his quiver.

Gessler who had watched Tell do so asked,'Why the second arrow?'. Tell waited with his reply. The tyrant urged him to answer: 'If you tell me the truth your life will be saved!'

'It was to pierce your heart', was Tell's grim answer, 'if my first arrow killed my son'.

Gessler, beside himself, ordered to jail the rebel at once. 'I do not go back on my promise but you will be jailed until your death in the prison of Küsnacht castle.' A boat was launched immediately at Flüelen. Tell was chained in it while Gessler and his soldiers were embarking. Not far from port a tempest broke out. The Föhn (a southernly wind) caused such high waves that the boat almost got lost or thrown onto the nearby rocks. The boat people became very frightened and shouted, 'Only Tell can save us!' Gessler ordered to free Tell who then took the rudder in a firm hand and steered the boat to the foot of the Axenberg Mountain, near a rock called the "Tellsplatte". All of a sudden Tell took a spear from a soldier, jumped from the boat onto the shore, pushing back the boat with his foot, then in a great hurry traversed the county of Schwyz. Gessler managed to survive the bad storm and reached Küsnacht castle that very night. Tell hid behind some bushes along an alley which led to the governor's residence. Soon enough Gessler and his people appeared and Tell killed him with an arrow from his crossbow freeing the country from an evil tyrant.

We continued our journey to the 800 year old village of Andermatt, then over the pass to Brig. We managed to find a campsite with a swimming pool. By this time we were hot and tired, so first the "kettle was put on" for a nice cup of tea, then we both headed for the swimming pool. Glenys climbed slowly down the steps and into the water. Now that's one thing I can't do, immerse myself slowly in water. So there was nothing else for it, but to dive straight in at the deep end. One, two, three and in I went. But, oohh, I've never felt water so cold! I think it must have come down from the glaciers. I belted to the far side of the pool and hopped out before you could say "Three Brass Monkeys". Glenys climbed out slowly via the steps again, 'Hmm' she said smiling, 'the water is a bit cold' she casually remarked as she headed for our van.

Up early on the following morning, we caught the train from Brig to Zermatt. Arriving at Zermatt station we were surprised to find there were no cars on the streets, only horse drawn carts. If you were staying at one of the five star posh hotels you were met by a footman and escorted to a beautiful horse-drawn carriage with two fine looking well-groomed horses waiting to take you to your hotel. If you were at one of the smaller hotels then you sat on the back of an electric milk float. If you had booked into a guest house then you walked!

High above the village stood the mighty Matterhorn. The lower half was shrouded in cloud whilst the peak poked its head out above. Somehow it seemed to be a lot higher than I had imagined. We managed to find the plaque of Edward Whymper – the first man to climb the Matterhorn. I couldn't wait to get above the snow line. We caught the cable car to Gornergratt. Now, this might sound a bit silly, but it was a beautifully hot bright summer's day, so we were both wearing sandals. We left the cable station and headed upwards. We soon found ourselves knee-deep in snow, but who cares! Yes, I know, as a mountaineer I should know better, but we weren't attempting the peaks, I just wanted Glenys to enjoy the height and views of the surrounding mountains. It wasn't too long before I realised that we were both experiencing mountain sickness, our brains were getting muddled and it was difficult to control our movements. With that, I decided to head back to the café by the cable station. We ordered black tea and lemon with lashings of sugar, which we drank by the gallon. We were then fine and ready for the descent down to Zermatt.

Unfortunately we never saw the Matterhorn in her full glory. We just caught sight of the peak poking out of the clouds, then that too disappeared, just as the lower half became visible! It was very frustrating for me; I thought to myself one day, yes one day, I might just climb and conquer that beautiful, elusive mountain. (Many years later I did conquer her...but that's another tale waiting to be told!).

From Brig we headed for Chamonix in France to see and enjoy the marvellous views of my very own Mont Blanc (which I had climbed and recounted my exploits in my first book "The Spirit of Adventure").The five hundred mile journey back to Cologne seemed to be very much quicker than the journey down. The old Bedford van took all the mountain passes and the long journey in its stride without any hitches. We stayed overnight at the Schultz family home, where Ernst introduced me to the litre pot of beer. I could hardly lift it up never mind drink it! It was time for us all to say our goodbyes, and there were a few tears as we left for our final trip home.

There were only a few people on the last ferry back to the Isle of Wight; unlike the following year, when thousands upon thousands of young people invaded our lovely tranquil Island!

28

Five Days That Shook The World!

They came by their thousands. Every ferry and every hovercraft was loaded to full capacity. Then queuing, queuing, and queuing for the special buses at six shillings per person, to rush the hordes of happy hippies on their way to the large compound that had suddenly appeared on Afton Down near Freshwater.

This was the dream of Ron and Ray Foulk (from Freshwater) and Rikki Farr ("The Fiery Creations"); The 1970 Isle of Wight Pop Festival was now on!

There was a never-ending stream of young folk who had spent their savings on the £3 weekend entrance fee and were determined to save every penny by walking the 20 miles to the festival site. Here they were on a hot summer's day in August, stripped to the waist, boys and girls, carrying their large backpacks and sleeping bags, with cuddly toys dangling from the rear straps. Hundreds of police placed every few yards covered the entire route.

Outside the compound was a sea of tents as far as the eye could see. Inside the barricade was the largest stage ever built in the world. This was Canvas City at its best! Signs appeared everywhere; "Snack Bar", "Soup and Salad", to the slightly more obscure "10 Downing Street", "Girls Wanted", "The Weasel Ripped My Flesh!", "Dodge City", "5 Acid

Gang", and so on! First Aid, Medical and Police tents were dotted amidst the mayhem. Looking around was amazing. The ground was littered with rubbish, paper, cans, bottles, and of course, more tents! There were bales of hay stacked around to form communes of hippies. Psychedelic vans, Flower Power painted cars, people drifting about in a daze whilst others simply laid about chatting or fast asleep. Music blared out over the whole countryside. The locals from all over the Island came to witness this unbelievable transformation of their lovely rural downsland, which was owned by the farmer Max Yasgur.

The roar of the huge custom-built motorbikes, all revving up to form a crescendo of noise, which could only be matched by an almighty thunderstorm, meant that the Hells Angels had arrived. They were eager and impatient to disembark from the ferry, ready to race along the road to the site, their mission was to take control of the security duties (for a fee, naturally!). Of course, it wasn't all "Peace Man" and the police had to take action when the Hells Angels decided they would impose their own brand of law and order. The French and Algerian anarchists, The British White Panthers, The British Hells Angels and the American radical splinter groups had already taken over the hill overlooking the festival site. This became known as "Devastation Hill" and provided a grandstand view of the stage, though it seemed to be miles away. At one time, the security forces made an attempt to clear the hillside. But they were no match for the thousands who had set up camp there. The promoter's security staff made a feeble effort to erect a ten foot high corrugated iron fence along the ridge. As soon as they had put up one section and moved on to the next, like the walls of Jericho, they came tumbling down – with a little help from the "toughies"! One of the promoters came up with the bright idea of using powerful ex-naval searchlights to simply blind the non-paying onlookers on the hill. I understand that somehow the power supplying these lights mysteriously failed!

The packed ferries ran a shuttle service day and night, and at a fare of five shillings and threepence, made an absolute fortune over the festival period. You may be surprised to learn that the performers were playing to an audience of over 500,000; half a million youngsters, that's more than Glastonbury and Live Aid put together!

Naturally, our teenage children Della, Vanda and Tony, and their friend Gerry, wanted to go. David Lever, a friend from Lancashire, came to stay with us on his way to the festival, so it was agreed that he would keep an eye on them and make sure they all stayed together. With that in mind, we arranged to take them to the site with all their camping gear, sleeping bags, tents, primus stove and plenty of food and water – oh, and not forgetting the many rolls of toilet paper! Everyday at 11 am we met up with them at the gate to ensure they were all okay. We had no trouble getting in, as the gate attendants knew we were just there checking up on our children, especially when they saw we were pushing our three month old baby daughter in her carrycot. I think Petra may possibly be able to take the claim of being the youngest spectator at the 1970 Isle of Wight Pop Festival!

It was quite funny, as we made our daily checks, to notice that the dark rings around their eyes were getting bigger and bigger through lack of sleep. But they wouldn't give up; oh no, they were determined to stick it out.

David, wearing his undertaker's frock-tailed coat and tall black hat, drifted to the stage to listen and watch his favourite groups, followed closely by Della and Gerry, and Vanda hanging on to Della like a leech, as she was frightened to death of getting lost amongst this seething mass of bodies! Tony, well he was fascinated with "Desolation Row", and all the hideouts constructed from bales of straw, but he wasn't far behind when the group was on the move.

The police were constantly raiding tents full of pot smokers, whilst the plain clothed drug squad were on the move trying to capture the pusher known as the "Acid Man". The First Aid tents were overflowing with youngsters suffering from drug related symptoms and the after effects of LSD trips. The toilets consisted of slit trenches which served as a mass open-air communal latrine. The stench was unbearable, but when nature calls you have to do something about it! It was quite amazing how private it was, no-one was caught peeping as there was a natural fifty yard "Stink Zone" in every direction, and you only ever ventured into that zone when you were on a "now or never" mission!

The priest, Reverend Robert Bowyer, had his work cut out organising the Voluntary Welfare Service. On one of the festival days he even conducted a hippy wedding at the local church. It was pretty obvious by the end of the festival that there were a lot of kids who had spent all their money, and didn't even have their fare left for getting home. The Reverend had a plan to help these youngsters. He appeared on stage to announce that Fiery Creations had agreed to provide them with enough work clearing the site to earn money for food and their fares home, all they had to do was meet in front of the stage at the end of the festival. But did he manage to get this message over? No! He was just met with boo's and catcalls.

Rikki Farr, one of the promoters, tried to calm the situation but the crowd continued to boo and hiss. In the end he picked up the mike, and told the crowd, 'To all the good kids who came here, I say goodbye; to the rest of you, go to hell!', then he stormed off the stage.

A funny incident happened in the nearby launderette. All the local women were sitting around waiting for their weekly wash to dry when a group of male flower-power hippies came in. Without a word, they stripped themselves down completely naked, shoved all their clothes into the machines and sat down on the vacant seats amongst the silently stunned women. There were a few red faces, but without batting an eyelid the local women kept their heads down and carried on reading their papers. Eventually, one by one, as the machines finished their cycles, they collected their washing together and casually wished the hippies a good morning and walked out. Now that's the Isle of Wight for you.

As the sun set, and darkness descended like a black velvet veil, there was an uncanny strangeness about the Canvas City. The sky was floodlit amidst the surrounding blackness of the countryside. The red and orange flickering of the campfires were like semi-precious gems glowing in the night. The hills were alive and vibrated with the constant non-stop beat of the music. It was like a giant monster, heaving and pulsating, as it attempted to be born, to announce to the world, 'Hey, look and listen to me, I'm alive!' But the rest of the Island, unimpressed and tired, just closed it's eyes and fell asleep.

Hundreds of thousand of music fans came from all over the world to enjoy the continuous performances from some of the greatest pop musicians of that time. Just take a look at the line up of the artists who had come to this special Island to entertain and enthral the young music fans:

The Bill (in alphabetical order) – Arrival, Joan Baez, Black Widow, David Bromberg, Cactus, Chicago, Leonard Cohen, Miles Davies, Donovan, The Doors, Emerson, Lake and Palmer (their debut performance!), Fairfield Parlour, Family, Gary Farr, Free, Gilberto Gil, Good News, The Groundhogs, Richie Havens, Hawkwind (played for free outside), Heaven, Jimi Hendrix, Howl, Jethro Tull, Judas Jump, Kris Kristofferson, Lighthouse, Ralph McTell, Melanie, Mighty Baby, Joni Mitchell, The Moody Blues, Open Road, Pentangle, Shawn Phillips, The Pink Fairies (played outside for free), Procol Harum, Redbone, Terry Reid, Andy Roberts Everyone, John Sebastian, Sly and the Family Stone, Kathy Smith, Rosalie Sorrels, Supertramp, Taste, Ten Years After, Tiny Tim, The Voices of East Harlem, Tony Joe White, and last but not least, The Who!

Jimi Hendrix came on stage and said, 'It'd be better if you stand up and start singing for your country.' Immediately he began playing "God Save the Queen", but with background sound effects of dive-bombers and explosions, and machine gun fire, and children crying! You felt as though you were in some kind of inferno of sound, with smoke literally coming out of the amplifiers. Some people began to leave. These were mostly women who said that they were frightened by Jimi. He played with a loudness and fierceness that surpassed all of his previous performances. He played as if he knew that this was to be his last live performance – and it was, as Jimi Hendrix died in London just eighteen days later.

On Sunday afternoon, one of the Foulk brothers said, 'For Christ's sake, open the gates and let's hear some music!' And suddenly it was the music that was important.

For five days the army of the young encamped on the hillside to join in this mammoth music extravaganza that was regarded as Britain's "Woodstock". Unfortunately a huge number of people wanted to enjoy the festival without buying a ticket, and they continued to break down the perimeter fences and create havoc for the police and staff. With nearly one million rampaging hippies taking over the Island, it was decided that enough was enough.

'This is the last festival, it began as a beautiful dream but it has got out of control and it is a monster', announced Ron Foulk on 1st September 1970. Later the same year the "Isle of Wight Act" was passed by Parliament to ban all future festivals.

Most of the youngsters, were now walking the twenty

miles back to the ferry, like an endless procession of refugees; their rucksacks and sleeping gear on their backs once more, and their favourite soft toys still dangling from their back straps. These people were too impatient, or too broke, to join the other thousands in the five mile long bus queue.

At the car ferries, kids were begging car drivers to let them hide in the boot of their cars, as they were completely without the ferry fare required. It was surprising how many of the cars travelling back to the mainland had a few extra stowaways tucked up in their boots, and I'm sure it was amusing to see them all tumbling out on arrival at the mainland terminals! The attendants at the terminals were good enough to turn a blind eye to the antics of these weary travellers, who now just wanted to get home.

So what is the point to it all? The point is that there is no point whatsoever, except that these were our children, who could tell their children,

'FIVE DAYS THAT SHOOK THE WORLD – OH YES, I WAS THERE!'

29

'Oh Hello! I Would Like To Buy Four Feet Of Your Land'

Just after we had moved into The Briars, I started having dizzy spells. We initially thought it was because of all the hard work we had been doing, which often went on into the early hours of the morning. I was feeling a little bit weary and worn out; I didn't know why, as I'd never had this sort of problem before. In the end the doctor came out to see me and ordered me straight to bed, and he proceeded to raise up the foot of my bed with the aid of a couple of bricks. After a while my neck started to swell up on my left side; up and up it went until it was the size of a small lemon. An ambulance was then called and I was rushed to St Mary's hospital. Once established, the specialist came to see me and wasn't very happy. So there and then I was taken to see the surgical specialist and within a couple of hours I was in the operating theatre.

In the meantime, poor Glenys had three little children to deal with and had been informed by the hospital that they thought it was cancer in the main neck artery. Here we were, after leaving all our friends and family behind up North, stuck on this little island with no one to turn to for support and help.

Thankfully, it all turned out alright; it wasn't cancer, it was a string of calcified nodules which had somehow wrapped around the artery and had become infected.

A couple of days later and I was able to go home sporting a dressing across my neck stuck on with cellotape! The nurse couldn't find any sticking plaster so she took some cellotape out of her drawer and cut off a couple of strips.

'Don't worry,' she said 'It'll do the same job!'

The whole incident made me wonder how I could have been infected with tuberculosis. I thought maybe I had caught it whilst in the army, but then I remembered when I was a youngster being told to go and sit with my two sixteen and seventeen year old cousins who were both dying of "consumption" as it was known then. My job was to empty their phlegm mugs – they spat out the green phlegm into these mugs after each bout of coughing. When the mugs were full I'd have to take them to the slop stone, wash them out with carbolic soap and return them back upstairs as quickly as possible. They were both ever so grateful, and were beautiful girls. They died within a very short time of each other with tuberculosis.

* * * * *

Whilst renovating The Briars I decided to have a go at painting a full size mural of a beach scene in the bathroom. I was very pleased with the result and thought I'd like to try my hand at oil painting. Of course, it had to be a picture of my dream mountain, the Matterhorn, with its snow capped peak. I painted this on a six foot by three foot sheet of hardboard. With the help of a palette knife I managed to create a living mountain with all its gullies, rock faces and snow fields. My masterpiece took pride of place in our lounge, where I built an archway around it as a centre piece on the main wall. Peter, the landlord of the pub down the road, saw it and asked if I would do a full size wall painting for him. The pub was called the Woodman's Arms, I created a woodman with a large axe on his shoulder standing over a pile of felled logs in the middle of a forest. It was fantastic (even if I do say so myself!) The landlord and his customers were delighted with the finished painting, and he paid me well over my quotation!

Sitting quietly watching television late one evening we were disturbed by a gentle tapping on the window. I looked at Glenys.

'Who on earth can that be, at this time of night?' she asked.

Opening the curtains I could see a man standing there with a roll of paper. I opened the door to him and stepped back in amazement when he said, 'Oh hello! I would like to buy four feet of your land.'

Isn't it funny how two taps on your window can turn your world upside down in an instant.

'Which four feet are you interested in?' I asked, imaging a square shape somewhere in the middle of our garden.

'I'd like to buy a strip right up the side of your garden. In fact, it's the ditch that you own on the outside of your hedge and into the lane.'

At this, bells started ringing in my head.

'Hold it right there. I think you had better come in and explain yourself.' The man came in and unrolled the large plan of the development proposed to be built on the old army cemetery at the back of our house.He had outline permission to build four rather posh houses on the land, but needed a minimum width of access to the main road, and he had found that the lane was just four feet too narrow – and that's where we came in.

Well, after a bit of haggling, he came up with an offer of a few hundred pounds, saying that he wasn't too bothered; he had an alternative, as the pub was interested in selling up and that would give him all the access required.

As you can imagine we didn't sleep very well that night. We dreamt about all the lorries churning up and down the narrow lane and all the noise of digging to put in new sewers. Our little bit of peace was about to be shattered. We decided this needed to be investigated further before any decisions were made.

In the end we found out that it was a Cowes based solicitor who was funding the project. So we promptly made an appointment to see him. Over the past few days, Glenys and I had come to the conclusion that it would actually be better for us as a family to sell our house, and simply leave all the upheaval behind – this decision was substantiated further when Bill, our friend, told us that Mr Wheeler, the farmer, was going build another huge barn straight opposite our house, ensuring all our lovely views across the Medina valley would also be lost.

As a house, The Briars was valued at a price of between twelve and fourteen thousand pounds, but we knew the potential for access and further building land. So I presented the solicitor with a crazy figure of £40,000 we would require for the sale of our home. He was taken aback and told us it was an outrageous amount. We weren't bothered as we had nothing to lose. However, he eventually came back to us with an offer for £30,000, and that was the maximum he was willing to pay. With a little further negotiating he increased the price to £36,000 and the deal was done!

Glenys and I looked at houses all over the place. New ones were for sale at Yarmouth for £18,000 each, and we even tried to find a caravan site which was for sale for £18,000 with a house and substantial land. We spent over two hours trying to find Sylvan Glade before giving up – we thought that if we couldn't find it, tourists probably wouldn't be able to either!

Finally we came across a newly built bungalow in Nettlestone. It was standing in its own grounds and was attached to a copse. Glenys wouldn't even get out of the car, as she said that the front of the bungalow had no character, and it was raining. I, however, ventured inside. Wow! I thought. I could live here! I persuaded Glenys to leave the dryness of the car and come and look around. She too fell in love with it and thought it had great potential.

In the drive was a huge cruiser day boat with a seventy horsepower engine. We agreed on the price of £18,000, but I cheekily remarked that it would have to include the boat as well. That took him back for a minute or two, but when I told him it was a cash sale, the deal was sealed. We were soon to be the proud new owners of a beautiful bungalow (with potential) and a good sized garden, plus a nice cabin cruiser thrown in.

All went smoothly until the completion date. Our solicitor informed us that the Cowes solicitor buying The Briars had not sent the money through, so the deal could not proceed. He said that we shouldn't worry, and he would arrange a bridging loan for us. The timing couldn't have been worse; I was in hospital again, this time having my nose chipped out, so yet again Glenys was left to cope with the bombshell. She agreed with our solicitor that interest would not be charged on the bridging loan. We thought everything was now in order – however, we had no money paid over.

When I got home I wrote a strong letter to the Law Society saying that I suspected our solicitors were in collusion in arranging the sale of our house, with the intent to hold on to the money. I hand delivered a copy to both solicitors and told them that if the money wasn't paid within three days then the letter would be sent. That afternoon I learned that our solicitor went over personally to see the solicitor in Cowes, and returned to his office with a cheque for £36,000!

From that moment on it was all go! All the family and friends joined in as we set about stripping out everything we wanted from The Briars (even my painting of the Matterhorn was dismantled and eventually built into the new extension at Inglewood).

All our established shrubs and roses trees were dug up and transferred in a fibre-glass dingy, used as a trailer behind my car. The star turn was the two large palm trees from the front of our house; I dug over four feet down and still hadn't reached the root bottom. Bill managed to borrow a tractor from the farm and wrapping a chain around each one, pulled it out bodily until it lay across the main road. Both were then loaded into the dingy and trailer, and were taken to the readily prepared holes awaiting them. Our move caused quite a sight on the roads from Northwood to Nettlestone. By tea time, we had a ready made garden at Inglewood!

The Briars was eventually demolished and Hogan Close was built on the land. I'm pleased to say they left the old ash tree from our front garden, which still stands today in all its glory at the entrance to the close.

* * * * *

The manager looked at me with a smile.

'Oh yes, sir' he said 'It's free delivery. Yes, free delivery.'

30

'Oh Yes, Sir, It's Free Delivery!'

Della was over the moon with her sixteenth birthday present. Standing in the driveway of The Briars was a bright blue, three-wheeler, two-seater Isetta Bubble Car. She couldn't wait for her first driving lesson. Ten minutes later we were going up and down Noke Common Road. I must admit she had all the confidence in the world and soon mastered changing up and down through the three gears. Of course it had no reverse, and was classed as a motorbike – it was therefore in order to drive it at sixteen years of age.

Before long she was off to the disco at the Halland Hotel at the bottom of Pier Road in Seaview. Two or three of her pals would be jammed in like sardines on the return journey home.

Another time they would be off to the Barbalu on Brading Road in Ryde. The nightclub building was originally the Control Tower of Ryde Airport. The airfield itself stretched from Westridge Cross over the land where Tesco now stands and across what it now Westridge Golf Course. When Westridge Construction Company started work on the golf course they found two World War II unexploded bombs, which had to be disposed of and blown up by the Army Bomb Disposal Unit. (I've often wondered, whilst playing on the course, whether the two ponds on hole six might have been created by those explosions).

When it was Tony's sixteenth I managed to get hold of another Isetta Bubble Car, this time white in colour, and like Della, it didn't take him long to master the controls.

It was about this time that the film "The Italian Job" was showing, and Vanda's sixteenth was just around the corner. Well, I must have scoured the whole countryside to get hold of red Bubble Car. I had visions of the three of them driving along in red, white and blue, just like the film! But I couldn't manage it.

I was, however, offered a British Racing Green fibreglass, three-wheeler, two-seater Bond Mini. Oh Boy! Now this was something different! If the starter battery was low you simply lifted up the long bonnet, stepped inside and kick started the motorcycle engine, and away it would go. Again this car had no reverse, but to compensate, the engine was mounted above the front wheel and the whole unit would turn 90 degrees and at right angles to the car. In a tight parking space you would turn the wheel to a full lock and the Bond Mini would simply glide out within the full length of the car. It was an amazing design and often gained an audience in the middle of Newport, as Vanda confidently climbed in and slid out of a tight spot.

Before we leave The Briars completely to the demolition squad, I must tell you about the old deeds of the land and property I have in my possession. They date back to Saturday 24th April "in the year of our Lord 1813"! This was the date of an auction which took place at the Bugle Inn in Newport.

The deeds, entitled PARKHURST ENCLOSURE, read:

> *"An Act of disaforresting the Forest of Parkhurst, in the County of Southampton, and for the inclosing of the open commonable lands within the said Forest."*

Thirty pounds was paid for a parcel of land – Lot 45, containing "one rood and seven perches". This was the piece of land that we had just sold for £36,000!

Ms King who owned an antique shop in Lugley Street, Newport, owned the old Albany Barracks' Burial Ground behind The Briars. We were originally told that this land could never be built on as it was consecrated land, and the only building allowed was the old Newport boxing Club which was classified "temporary" as it was made out of timber.

But that didn't stop the developers building twenty properties now known as Hogan Road and Hogan Close.

Another interesting document was about the owner of Dale View, which was renamed The Briars after intensive reconstruction work, including demolishing and rebuilding the front and side walls whilst leaving the roof propped up with beams! Morris Morgan Senior to whom Dale View belonged died on 8th June 1862, leaving half of his property to his daughter Anne Sibley and the other half to his son Morris. According to the death certificate I have in my possession with the land deeds, Morris died on the 8th of May 1878 in the Colony of Victoria, Australia. William Morris Morgan then took possession of Dale View. Unfortunately it seemed he was a bit of a villain and he died "at the age of 38 years in Her Majesty's Gaol, Nottingham on the 13th October 1878."Charles Morgan, brother of William deceased, then came into possession and sold the property on to Walter Sibley of West Cowes on the 22nd September 1880 for the handsome sum of £130. The rest of the documents up to date are beautifully hand written with old stamps paid as duty and sealed with wax.

Moving on from the deeds, whilst searching my document collection I also found my First Edition of the Daily Express dated "No.1...London, Tuesday, April 24th 1900". There's a lovely article on the front page set apart from all the reports of the war in South Africa, written by their Dublin Correspondent about Queen Victoria.

> *"THE QUEEN WINS IRELAND'S LOVE AND BETTER HEALTH THROUGH HER IRISH SOJOURN... Ireland certainly suits the Queen. Everybody is saying how wonderfully well she looks – fresh and bright and alert, with a quick eye for every peasant who stands bareheaded by the roadside, and a sympathetic interest in the welfare of all the homely warm-hearted folk who, for the first time for so many years, are taking care of their Queen.*
>
> *Her Majesty goes everywhere. Nor hail, nor rain, nor blizzard robs her of her afternoon drive. It may curtail the excursion; but it never postpones it.*
>
> *'An' that proves,' said the carman, with Hiberian logic, 'that if she had always lived here she would have been a wonderful healthy ould lady.'*
>
> *I submitted that her Majesty's health was rather wonderful as it is.*
>
> *'Yes, that's thrue,' he rejoined, 'but if she had always lived in Ireland she would not have required to come to Ireland to improve it.'*
>
> *There was no answering this."*

How lovely!

* * * * *

I now leave The Briars and lot number 45 to the developers, as we move into our new home "Papplewick" which we immediately renamed "Inglewood".The building itself from the front was very unimpressive. Our first job was to give it some character, and straight away I changed the front glass-panelled door to a beautiful Spanish-style carved Mahogany one. My next project was to build a natural stone archway over the plain front.

We were out for a ride one nice sunny Sunday morning, travelling from Carisbrooke to Brighstone along Clatterford Road, when I spotted a field on my right containing an old dilapidated stone barn. Most of the building had collapsed and the roof had completely fallen in.The old farmer with his corduroy trousers and tatty jacket was leaning over the five barred gate, his faithful sheep dog perfectly still at his side.

I pulled up smartly on the grass verge and hopped out. Glenys looked at me in surprise.

'Where are you off to now?' she asked.

'I won't be a minute,' I replied and strolled casually back along the road.

'Morning, Sir,' I said to the farmer, 'so how much do you want for four yards of that old stone over there?'

For a second or two he didn't move or look up. Then he slowly took the piece of straw from his mouth.

'Morning to you! Now what would you want with a yard or two of yon Island stone?'

I went on to explain that I wanted to build an imposing archway on my newly-acquired bungalow.

'Ah, well, then. It all depends on whether you 'ave transport to shift it or not then?'

'Er, no,' I replied.

'Well, then, if you give me fifty quid I'll drop it off on your doorstep for you.'

'If I had fifty quid I'd give it to you,' I muttered to the farmer, 'but at the moment the best I can do is about thirty quid.'

'Nay! That won't even pay for me petrol, let alone the blooming stone!' he laughed.

'Ok…' I thought for a moment. 'I think I can find another ten pounds out of my holiday money. That means I will have met you half way. So if you come down another ten quid, we'll both be happy!'

He looked at me as a wide grin spread across his face. 'You should become a farmer, young man. You'd do well at the auctions!' And he held out his hand.

The deal was done and the stone delivered the next day as promised.

There were some whacking big stones among the pile delivered which made an ideal base course for the archway. I sorted and laid one course of stone every night when I came home from school. It took me three weeks to complete the magnificent stone archway which then lead us grandly into our new home. I felt really proud of my handiwork; I had never tackled stonework before.

Inside the house, the roof space had been designed with floor joists, and just cried out to be developed into a separate living unit, accommodating two bedrooms, a bathroom, a lounge and a small kitchen area.

Later that year we were visiting Mildred and Derrick, our friends in Lancashire, and I offered to help them replace their kitchen units. At the plumbers merchants Mildred choose the units she wanted whilst I had a good mooch around the showroom. Then I spotted it... It was a fantastic corner bath, complete with gold taps and fittings. I'd never seen anything like it before!

Two young chaps were dismantling the stunning display. I casually asked if the suite had been sold.

'Oh no!' the young one chirped up. 'Why are you interested? 'Cause the boss usually lets the ex-display ones go cheap.'

'Shurrup!' the older lad piped in. 'He might not let this luxury one go cheap.'

I gave it a good looking over, but couldn't find any marks or chips which would give me a bit of leverage in negotiating a fair deal.

I was then approached by the manager.

'Hello, Sir. Can I help you?'

'Hi, I'm Derek, and you are?'

'Oh, hi. My name's Pete, I'm the manager.' We shook hands.

'Now,' I continued, 'what's all this about selling this old showroom display off cheaply? What discount can you give me as I'm in the trade?'

'Well, I must admit we don't sell many of these luxury suites around here. In fact, they couldn't even get this lot in the front bedroom of half the terraced houses in this area – and even if it did fit they probably wouldn't manage to get the bath up the stairs!' He started laughing. 'So then, do I have a customer for this little lot?'

'Maybe,' I replied. 'If the price is right.'

'I think I can do you a good deal.'

I looked up at the big sign hanging from the roof of the warehouse; "All items over £100 delivered FREE." 'And do I get free delivery then?' I asked, pointing to the notice.

'You do, Sir! It's free delivery. Oh yes, Sir, it's free delivery.'

After a bit of wrangling he said he would give me 20% trade discount plus a further 20% as discarded showroom display discount.After I had snapped his hand off, he started to fill in the delivery details. Casually, keeping a straight face, I started to reel off my Isle of Wight address. He wrote it all down then frowned a little.

'Hmm, I don't know where that is. But I'm sure the van driver does. He knows all the back streets around here!' He looked again at the papers and scratched his head. 'So, where about is the Isle of Wight then? I've never heard of the place.'

'Well,' I said, with a smile creeping across my face, 'when you leave Bolton you just keep heading south until you come to the sea at Southampton. Then you keep going another four or five miles across the sea and you're nearly there.'

'Bloody 'ell, mate! We don't deliver that far!'

I pointed to the sign again. 'It doesn't say anything about restricted area, and we did shake on FREE delivery!'

'Ah, yes. But, but…' he spluttered.

'Look, Pete. Can you drive the van? And are you married?'

'Er, yes.'

'Then why don't you drive the van down, and you and your wife can stay with us for a long weekend? Of course, don't forget to bring the bathroom suite along too!'

'Right, hang on a minute,' he said, and disappeared to use the telephone. I could hear snippets of the conversation; 'Yes, yes. The Isle of Wight. No, not the Isle of Man! It's down south somewhere. Yep. Ok, love. You sure? Yep, I'll tell you all about it when I get home, then. No, he's a nice chap, you'll like him. He's from around here originally. Okay, yes, see you later, love.' He placed the receiver down gently and burst out laughing.

'We'll do it!' he shouted.

With that I was treated like royalty. We also selected some beautiful Italian tiles; I had to guess the amount we would require!

The next weekend we met them at the East Cowes Ferry Terminal. Pete and Christine, his wife, followed us back to our house in the large bathroom-filled van. We all had a really great weekend and we took them all over the Island. They were smashing company and really appreciated everything. I offered to pay for delivery.

'No! When it says FREE delivery, it means FREE delivery! But, we have now changed the sign to read *anywhere in the Bolton area!*'

I fitted the suite and about a month later realised I needed about a dozen extra tiles to finish the job.I phoned Pete and asked them if he could send me some down by post or carrier.

'Well, they may get broken. So it's probably best if me and the missus bring them down. And yes, before you ask, it's FREE delivery – but only to our very special customers on the Isle of Wight!'

31

One Christmas Day At The Briars

Isn't it funny; the minute you get a piece of land, you fancy yourself as a smallholder growing your own vegetables and collecting your own eggs for breakfast, and maybe have the odd animal wandering about.

Well, not this time! We'd done all that at The Briars. I must admit, I was very proud of the bowls full of ripe juicy red tomatoes that lasted all throughout the summer months. I wasn't so lucky however with the vegetables; the woodlice shifted the lot of them.

I then picked up an old wooden dinghy, drilled holes in the side and filled it with good quality soil and planted it up with fifty healthy looking strawberry plants. They grew to a tremendous size and eventually produced a mass of succulent rosy strawberries; success at last! But once again, it wasn't to last. The woodlice and grubs had invaded the boat and after eating their way rapidly through the old timber, decided it would be nice to have strawberries for tea, and shifted the lot over one weekend! I'm afraid the old dingy ended up on the bonfire and I tossed the strawberry plants onto the compost where they seemed to thrive year after year to provide the dessert course for the ever persistent woodlice.

Of course, the final straw came at Christmas time. We only had one hen left in the ark. When I came to move the structure a huge rat, bigger than a cat, scurried out across the garden and disappeared through the hedge. I had often wondered how one hen could eat so much food each day. Well, I thought to myself, the one thing I don't want around the house is a rat. Being Christmas, and as Snowy our hen was getting on a bit and her supply of eggs was diminishing, I decided she would make us a very tasty Christmas dinner.

We opened all our presents; Father Christmas had supped his traditional Harvey's Bristol Cream, and demolished the whole of the mince pie left in the hearth of the fireplace the evening before. The kids sat around the table with knife and fork at the ready. They were starving after having been up so early. Glenys served up the vegetables and placed a large dish of gravy in the centre of the table. I opened the oven door and out came a beautifully basted golden roast chicken. I had the job of carving. As usual everyone wanted a leg, but as we weren't serving up octopus there were a few disappointed faces. (But that was soon put right, as the ones without a leg got a little extra meat.) Naturally as I was carving, every now and then a little would fall off the plate and somehow jump up into my mouth. I thought to myself that this was one of the nicest tasting chickens I'd had in years. The kids poured on lashings of Glenys's rich, dark brown gravy. I made the toast – 'Happy Christmas Everybody!' And we settled down to enjoy the sumptuous meal before us.

'This isn't Snowy, is it?' Vanda piped up suddenly, with her fork full of chicken.

Deathly silence.

'Is it heck!' I said. 'Don't be daft. Enjoy your meal.'

But that was it; not convinced, Vanda jumped up and ran outside. She saw the empty food and water dish in the ark and came hurtling back inside.

'It is Snowy!' she cried. 'I'm not eating Snowy. I'm not going to eat her.'

The other two then put their knives and forks down.

'We're not eating Snowy either!' they chimed in.

Glenys looked at me with that "I told you so" look, and quietly stood up and cleared all the meat off hers and the kid's plates, and came out of the kitchen with a tin of trusty corned beef. I took another mouthful of chicken, but the silence was deafening and all eyes were on me. I lost my appetite and resigned to open up the corned beef. I cut it up and placed a couple of slices on each plate, including my own.

* * * * *

Well, it was Christmas time again at Inglewood. The dinner was cooking merrily on the stove. I ran down the steps into the garden and shouted back to Glenys.

'I think the carrots should be done by now.'

Pippa and Squeak, Petra's pet rabbits, pricked up their ears. Oh no, they probably thought, I hope that cruel chap isn't going to do the same to us as he did to poor Snowy. They hid behind their hutch inside the run and waited, as a shadow passed across in front of the hutch.

'Come on, come on,' I encouraged. 'I've got a nice juicy carrot for you, which Rudolph didn't fancy.'

Pippa was tempted by the sweet aroma of carrot and cautiously crept out of his hiding place. Nearer and nearer he came. I put my hand out to stroke him. Ah, to hell with that, he thought, I'm not being your dinner, and promptly bit me. I jumped back; that was the first time he'd ever reacted like that. He scuttled into the hutch dragging his prize carrot behind him.

It was only really a friendly nip, but it had broken the skin. I tried to ignore it, but there was to be no peace. All the family were on to me to go to the Casualty Department at Ryde Hospital and have a tetanus jab. Della phoned the hospital.

'Yes, he needs to come straight away. It is advisable to get the jab immediately,' was the reply.

On entering the unit I was met by two rows of people up each side of the corridor. One chap looked as if he was bleeding to death. Blood was running through the substantial bandage he had wrapped around his damaged arm. In fact everyone there looked in dire need of urgent attention. I gingerly reported to the reception.

'Ah, yes. We're expecting you. Nurse,' she shouted across the room, 'Mr Feldon is here for the injection.'

The nurse appeared from behind a screen.

'Well, what are you waiting for? Come this way,' she ordered.

I ambled forward, feeling a fraud amongst all these urgent cases. I thought to myself, well at least they don't know why I'm here. Behind the screen and out of sight the nurse then said in a loud, clear voice, 'Drop your trousers. Bend over and touch your toes.'

I tried to explain that that was one of the things I cannot do – I have great difficultly in touching my toes without bending my knees.

'Now, you are the chap who was bitten by a *(pause)* rabbit!' she announced loudly

Well, there was an uproar of laughter at the other side of the screen. I didn't know where to put myself; I was so embarrassed. I tried to redeem my dignity.

'No, no. It was a lion! It was a lion that bit me!'

The nurse started laughing.

'Come on then. Pull your trousers up, and off you pop home. I've got some real work to do now!'

I sidled out from behind the screen. My face was as red as a beetroot.

'It was a lion,' I muttered, rubbing my backside. 'It was.'

Everyone looked at me and someone tittered, 'Bit by a little bunny, ahh!'

I shot through the double doors as quickly as I could.

* * * * *

Our little estate at Inglewood was certainly fit for a peacock, and as luck would have it, they were selling peacocks at Calbourne Water Mill. The chap took us into a barn. There were dozens of young peacocks everywhere. He grabbed hold of a beauty and jammed it into a sack and fastened it.

'You'll need a couple of hens to keep this fellow at home,' he said as he placed two more birds into sacks.

We drove home carefully back to Nettlestone, with the three bagged birds on the back seat. Every now and again they would be a squawk and one of the bags would jump up into the air. What a journey! The bags took on a life of their own. As we approached Newport one of the bags leapt up and banged into the back of my head. I was a bag of nerves for the rest of the way!

At home I had prepared a dark shed to keep them in for a week and fed them regularly, as instructed. After a week of getting them used to the feeding place, I was then to let them out into a netted pen, so once again they could get used to walking about the area, whilst still knowing they should return to the shed for food and shelter.

It sounded so easy. The man said it would be alright to make the enclosure out of string netting, like the type used to cover fruit trees. The day came when I let them out into the daylight. They strutted cautiously around, poking here and there. Then without warning, the cock, who was later to become known as Tarzan due to his extremely piercing and high pitched call, suddenly took off like Concorde. He shot off, rocket-like, straight through the netting and disappeared, and we were left peacock-less as the two hens pecked about contentedly on the ground by my feet.

A week later the phone rang.

'Mr Feldon? This is Ian Brett. Have you by any chance lost a peacock? I have one in my mother's greenhouse in Seaview!'

I had quite a job catching Tarzan and getting him back in a sack, but eventually we got him home safely.

Needless to say, the cage was now made out of wire netting.

They all settled in nicely and strutted about the place as though they owned it. We even had a couple of chicks hatch out, which was very rewarding.

They all became very tame and would eat out of your hand, and were even known to pinch ice cream out of the kid's cornets!

Tarzan's favourite trick was to come into the porch early morning and sit on our windowsill, and then he would tap at the glass with his beak until we opened the curtains. Then he would do his formidable call to demand his breakfast. Initially we thought his antics were rather funny. That was until we realised that he also used the porch as his own personal lavatory.

Whatever we tried, we couldn't get him to go elsewhere! We would clean up the large, juicy droppings every day. Whenever we had visitors we had to dash to the front door to warn them of the mess, and without fail would find another pile waiting for us on the front door step.

It finally got to the stage, whether we liked it or not, that the beautiful, but extremely messy peacocks just had to go. A friend of ours agreed to take them on to his open land at Thorness.

It was a shame. We really missed them; especially Tarzan who was stunning when he opened up his fantail and paraded around our patio. In reality, he did become the lord and master of Inglewood – well, for a few years anyway.

* * * * *

Have you ever had that strange feeling that somebody was watching you?...

32

We Were Being Watched By An Etheral Figure

It didn't take long to realise the outside pool that we had brought with us from our old home wasn't the ideal type for Inglewood, nestled within the lovely Longlands Copse. It looked attractive and you could dive straight into it from the patio but I had a heck of a job keeping the filter clean, due to the everlasting falling leaves from the surrounding trees.

'That's it!' I announced one morning, after having spent over an hour fishing leaves out with a long-handled net. 'I'm going to build an indoor heated swimming pool! We can use it winter or summer, rain or shine. I had this wonderful vision of getting up early every day and having a quick dip before going off to work.

I called in at Gordon Lowe's, the plastic fabricators at Cowes and ordered a pool liner that very morning. Everyone laughed and told me, 'You can't just build an indoor pool just like that!'

'Too late,' I said. 'I have committed myself and bought a liner.'

From that moment, everything started to just fall into my lap.

A set of girders was acquired from a building at school which had been demolished to build our new Technology Department; I managed to buy them at scrap price.

A few days later I spotted a gas hot air heater which had been taken out from one of the new bungalows across the road, and was standing patiently on their lawn awaiting dispatch to the scrap yard. I bought it from them for £10. It was in perfect working order.

Our friends Colin and Monica came over and helped to dig out the footings. Then Tony Brett, the local builder, loaded his dumper with ready mix concrete and drove down the lane next to our land and into our back garden through the hedge – and within a day we were ready to start the building work.

Colin, who was a Structural Engineer, worked out the snow loading for the roof and the sizes of the girders and fibre-glass double-layered roofing we would need.

I couldn't resist having a quick scout over the ground, which we had cleared when making room for the dumper truck to get through the hedge, with my metal detector. To my surprise, the machine soon "peeped" and I dug up a Second World War General Service Medal with the name Private Skipper engraved around the edge. I took the medal along the road to a family we knew named Skipper, but they told me they didn't know of anyone who had been in the war. Another beautiful find was a silver cane handle top, shaped like the head of a bird. The discovery of these lovely objects rekindled my enthusiasm in detecting – but more of those adventures later...

I concreted over the 25ft circular base where the old outdoor pool had stood, and cast a series of upstanding pillars around the outside edge to form an Italian-style sunken garden with a pond and fountain in the centre. Keith, our friend the builder, created a nice set of curved steps to lead down from the high patio into the new garden.

He also finished off the surround and steps of the new indoor pool. With the help of Jim (our son-in-law) and Colin, we all managed to man-handle the long roof girders into position, and in no time, the fibre-glass roof sheets were in place. It was very successful with the room heater, the sand filter and the gas water heater I fitted up in the garage. The pool was easy to maintain and a joy to keep clean!

After a couple of years I decided to do away with the liner, and splash out (so to speak) by having the pool redone with reinforced concrete and rendered in marbleite. However, on viewing the finished result I was rather disappointed in the colour which was more putty-like than marble. So I took on the challenge to tile the whole lot out with blue mosaic glass tiles. Every night after work, I would get changed and climb into the pool, mix up the tile adhesive and lay two lines of the foot square tiny mosaics. I must say it needed discipline, but by persevering, after just two weeks I had completed the walls and base of the pool. It looked fantastic and I was very pleased with the finish. The pool was refilled and the water heated. Then everyone jumped and dived in to the crystal clear sparkling water. And so my dream had come true!

Talking about dreams, around this time, I had a reoccurring dream about a sword which was buried in some woodland we knew, where many a skirmish had taken place.

Monica and I had previously detected in this area and had found some very nice artefacts: a solid silver cloak fastener, silver spoons, a pewter shoe and many other weird and wonderful knick knacks, and we had amassed quite a selection of lead musket balls.

One evening, after we had been detecting, just as it was going dark, we were heading back to the car with a pocketful of coins and a few more musket balls. My detector was still switched on but I wasn't really concentrating, when suddenly there was a loud "ping" in my headphones. Not the sweet sound of gold or silver, just a loud dull tone. Monica and I dug around, and eventually unearthed the handle of a sword, but there was a snag; the sword blade went straight downwards and was firmly implanted in the hard earth. We struggled and struggled, trying to pull the sword out, just like Excalibur. It meant we would have to dig down a couple more feet with the small trowels we had with us. So we made the decision to leave it and made our way along the nearby beach to go and fetch Colin, and a spade. I then spotted a piece of galvanised iron tubing and back to the site we trudged. Eventually we managed to dig down far enough to get the pipe through the hilt of the sword. We both pulled and pulled but it wouldn't budge. We had almost decided to give up when on our last pull it moved slightly. Up and up it came, as we slowly eased the long-lost sword from its resting place – and another of my dreams had come true!

* * * * *

Do you believe in ghosts? How about this for a true ghost story...

Glenys, Colin, Monica and I were messing about one night with the old wine glass and ouija board. We had all had a few drinks and were larking about when the wine glass shot round the table and spelled out the word THOMASY. The glass continued on its mission and went on to inform us that Thomasy was a monk; he told us of ancient coins that were underneath the roots of an old fallen tree, and he told us where to find the tree.

A few days later after work, Colin and I decided for a laugh that we would go and search for these ancient coins. It was a dark evening and the light was fading fast. We both thought it was rather creepy as we made our way through the overhanging trees in the dense woodland. On reaching the spot, I tuned in my detector and made a sweep across the ditch around the dead roots of the old oak tree. Nothing! We looked at each other. Colin shrugged his shoulders.

'I thought it was a load of rubbish! Messages from an old monk! Ha!' We must be out of our minds to think you can get true messages from a wine glass and odd bits of paper!'

I agreed, and said that the only spirits we could rely on was a nice tot of malt whisky when we get home, to warm us up! The light had all but gone, and a mist had started to build up and drift through the trees. I didn't feel afraid, as such, but I was certainly very uncomfortable. The dampness seemed to penetrate my very soul. Nothing stirred and not a leaf moved.

I gave one final sweep with my machine; did I hear a faint tiny "ping" in my headphones? No, I was probably just imagining it! Colin had already turned to go, when I shouted to him.

'Colin, bring your spade! I think I have something. Just down there,' I pointed.

He dug out a large spade-full of soil and dropped it at my feet. Over the spoil I went again, and yes! This time I heard a positive clear rounded tone. I was half expecting the usual ring-pull but to our surprise a nice small Roman coin appeared. Believe me, that one tiny coin sent shivers down our spines.

Before we knew it, we were totally shrouded in darkness, like a black velvet cloth. The incandescent moonbeams shone through the trees giving off an unnatural ghostly light as it penetrated the cold dank mist swirling all around.

We both jumped, as a pure white owl swooped low over our heads and let out a loud "twit-ta-woo". By this time we had unearthed a further four Roman coins.

Suddenly the hairs on the back of my neck bristled and I had the strange feeling that we weren't alone in the dark dismal forest. I looked up warily; everything seemed normal, but then, out of the corner of my eye, I spotted something. We were being watched by an ethereal figure standing not fifteen feet away. I turned my head slowly. There was no mistake. The figure remained stationary with the moon shining behind giving an unusual vision of something strange yet very real. I saw Colin glance up, then he looked behind me. He lowered his head then looked up again. His eyes nearly popped out of his head. He shuddered and whispered to me.

'I think we'd better be going. It's getting really late now.'

I immediately agreed, but the detector was still pinging away merrily.

'Colin, put your cap down on the ground.'

He looked at me oddly, but hastily removed his cap and put it down next to me. I grabbed a large handful of earth from where the multi-sounds appeared the loudest and filled his cap to the brim.

'Right, let's go!' I said, as he grabbed his cap.

We scampered past the lone figure still standing watching us in the cover of the menacing trees. We made our way through the dense woods, falling and tripping over roots and dead tree branches, increasing our speed as we went. We were now running, like a couple of schoolboys who had been caught pinching apples, glancing behind us every now and then to see if we were being followed. Twenty minutes later we threw ourselves into the car. Colin revved up and we were off like a shot. I looked at Colin; he looked like I felt. Sweat was pouring down his face, he was bright red and he was visibly shaking.

By the time we had driven home, we had both calmed down somewhat. Entering the house Colin said to Mon, 'Get us a couple of double whiskies, quickly!' We downed them speedily then proceeded to empty Colin's mud-filled cap onto a sheet of plastic. In all that soil, besides the worms, woodlice and mulch we uncovered another thirteen Roman coins.

Colin was quiet for a moment.

'You saw him, didn't you?' he asked me softly.

'Oh, yes! I saw him,' I replied. 'He was…'

'He was smiling!' Colin interrupted. 'Thomasy the monk was smiling at us, wasn't he!'

'He certainly was,' I confirmed. 'He was smiling, as if to say, I told you so.'

'Thank Goodness for that,' Colin gasped. 'I thought I might have seen a ghost!'

Of course, we always had permission and agreement with the landowners to detect on their land.

But the next time I was all alone, and had an uncanny feeling someone, or something, was watching my every move.

33

A Strange Supernatural Tale Of Long Ago

It was a tradition; every New Year's Eve we had a family party. After a meal, and swim, all the grandchildren would sit around the old story teller (that's me!), and I would tell them about the time I met a ghost.Often, after the story we would wrap up well in our hats and coats and head off to the place where the ghostly meeting had taken place. I timed it, so that we would arrive on the exact spot as the clocks reached midnight. After the adventures we would return back to Inglewood. All the kids slept over and looked forward to one of Glenys' Full English Breakfasts bright and early on New Year's Day.

However, I remember one specific night of storytelling, when no one was game enough to go off at midnight down the haunted lane I described in the chilling tale. (However, they did vote on going the next morning, in the crisp, winter sunshine).

I spoke quietly and slowly.

'Turn the lights low and snuggle cosily into your armchair. Listen to the moaning of the wind outside as the raindrops tap at the windows, like goblin fingers… I promise you, my friends, tonight you will hear a tale that will send cold shivers down your spine.

From the earliest times, there have been uneasy whisperings of unbidden guests and weird happenings and hauntings, which, by the laws of common sense, are impossible. Now allow yourself to imagine there is no time and no space boundaries, as you drift back through the years to the beginning of the reign of King Edward III. Mentioned in the Doomsday Book is a small town called Woolverton, which lies snugly below the downs of Culver, on the road from Bembridge to Brading.

The old road passed right through the gates of Ye Olde Towne of Wolverton and continued across the ancient causeway to Brading. All that remain of this once thriving little community are the earthen ramparts and fossitts which proclaimed the importance of the place in days long passed.

Now at the crossroads of the old town was a Holy Well. It was a plentiful spring of the purest water, which rose up through the ground in a small basin about six feet across. It was without ornament of any sort just a few stone steps down and a sturdy piece of English Oak with a v-notch in the top to carry the bucket pole. In short it was nothing but a hole in the ground. The water was known to be pure, sweet and crystal clear, and some say, with magical healing properties. On the small knoll immediately above it, stood a rude, rough stone cross. On this cross were these unusual verses carved deep into the stone:

While the oose flows pure and free,
This Burg and Towne shall happy be –
The net be heavy in the sea
And wheaten seed shall yield plentee.
When stained blood in the burn shall well
It shall light a flame so hot and snell –
Shall fire the towne from lock to fell
Nor sheeling hide its place to tell –
The Culver Ness shall ring its death knell.

This uncanny story had been carved on the arm piece of that Holy Cross. The well waters were known as the 'fountain of life' by the holy people who came from far and wide to collect samples of this special water to mix with herbs and plants for medicinal purposes.

That well still exists to this very day, as Colin, Mon, Glenys and I relocated it by dowsing over a map then using dowsing rods in the woods.

Once a year an old Holy Man (commonly known as The Pilgrim by the local townsfolk) visited the well, dressed in dark grey woollen cloth with a hood to match. It is said that his face was wrinkled and dried out like an old prune and his fingers were gnarled and bony, but his eyes were piercing and alive, kind and full of understanding wisdom. He spoke with a gentle foreign accent. Some say he travelled from the Holy Land to collect samples of plants that only grew in the remote marshy parts of this special island.

Over his left shoulder he carried an old battered, leather saddle bag fastened with two large bronze buckles. It was said by some that this saddle bag was full of gold and silver pieces.

On a fateful summer's day long ago, the Holy Man stooped low over the sweet magical waters to fill his silver flask, unbeknown and unaware that he was being watched. Two nasty scruffy-looking vagabonds crept up behind him and struck The Pilgrim on the head with a vicious club made from the roots of an old Oak tree. They say his frail head split open from the crown to the neck. As he fell forward into the water the villains grabbed the bag and made off down one of the darkened alleyways of the old town. The only things they found in the saddle bag were dried herbs, plants and some very unusual star-shaped dark yellow seeds. The vagabonds looked at each other in dismay; they knew they had broken the spell above the well, which they believed would bring ruin to their much-loved Towne. They fled from the town. Grabbing a boat they swiftly sailed out of the haven and headed out to sea – they were never seen or heard of again.

In the meantime the old Holy Man's life blood was flowing freely from the gash in his head turning the once crystal clear waters of the well into a vivid glowing bright crimson red. Immediately the blue skies clouded over and large black clouds formed overhead. It became darker and darker as if some evil hand had torn the sun right out of the sky. Thunder and lightning pounded the old town and hailstones as big as pomegranates hurled down. People scattered for shelter, scared and confused, as the storm increased to wreak revenge on the inhabitants of Woolverton. Everyone knew that the curse of the well was now truly upon them and their beloved Towne.

The villagers were grief-stricken at the fate of The Pilgrim, and carefully wrapped his body before taking it to Saint Urians Chapel on the outskirts of the town. There he was buried with dignity beneath the branches of the large Yew tree, the year being 'thirteen hundred and forty in the Reign of our dear King Edward III'.

Over the years the town had withstood the many raids of pirates and vagabonds who came into Brading Haven waters as they moored at Woolverton Quay, then known as 'Ye Olde Lock'.

Another unforgettable day saw a French fleet of large Man-o-Wars appear on the horizon and head towards Sandown Bay. The old Culver hermit who lived in a cave on the cliff face spotted them and immediately ran down to warn the inhabitants of Woolverton. If the ships had entered Brading Haven they would have been seen easily by the lookouts and the town lock-gates would have been securely closed and barred and the ramparts overlooking the waters would be defended by every able bodied man, woman and child. But, as far as the townsfolk knew the French were only attacking them from the landward side, so the gates at the lock had been left open in case they themselves had to make a quick exit.

Now an old fisherman named Edgar pulled his boat high among the bushes. Hid his money and fishhooks under a stone, and hid his pots, pans and drinking vessel with equal care. He took his crossbow and worked his way up the stream towards the town gates. A large party of the enemy, the French, passed the lane close to Edgar's cottage, which stood by itself a few hundred yards from the walls of the town, but hidden from view by the trees.

The Culver main gates of the town were closed just in time. The enemy were exposed to a galling fire of crossbows from the ramparts. But to no avail. Under the cover of their shields the French using a battering ram, smashed through the sturdy gates.

All seemed lost, when a shout of 'A Russell. A Russell', was heard. The true knight of Yaverland, Theodore Russell, came with his reinforcements. He had a complete suit of armour with a plume of red and white feathers in his helmet. The brave knight led the charge but unfortunately his pony was soon struck down by an arrow. The pony stumbled and the knight fell in the mud; before he could get up he was knocked on the head by a Frenchman's battleaxe. His death was instantly avenged by Edgar's crossbow arrow.

Unbeknown to the inhabitants, at the same time another contingent of French had landed at the rear. They made their way from Brading Haven and up the River Yar, which ran close to and under the undefended walls of the town.

That day the town was pillaged. The houses were made out of wood and completely destroyed by fire – never to be rebuilt again!

The curse of the Holy Well had truly come to pass.

It is said that The 'Grey' Pilgrim is often seen to walk at night'; always accompanied by the uncanny sound of a dog barking. He is even to this present day sometimes met late in the evening in a place called Pilgrim's Lane. Nobody is comfortable entering this lane at night. Rumours say, if you happen to be passing by on a dark, dank night often one could hear the wailing and cries of terror, which sends cold shivers down the spine. Some folk have even reported seeing fires burning brightly as if the whole woods were on fire.

The new road was laid to skirt around Culver Cliff and a new bridge built over the River Yar to avoid going near this cursed and haunted spot.

Edgar's cottage was neither sacked nor burnt by the French, as it lay in a hollow not a hundred yards from Ye Olde Towne.

But what was the fate of poor Edgar? Eventually he was captured, and thrown alive, along with the other prisoners, into the blazing inferno.

It has been said that on hearing the French were approaching, Thomasy the monk, collected all the silver from the chapel at St Urian's and buried it in a secret place. Later, the monk, although of French origin, also suffered the same fate as Edgar and the rest of the inhabitants.There is a wealth of treasure still lying in that town which has now overgrown into a copse. Some now call it Centurions Copse, as Roman artefacts have since been found on the site.

It was a cold, damp, misty day when I was metal detecting in a field near to Ye Olde Towne. Walking slowly over the ridge of the hill concentrating on the slight buzzing sound in my headphones, I was suddenly aware of a chilly feeling running down my spine. The hairs on the back of my neck and hands bristled, and I had the strange feeling that someone or something was out there in the mist watching me. I slowly removed my headphones and listened in silence. I felt as if time had stood still and I could smell the disturbing stench of burning meat. I turned slowly around, and to my amazement stood beside me was an odd figure. I half expected it to be the old Pilgrim – but no!

Standing beside me, not two feet away, was this person – a man – with untidy, black, curly hair and a windswept look on his face, but his eyes were so dark I wasn't sure if they were just empty sockets, it was very difficult to tell. He wore a smock of rags, tied around the middle with a hemp rope and fastened with a small boat hook. His sack-like trousers were tied just below the knees, and old worn-out tatty canvas shoes were on his feet.

I was shocked – nay, more like afraid – nay, more like petrified! Was I dreaming? Was this a real person from the past or just a scarecrow? I felt as though I could reach out and touch this uncanny person. I thought to myself, I wonder it he would be solid or would my hand simply pass right through him? Then the bizarre figure spoke slowly.

'I be Edgar. Who might you be?'

'Er, I be Derek', I replied, and without further ado, held out my right hand.

Edgar smiled as he placed his hand in mine. I realised I couldn't feel his hand and my hand clutched at thin air as there was nothing but empty space. My heart missed a beat, then started to beat rapidly. I felt as if I wanted to flee from this spot, but my legs had turned to stone.

Then Edgar turned away and casually muttered, 'I be off now to feed the Master's ducks.'

He ambled across the fields and disappeared slowly in the cold mist.

My gaze followed his steps. I was stunned and couldn't move for quite a few minutes. It was if I was in a time warp, as if I had been transported back in time. Then with a jolt I came to and found myself alone with my detector in my left hand, whilst my right hand was still clasped tight. I'll tell you what, it didn't take me long to scarper across the field to the lane. Walking hastily up the long lane, my mind was all mixed up; had I actually seen the figure, or was I just imagining things?

A few steps later a familiar and friendly figure stepped out of the copse into the lane in front of me. It was the gamekeeper with his shot gun looped over his shoulder and a dead rabbit slung over his back. He stopped when he saw me hurrying up the lane, as if there was no tomorrow.

'Hey, slow down. You'll meet yourself coming back, if you carry on like that!' he said with a grin on his face.

'Thank goodness it's you!' I burst out. 'You won't believe this, but I've just met a really queer person, over there in the mist.'

'Oh, you needn't worry about that. I've met all sorts of odd folk around here, men, women and children. And, one day I came across a couple of foreign-looking pike-men – now, those two really scared the living daylights out me! But they always just melt away as soon as I tell them that they are trespassing on private land. Oh, yes, I could certainly tell you a tale or two about the happenings that take place around these parts, especially when the sun goes down. Now, the chappy you met in the field, I've met him a couple of times; he's harmless. That'll be Edgar, or so he tells me, and he always comes up with the same old tale, "I'll be off to feed the Master's ducks." "Good Luck!" I always say to him; as there haven't been any ducks or duck pond, for that matter, since Edward was on the throne.'

The gamekeeper dug into his pocket and held out a piece of pottery. It was part of a 14th century jug handle.

'Here, you can have this. It will remind you of when this used to be a thriving little town, when all those poor souls were happy and content to live quiet, simple lives in peace...

before the days of that curse.'

I found it difficult to open my still clenched right hand to take the pottery. With great effort and will power, I prized my hand open and to my surprise found a tiny pile of grey powder in my palm. Then before my eyes it melted and turned into a green liquid, and the next minute, puff! And it was gone; simply evaporated into thin air.

'Whoa!' I yelled. 'What the heck was that?'

The gamekeeper, with a twinkle in his eye and a broad smile on his face, answered my question.

'Aha! That, my friend, means you too have shaken hands with a *real* ghost!'...

Silence; no one spoke or moved.

I waited a few minutes then continued.

'Now, my little friends, I want you all to wrap up warm and I will take you down the haunted lane, and who knows, you too may shake hands with a real ghost from the past. As the clock strikes midnight, you may hear that strange uncanny voice speaking to you from way back in time; "I be Edgar, who might you be?"'.

The brave ones gaped at me in horror and disbelief, whilst others covered their faces with the cushions clutched firmly in their hands.

Then I heard a little voice whisper from behind one of the cushions.

'No way! I'm not going down that haunted lane to shake hands with a ghost.'

All the others nodded their heads in agreement.

At that moment a dog barked loudly outside from the main road. All the grandchildren jumped out of their skins, belted through the door and up our spiral staircase and were hiding under their sheets in two minutes flat. I stood at the bottom of the stairs.

'Goodnight and sweet dreams my little ones!' I whispered. Funnily enough no one replied!

* * * * *

Sweet dreams? Oh yes, I had a dream when I was about their age, in which I opened up a faded, battered, old copy of a Geographic Magazine, and behold, before my very eyes was a black and white photograph which would haunt me for the rest of my life.

34

Dreams Are Made Of This

The clatter of pots and the nagging of the dinner ladies continued as we picked up a plate from the top of the pile.

Wow! We started to juggle with them; they were red hot! The fun started as we passed them quickly up and down the line. The idea being if you could manage to throw a plate to the next lad who already had one, he had the choice of either burning his fingers or dropping the first plate to catch the second! Of course, you always had the clever ones who would shove the plate under his arm pits and pass the next one down the line.

Clatter! Bang! The first plate dropped and smashed to smithereens, amidst a loud cheer and a shout of 'Butterfingers!' At that moment the bell rang three times – oh, no, not another wet break. After dinner we all traipsed slowly back to our classrooms, fed up to the teeth; this was the fourth wet break this week.

Outside the hailstones continued to pelt down and they bounced off the flagstones like jumping beans. All the windows steamed up with the forty sweaty bodies lounging around on the desks.

Two boys were playing noughts and crosses on the smaller panes of glass, whilst a couple of the "bullies" Butch and

Weasel were drawing rude pictures until Miss Rouse, our form teacher, looked up from her knitting. We all tittered as Butch held on to the cuff of his sleeve and wiped over the glass quickly with his forearm.

Miss Rouse must have been at least ninety, as all our young men teachers had gone to war. All our teachers were either old women, old men or young men with an arm or leg missing, who had been shot down in their Spitfires or Lancaster Bombers and were lucky enough to escape with their lives.

That's the war for you.

Our geography teacher came back from the war with one leg missing. He was a cheerful chap, always telling us jokes and tales about the dogfights up in the air over the Channel. One dinnertime he came in followed by Willy, the caretaker, who was carrying a large cardboard box. Willy placed the box down on the front desk, saluted, and walked out of the room. We all looked up as our teacher announced that he'd brought us some intellectual reading matter. We gawped in amazement. Then one boy at the back spoke up.

'Sir, what's that intellect thingamajig, or somat like that?'

Our teacher surveyed each and every one of us.

'Well, it's like this. I know you get bored at playing noughts and crosses and hangman all the time, so I thought what you need is some exciting reading matter.'

'Oh, not more homework!' we all groaned.

'Oh, fine. I'll take it back home with me then, and give it back to my pal, who's come over from America.'

With the word "America" we all looked up with renewed interest. He put his hand in the box and pulled out a pile of American comics, and assorted magazines from his own collection at home. There was a mad scramble as lads climbed over desks, pushing and shoving was the order of the day; first come, first served. The teacher laughed out loud.

'Okay, okay! Just take one, and then back to your desk.'

We were entranced; you could have heard a pin drop during that wet lunch break. We all jumped out of our skin when the bell rang to start the afternoon lessons. All the comics and magazines were placed gently back in the box, as we all looked forward to another wet dinner time – it was great!

During one of these sessions I was mooching around in the box, and came across a pile of Geographic magazines. Now, we had just come back from a potholing trip to Castleton in Derbyshire with Mr Hughes our headmaster, and I was smitten with the "mountains". Leaning back on my seat, I casually opened the book in the middle. I gave a gasp and nearly fell on the floor; there right in front of my eyes was the most amazing black and white picture of... I closed my eyes and slowly reopened them – I just couldn't believe that there was such a high snow-capped mountain anywhere in the world. It looked like a giant steep pyramid which seemed to tilt over at the top. The rock face looked steep, rough and menacing. This mountain stood out and seemed to tower above everything else. I thought to myself, this must be Everest, as I had never seen anything like it in my life. Before I knew it, I was working out possible routes up to the top. Some routes got me near the top then I realised the top triangle was tilting outward. Well, that can't be done. So I imagined I would go around to the right side, but that was extremely steep and covered in ice; if you came off there you would fall directly on to a glacier below. The bell rang loudly. I was determined to keep these centre pages, so I carefully tore the paper through the cotton and hid the sheets in my exercise book.

The next time we had geography with Hopalong (we used to call him that, as he had a tin leg and hopped along the corridor), I showed him my picture.

'Ah! The Matterhorn. Now that, my lad, is a real mountain, if there ever was one!'

'Do you think it could ever be climbed?' I asked.

'Oh yes! It has been conquered by an Englishman called Edward Whymper.'

'Wow! And did he…'

'Hold it there. I tell you what, I've a little book at home which tells you all about it. Would you like to read it, Derek?'

'Oh yes please, Sir!'

'Then I shall bring it in tomorrow morning.'

I couldn't sleep that night. I had my torch under the blankets shining on that wonderful picture. The snow shone and reflected from the light of the torch. But those rocks – those rocks looked more menacing, frightening, dangerous and steeper than ever! I was just over half way up when I fell into a deep sleep. There was little oxygen at this height and I was short of breath. My chest hurt as I lay on a slab of hard rock. It was a real nightmare; I tried to shout but there was nobody in sight. I felt a tugging, and suddenly daylight surrounded me. My mother pulled back my blankets and wanted to know 'what the heck I was doing' face down on top of my torch with all the covers tucked tightly over my head.

'It's a wonder you didn't suffocate!' she said.

'Oh, thank goodness, it's you.' I said. 'I was half way up the Matterhorn when I just fell asleep and…'

'Enough! Come on it's time for school,' she said as she turned to walk through the door. 'Up, up – Now!' Just as I was settling down for another ten minutes kip, 'And don't forget to wash behind your ears and the back of your neck.'

It was no use arguing with her about the waste of soap, especially as there was a war on and the soap was rationed. When she was in one of those moods you just did as you were told, because I knew from experience that there would be a full inspection before I could have my breakfast – And today I wanted to get off to school extra early so I could catch Hopalong. He always came to school on a ladies bicycle, because it had no crossbar. It was quite funny watching him ride the bike, which Willy Wanker, the caretaker, had converted for him. One pedal was stationary at the bottom where Hopalong would rest his tin leg and his tin foot was jammed on to a special clip on the pedal. The other pedal was in a fixed gear so it would come up to the top by itself. I never fancied having a go on that contraption. I had once had a go on a fixed gear, down a steep hill. Half way down I decided to stop pedalling and suddenly found myself being lifted up in the air. I then panicked and jammed the front brake on – Whoosh! I shot over the handlebars like a man on a flying trapeze.

I waited at the school gates in my navy blue gabardine raincoat hitched up over my head. It was raining cats and dogs, and there was a perishing cold wind, which didn't help. But I stuck it out until I heard the familiar whistling of old 'Hoppy'. How he managed to keep so cheerful, even in this foul weather, I'll never know! Smiling to himself, he turned into the driveway and nearly came off his bike, as I pounced out in front of him.

'Sir! Sir! Did you bring it?' I asked eagerly. He looked at me in surprise.

'Bring what? he asked.

'That book about the Matterhorn,' I continued.

'Oh dear me, I forgot all about it,' he replied.

My heart dropped straight down to my clogs. My shoulders drooped as I thrust my hands deep into the pockets of my soggy raincoat, as I slouched towards the school entrance. I could hear him start to laugh as he shouted me back.

'Hey, come back! Will this do?'

I turned around; I'm afraid I was in no mood for jokes. I looked up at him. The rain was washing down my face mixing with the little tears running down my cheeks. He stood there holding his bicycle handlebars in one hand, whilst in the other outstretched hand was a little book about the Alps by Edward Wymper.

My mother always said 'I think you must have mountain blood running through your veins'. Little did she know what words of wisdom she had spoken. I only felt at one with the world when I was climbing a rock face or standing on top of a mountain. There was something spiritual, a deep down feeling of being in touch with my ancestors.

Funnily enough, it was only when I was researching the name of FELDON, during 1996 and 1997 that I suddenly understood who I was and why I had this magnetic love of mountains. Only then did I become aware that it was my true nature and that I did, in fact, have mountain blood.

* * * * *

The Family Name of
FELDON

The distinguished name of FELDON is one of the most notable Anglo-Saxon surnames, and its historical trail has emerged from the mists of time to become an influential surname of the middle ages and even continues to the present day. It is recorded in the Anglo-Saxon chronicles that the Feldon's were notable members of the third order "The Thanes", or Ministers to the king. The first order was the King himself and the second order were The Earles. The third order were The Thanes, however, they were by no means less important! They served the King in times of war with the swords by which they were girt, and were therefore called the King's Ministers.

The Thanes were all landowners; and let it be known that no individual, however notable he may be, could sit amongst them, unless he was entitled to land. Hence the notable names held by these distinguished and privileged people. The Thanes landowners became known as Field, Fielden, Feld, Feldon, Fildying, Fylde, Fylden and even Velden. The land-owner Thanes were recognised as an elite group of King's Ministers. To possess the qualification of "Land Thane" each Thane was to own and manage forty hydes; with each hyde containing one hundred and twenty acres, it meant that each Thane's minimum holding was 4800 acres of land.

Of course, he was totally responsible for the defence of his land – for the upkeep of the defensive systems in case of invasion – and also to provide a minimum number of fighting men under his command in the case of war.

He was also responsible to build fortresses in strategic positions. These were known as "duns", hence the name of "Fieldun". The Anglo-Saxon word for mountain was "don", so the mountain men became known as the "Feldons".

Though the Anglo-Saxons possessed the best parts of Britain, the North-West side of the country was retained by the Ancient Britons. Principally those districts where the natural fortifications of moors, fells, mountains, lakes, and dense woodland, enabled them to withstand the Anglo-Saxon invaders.

The original homeland of the Feldon's was the County of Lancashire. The county was protected in the North-East and Southern borders with fortresses (Felduns) of the true Britons known as the Duns, and defended by the Fielduns, Felduns, etc. The ridge of mountains running down the Eastern side were not inaptly termed the British Appenines (now the Pennines) which separated them from Northumbria, Yorkshire.

Now this is where the surname of Feldon comes into being. The Anglo-Saxon word for mountain was "don", and therefore the ferocious and unmericiful Men of the Mountains were known by the Anglo-Saxons as Fieldons, Feldons and Fyldons.

The Anglo-Saxons never penetrated and conquered the Mountains of the Appenines. They tried many times but to no avail. The sea was the natural defence on the West side and any invaders from that region were dealt with unmercifully by the Fyldes, Fyldemans and Fieldmans.

It is interesting to note that the area around Blackpool is still called The Fylde to this very day!

These brave and determined people were never conquered by the Anglo-Saxons. They became Anglo-Saxonised not by defeat but by naturalisation, and that is when they recognised the benefits of the Anglo-Saxon system of government and ruling.

The crest on the Feldon coat of arms is a "Wild Man Proper".

In the Anglo-Saxon language the word "man" was used to designate a human being; a good man, a God man or man of God. They had firm convictions that the soul did not perish with the body. Of their conception of the essence of Divine Being the Anglo-Saxon language affords a singular testimony, for the name of God signifies "good". He was goodness himself.

The "wild" signifies ferociousness towards the enemy, and as above, we now know that "man" signifies a good man. The Anglo-Saxon terminology for "proper" states: "a proper man was less corrupted than the more polished Romans. A proper man was faithful, chaste and honest, turning towards the light and seeking amendment." (Ref: History of the Anglo-Saxons).

Family names or hereditary surnames did not come into general use until after the Battle of Hastings and the Norman Conquest of 1066, when King Harold came to the throne. The Normans introduced the Poll Tax (poll meaning head), and in consequence the need for surnames became law for identification purposes.

The first court recorded spelling of my family name is shown to be that of William de la Feldon, which was dated 1286 Calendar of Investigations after death.

All surnames of every country have been subject to changes owing to dialect, war and spelling. Many reasons were revealed for these spelling variations but it is mainly due to church officials and Norman scribes spelling the name as it was *told* to them.

In the 1990's it was recorded that there were only 396 Feldon's in the world! (Ref: Burkes Peerage World Book of Feldons).

This was broken down as follows: 208 in Great Britain, 125 in US, 17 in South Africa, 15 in New Zealand, 15 in Canada, 13 in Australia and 3 in Germany.

Total families are estimated at 167 in the world. Over 220 million name and address records were searched throughout the world. In Great Britain alone, 22 million households have been researched, and those households represented 56 million people. All these were researched and reviewed to find as many Feldon families as possible. (Thank goodness my family name is not Smith!)

Kinsmen of the family name of Feldon were amongst the many who sailed aboard the armada of small sailing ships known as The White Sails, which plied the stormy Atlantic. These overcrowded ships were disease ridden, sometimes as much as 30-40% – which meant that between 30-40 people out of every hundred never reached their destination due to sickness or the elements.

Looking at my family tree, I do know that my grandfather, Charles Ramage Feldon, had a twin called William Feldon who sailed to America. He married and had a daughter. During the Second World War she came to England to take myself and my sister Sylvia back to America for safety. My father, however, refused as he wanted to keep our family together as one unit. I have never been able to find out her name or where she lived. Just as a matter of interest my father, Charles William Feldon, was named after the twins.

(Over the years we have seen many films starring an American actress called Barbara Feldon – she was the youngest daughter of Roy and Julia Hall, and in 1958 she married Belgian-born Lucien Verdoux-Feldon).

Many of the Feldon hill men emigrated to the colonies where their leadership and land skills were used in developing and protecting sheep farms in Australia, New Zealand and America, with the same determination and persistence that won them the honours to "bear arms".

The noblemen have defended their country and have seen and taken part on many expeditions and battles in foreign lands. Battle tapestry of the knight bearing arms show the Feldon are a proud and ancient family, being one of the first arms to be presented and acknowledged by the Court, this can be recognised by the simplistic design of the arms.

The most ancient grant of a Coat of Arms for Feldon was a silver shield (known as an Argent, which represented Serenity and Nobility), with a blue horizontal stripe (called a Bar, which means One of The Honourable) bearing three gold diamond shapes. The stripe or Bar, is also known as The Ordinaries; in heraldry this is believed to have originated from bars of wood or iron that were used to strengthen, or fasten, the early shields.The blue (azure) colouring of the Bar represents Loyalty and Splendour. The three Golden Diamonds (Lozenges) on the shield announce the knight's achievements in battle, to tell others that its bearer achieved some notable feat and provide a clue to a persons being. They commemorate three honourable deeds and were presented to the Feldons as a gift from the crown for Brave Deeds in

Battle. They represent Bravery, Determination and Honour. As mentioned the crest was a Wild Man Proper, and the family motto was "Virtutis Praemium, Honor" – First Bravery then Honour.

In 1419 King Henry V of England forbade anyone to take on arms unless by right of ancestry. It was very exciting to research this history and find that my family has the right to bear this ancient Coat of Arms!

So you can see, by nature, I AM a Mountain Man!

It's like the song from the musical South Pacific – "You've got to have a dream. If you don't have a dream, how you gonna have a dream come true."

Well, I had a dream, but I must admit it took nearly forty years before it came true...

35

Hot Food? 12 'Til 2pm Only!

Sitting quietly listening to the background music of my favourite orchestra leader Mantovani, with a freshly made cup of coffee resting on my knee, the aroma and gentle music lulled me into a semi state of hypnosis. My eyes slowly drifted across the room and rested on the large oil painting of my dream mountain, the Matterhorn. I thought to myself, I wonder if I would still have the nerve to step out on to that final ice pitch and continue up the knife-edge peak of that wonderful mountain.

I had just celebrated my 50th birthday and needed a new challenge to get myself out of the doldrums I currently felt myself in. I needed a change; I needed a kick up the backside to get me back on track, to be able to face the world and say 'This I have done!'

It was Mon who broke the silence.

'What great things are you day dreaming about now?'

'I was just wondering if I have the nerve to tackle that mountain over there,' I said nodding towards the painting.

With that, Colin, Monica's husband at the time, butted in.

'Hey, if you're thinking of having a go, I'd like to join you.'

I looked up in surprise at him, 'What? But you've never even climbed a mountain before!'

'Well, no… but you could teach me to rock and ice climb.'

'Why the sudden urge to do a daft thing like that?'

'Well, it's the 50th anniversary of the Isle of Wight Round Table, and they have made a number of wooden island-shaped plaques as a challenge to members who can place them in the most unusual places. I've been racking my brains about what I could do. This would be just great!'

Well, that was it, the ball had bounced and started to roll gathering momentum as it went.

I contacted the Swiss tourist board in London. They gave me names of hotels and 'pensions' in Zermatt. They provided me with people to contact in the Swiss Mountain Guides Office, and they were kind enough, (when they learned what we planned to do and why), to provide us with a full travel itinerary together with prices for air and rail fares and also suggested which accommodation would best suit our budget.

Colin and I then went into strict fitness training. Everyday I would stop at the Smallbrook running track on my way to school, strip down to my shorts and t-shirt, pull on my running shoes and clog round for a minimum of six circuits – no matter what the weather; rain, hail, ice or snow.

Come November, I decided to phone the warden up at Idwal Youth Hostel in Wales to see what the weather was like up there.

'It's bloomin' cold and there has been a couple of snow showers. By the way Lyn Ogwen has frozen over, just to give you an idea of the icy temperatures we're having at the moment. Oh, and Idwal Slabs has a thin coating of ice,' he replied.

I asked about 'Faith, Hope and Charity' – three very nice climbs in summer.

'Oh, you'll want to keep off Faith and Hope. Charity might be a little more forgiving.'

'And what about Tryfan?'

'The East face is white with driven snow. The Milestone is more sheltered and I would think still climbable at the moment.'

I thanked him, and said that we hoped to be up there soon.

Armed with this information, I had a chat with Colin and we decided to go up the following weekend. I didn't ask the warden about accommodation, as we might have to stop on the way up.

Ropes, ice axes, rucksacks, the lot were checked over, and we were ready to go. Colin had just bought a new Morris Maxi and reckoned we could do the 217 mile journey to the mountains in North Wales in about 6 hours, including a stop off for dinner. Now, I had my doubts, as Lew and I had done this trip before in the Bedford Dormobile loaded with gear and lads, and it seemed to take forever! But who was I to argue with the driver…

It was raining and overcast as we drove the car up the ramp on to the ferry. We were first in the queue at the bar and each ordered a Full English Breakfast with a mug of hot steamy coffee – well, that's what the chap behind the counter called it! On studying the map, I reckoned we could do the 100 miles to Gloucester and then have a break and a spot of lunch.Believe me, the drive up there was no picnic, it rained and rained and rained all the way. The wipers had a job keeping the windscreen clear at times, especially when we were stuck behind heavy goods lorries as the water sprayed up off the roads at us. Driving? It was more like waterskiing behind a slow-speed boat!

By the time we reached Cirencester we were both ready for a cuppa, so we pulled into a lay-by next to a little cake shop and café. There we indulged in a couple of pies and a large pot of tea.

At least in Colin's new car the heater was great, and we were very comfortable in the nice wide seats. Between Gloucester and Hereford the rain stopped. It was still dark and overcast but it was such a relief. But I had an uncanny feeling that this was just a respite and that even worst weather was awaiting us. We had just about covered half the journey now and Colin picked up speed slightly and we motored along for the next 70 miles or so. We then arrived at Oswestry and came to the assumption that it must be market day here, as there were sheep everywhere! It took us almost an hour to get through and back on the road again towards Llangollen, where I suggested we could stop for another break and a hot meal.

Touch wood, everything had so far gone to plan, though it was now getting late and I wanted to find somewhere to sleep in the Ogwen area by about 4 O'clock. We came out of the bar at the rear of the hotel in Llangollen after only managing to feast on a cold snack – 'Hot food – 12 'till 2 pm only'! The bar man had told us it was snowing up in the mountains and he didn't fancy our chances of getting to Capel Curig by this time tomorrow! We laughed at his comments and ambled across the yard to the toilets. Much better, now where was I? Oh yes, it was then, that I thought I was seeing things. But there was no mistake; fine, powdery, snow was swirling around in the enclosed yard. Colin just stood there with a great big grin on his face. I looked up at the dark menacing clouds racing across the sky and thought, yep, this is what we came for!

As we approached Bettws-y-Coed we ran into a blizzard, with snow flakes the size of prawn crackers whipping across the road. The light faded completely as we drove on to Capel Curig in complete darkness. The road had disappeared under a six inch layer of soft snow, but what we didn't know was that there was also a frozen sheet of ice already covering the road beneath. Going down one of the hills, Colin touched his brakes as he approached the bend. The car continued moving in a sideward waltz back and forth, eventually stopping about a foot from an old stone wall. Even with the headlamps on dip we still couldn't see through the blinding wall of swirling snow. As Colin was concentrating on keeping the car moving in and out of the huge drifts of snow which had built up against the edge of the roadside, it took ages to cover the six miles to Capel Curig. Every time Colin stopped I had to whip out smartish and clear the windscreen with my arm and hands. I'll tell you what, it was absolutely freezing and my hands soon became numb. Back inside the car again, I sat on them to get the circulation going again, but the pins and needles gave me gip each time my hands slowly came back to life. On the odd occasion I took my eyes off the road and looked over at Colin, I could see sweat pouring off his forehead with the intense concentration, but the big grin never left his face; he was thoroughly enjoying himself, I think he fancied himself as a rally driver. I must give him credit, by the time we reached the junction at Capel Curig the number of manoeuvres we had made would make a professional rally driver stand up and clap. He had been absolutely brilliant, and I knew from that moment on he had the nerve to have a go at the ascent of the Matterhorn.

Finally we turned in the pitch black and headed down towards Lyn Ogwen. I knew there were one or two options open to us for accommodation; Mr Williams' farm 'Gwern Gof Isaf' where we stayed when I had taken the boys from school on a mountaineering trip, or there was the Youth Hostel at Ogwen, and even possibly the Climbing Club Cottage, where I had stayed a few times in the past, would probably be available to us at this time of the year.

'Where the heck are we going?' Colin enquired. The weather had deteriorated even further and we had trouble seeing even a yard in front of us, as the dipped headlamps just reflected back a solid white wall. Much to our surprise we could make out a brilliant light shining straight ahead, and as we approached we came to a Motel-type of building, which I had never seen before.

'Quick! Turn in there,' I shouted.

Colin swung the wheel around and pulled up to the entrance. This was to be our base camp from now on, for our expeditions up into the snow-capped mountains of North Wales.

It was a very warm and welcoming sort of place. The manager arranged a good hot meal and the chalet-type of accommodation was quite adequate, with two twin beds, a wash basin and shower unit, and more importantly, a nice hot radiator. We were fast asleep by nine o'clock.

Breakfast consisted of porridge, eggs, bacon and black pudding. I think this took Colin by surprise.

'What's this black pudding then?' he asked.

'Just get it down you!' I replied.

He nibbled around the edges, then whoosh, it was gone! We had an early start and were well nourished for the tough day ahead.

The heavy black clouds raced across the sky. I looked up and remembered the wise words uttered by Jake the Youth Hostel Warden in Castleton, Derbyshire, when I was on a school trip at the age of twelve; 'Now, my lads, anytime you are in the mountains, always take note of the weather. If the clouds look menacing, believe me, they are – and sooner or later they will hit you with all they've got – hail, rain or snow!'

Tryfan looked more like a bride on top of a wedding cake, dressed in white with a veil enveloping her head. Adam and Eve, the two sentinels guarding her honour, were completely covered in cloud. Boy, what a day to be out! Well, this is what we came for – this was Colin's initiation into mountaineering.

We set off slogging through the thick snow. There was an icy wind tunnelling down between the mountains from the Capel Curig direction. Fortunately for us, this was behind us as we headed towards Tryfan and the start of the Heather Terrace. Puffing and panting we stopped part way up the terrace. I took the rope off and laid it on a large snow-covered boulder.Colin looked at me with a surprised expression on his face.

'I think I can manage without a rope,' he muttered.

'Right,' I said. 'This is where we start the real climbing.'

I pointed up the first pitch of the North Buttress Route – a vertical pitch disappearing straight up into the clouds.

'Oh!' said Colin. 'I thought we were carrying on up this rough old pathway.'

There was no resistance as we roped up for the difficult ascent of Tryfan. The climb is classified as 'Difficult in fine weather' – and today, believe me, it was tough. A lot of the holds were covered in snow, but luckily there wasn't much ice on the rock face. I kept my eye on the escape route across to the gully. I must admit the gully didn't look very inviting today; the dripping water had frozen into sculptured icicles, some were four or five feet in length. To be quite honest, I didn't feel like abseiling or climbing down in these horrible unsafe conditions. It turned out to be a slow, exhilarating climb. Although I had climbed this route many times with Tommy, my pal, I still had difficulty staying on the route due to the cloud which reduced my visibility down to a few feet in front of me.

It was nearly dinner time when we came to the broad ledge just before the last pitch to the top. I kicked and scraped the snow off over the edge. Funnily enough, it seemed to land right on top of Colin.

'Whoops! Sorry Colin, I didn't know you were there,' I said in answer to his protests.

After a moments silence he replied, 'You rotten sod! You did that on purpose!'

'Who me? Would I do a rotten thing like that, knowing you were tied to a rock and couldn't get out of the way,' I laughed.

The next minute, the Abominable Snowman thrust his head over the ledge I was standing on. Talk about covered from head to toe in snow, poor Colin was still spitting out the odd icicle or two. As we both rested our weary limbs, sitting with our feet dangling over a couple of thousand feet of fresh air, to our amazement, the cloud started to lift and weak sunshine bathed the valley below in a pale golden tint, which reflected off the snow giving it an unnatural picture postcard effect. In fact it looked just like the icing on a Christmas cake. We finished the climb, clearing each hold of the white powdered snow before making the next move. Finally we reached the ridge and scrambled along to the top of the central peak, where the two monolithic boulders stood in defiance of all weathers. Now, you haven't climbed Tryfan if you haven't made the leap from Eve to Adam. There was a thin coating of ice on Eve, but Adam seemed to be reasonably rough and dry as a landing ground.

Well, Colin can certainly say that he truly has climbed my favourite mountain in great style, and yes, he made that famous leap to complete his first real ascent of a Welsh Mountain.

We ate our sandwiches and drank the traditional mountaineer's rum-laced coffee before we descended down to Lyn Bocklewed and abseiled down into the Nant Franchon Pass. We passed Mervin's Coffee Stall by the bridge, but much to our disappointment he was nowhere to be seen – I think he was still tucked up in bed, awaiting the influx of visitors in the spring.

The following day we managed a nice ridge walk and then descended down to Llyn Ogwen. Crossing the road, we clamboured over the large boulders up to the foot of the Milestone Buttress. I tell you what, I wish I had a pound for every time I had climbed the Buttress. We roped up and were once again met with ice-covered holds. Fortunately there wasn't much snow on this side of the mountain. We sat in the scoop, sheltering from the wind, and out came the flask – with a cup full of Derek's Special Coffee inside us, the world was our oyster! I climbed over the 'Garden Wall' onto the ledge below and traversed slowly along to the cave. In the cave I paused, belayed, and shouted to Colin to follow me, making sure I kept out of sight as he climbed over the wall and on to the ledge.

'Oh, bloody hell! Where are you?' he shouted, as he gazed down at the road way, way below, stretching out like a fine black ribbon laid out on the white layer of snow.

The small ledge was actually rather slippy in places and not really the ideal place to stop and admire the view. Colin almost threw himself into the cave next to me, gasping and spluttering. After a few minutes I went up the chimney. Colin followed and we completed the climb without further ado.

We were pleased to find that the roads had been well gritted and cleared, and we made our way home the following morning, after a wonderful exhilarating weekend in the Welsh Mountains.

* * * * *

Think of a mountain. Chances are excellent that your imaginary mountain will stand out tall and forbidding in your mind's eye; immense and ponderous, reaching up to the heavens and shrouded by perpetual snow plumes borne on a relentless wind. It is hard to visualise without feeling an attendant chill of forbidding excitement.

Mountains are the stuff of legends, about fearless adventurers who seek to know the solitary secrets of the Earth's highest places.

For as long as man can lift his eyes to the hills, he will always find fresh challenges there.

* * * * *

STOP PRESS – STOP PRESS – STOP PRESS – STOP PRESS – STOP PRESS – STOP PRESS

Sunday 5th August 2007 – I had just celebrated my 79th birthday. The next day I received a telephone call from Nick Cox, my Godson, to say his dad, my friend and teaching colleague, Lew, had just died.

Now, Lew and myself, had spent many a happy day taking the lads from school on mountaineering trips up to North Wales, and by the time I had finished with him, Lew was an expert at leading the lads on the Milestone Buttress climb.

Lew was also a member of the Crazy Concreting Gang and we did a lot of sailing and canoeing together around the Gurnard area.

One thing that sticks in my mind and makes him stand out from the rest is that he was fearless. At school you always used to get the odd ex-pupils who were unemployed, who used to drift up to the school gates looking for trouble – you could always rely on Lew to go and sort them out. He would pass my department wielding his Triumph car starting handle in his hand. If there were more than two or three thugs, he would pop in, beckon to me with his head, and I would join him with my twelve inch adjustable spanner! He didn't stand any messing about. It was a case of the old ex-para jump master's order of 'Go! Go! Go!' – and, funnily enough, they went! Of course, Lew was ex-RAF so they were called Dispatchers. He was the one who shouted, 'Action Stations!

Hook Up! And Go! Go! Go!' then simply shoved you out of the old Dakota plane.

Both Lew and Mary were great pals of ours. We were very fond of them and we have some wonderful memories to reflect on.

God Bless you both.

36

Some Climb Mountains Whilst Others Sit And Dream

For ages men have strived for goals that seem impossible: the North Pole, the four-minute mile, flight into space, landing on the moon. Then suddenly they break through the barriers into higher realms of achievement and the 'unattainable' soon becomes common place.

We flew to Geneva by Swissair then caught the train to the small town of Brig, where our journey continued on the cog narrow-gauge railway up the Zermattertal (gorge). Finally, after a stunning ride, we pulled into Zermatt's Bahnhof, which is protected from avalanches by sturdy sheds along the platform. Although it was July, there was a chill in the mountain air which is clean and free of any car fumes and noisy motor vehicles. The only way into Zermatt is either by helicopter, foot or the cog-railway.

Milling around the forecourt of the station were sheep, goats, people and beautifully painted horse-drawn carriages awaiting clients for the posh hotels, and for the lesser nobles, like Colin and myself, there were electric shuttles (very similar to the electric milk delivery vans). We arrived at our small, friendly, five-storey, timber clad, Swiss chalet-style hotel called 'The Alpina'. After a quick wash and bite to eat we went outside and gazed across the landscape to the mighty Matterhorn. It seems to just sit there, aloof from the other meaningless mountains, commanding respect and awe by its domineering presence alone. For a few moments we pondered in silence and wondered if we'd bitten off more than we could chew!

The frosty cathedral-like bulk of the Matterhorn's citadel loomed, almost unbelievably, dominating everything in the vicinity and standing starkly alone and supremely elevated above everything else around it. Just the sight of it haunting the skyline, like a mysterious spectre of stone, made our hearts beat faster.

Colin looked at me and whispered, 'I thought you had exaggerated in that painting you've done of the Matterhorn at home, but, my god, it's incredible. Do people really climb to the top of that?!'

'Oh yes!' I replied. 'And one day soon we too will be standing on the very top of that fantastic mountain'.

As we both stared transfixed, I seemed to drift back in time...

It was raining as I waited by the school gates for peg-leg to appear on his one-pedal bicycle. Then I was in the classroom lifting out the Geological magazine from the American comics. Then I had a flash back of the entire centre page, a black and white picture, of the Matterhorn.

With my heart beating faster, I opened my eyes and knew in my very soul why I was here and what I was going to do.

Dreams do come true! I knew it was time to relive my haunting dream – and now was the time to make my dream a reality before it was too late. This is what I came for and this was what I was going to do.

I didn't think this was the ideal time to tell Colin that over 450 climbers had already died attempting to climb the Matterhorn, or that the route we would climb, the Hornli Ridge, is far more technically difficult than the normal routes up Mount Everest or Mount McKinley.

Another thing I thought it wise to leave until after we had climbed the mountain was a visit to the Zermatt cemetery, which is in fact a very interesting place, as it is known as the graveyard of the Matterhorn. There are tombstones with real ice axes and crampons bolted into the stone. There is one amazing tombstone on which a crucified Christ is adorned as a climber with an axe and rope hanging from his body. I personally thought that was going a bit far; rather too theatrical. Here can be found just a few of the graves of the young people who attempted the Matterhorn and paid dearly with their lives. The one sculpture that impressed me the most was carved out of granite stone of two hands hanging on to a narrow ledge; simple, but with a powerful message.

Edward Whymper, the first man to climb the Matterhorn, ends his book with this advice:

"Climb if you will, but remember that courage and strength are nought without prudence, and that a momentary negligence may destroy the happiness of a lifetime. Do nothing in haste, look well to each step and from the beginning think what may be the end".

These words of mountain wisdom have been firmly engraved into my memory since I first read them as a twelve year old school boy.

Our acclimatising had begun. In the early morning we climbed slowly up through the pine forests. Our boots sank into the thick layer of pine needles making it really hard going, but this was only the beginning and we were refreshed after a good night's sleep. After a couple of thousand feet, we broke through the last of the trees and faced a long slog up the scree. Two steps up and one step down; we made slow progress, but kept going with determination to brilliant white snow fields, reaching down to us with ever pointing fingers. By now we had quite a sweat on. Strapping our jackets on to the top of our rucksacks we proceeded carefully on to the first layer of snow. It sounds ridiculous, but we were climbing in shirt sleeves and were still very hot. With the sun beating down on us from the clear blue sky above, the heat and light were reflected back at us from the snow – this was the stuff to give you a really weather-beaten mountain tan!

The ridge walk was amazing as we headed towards Monta Rosa, the highest peak in the area. The view up was absolutely stunning. We were surrounded by snow-capped peaks, but above all stood the majestic Matterhorn with its peak disappearing into the clouds, which seemed to be magnetised towards the mountain. It was then that we realised why the guides for the climb started off at some unearthly hour, to reach the top by sunrise and be off the mountain by noon, as each and every day the icy clouds surround the mountain at midday and swirl around the peak with either snow or hailstones. Eventually we reached, and stood, above the Monta Rosa Glacier and were rather surprised to see two bright orange tents pitched right in the centre of the maze of crevasses. We came to the conclusion that they were doing the full ascent of the glacier which includes a nasty looking ice wall at the top. I thought to myself, good luck mates! I knew just what they were going through, as I had climbed the Mer-de-Glace in the French Alps, and believe me, that was no picnic!

We returned along the ridge, still in the region of 12,000 feet. It was great fun as we sat down on the frozen snow. Holding the ice axe between our legs we slowly eased ourselves over the edge of the ridge. Inside two seconds, we were speeding down the steep slope, using the ice axe as a brake to control our descent. Well, in no time we had descended over 2,000 feet from the ridge to the snow fields below.

Now, at 11,000 feet I knew that both Colin and I had a tendency to mountain sickness. This is a very strange sickness brought on by altitude. It makes you feel as if you are in a dream. You feel light-headed, even slightly tipsy, and the lack of oxygen brings on a mental blockage, which stops you from thinking straight, it simply clouds the mind, and all you want to do is sit or lie down and go to sleep. It is a great danger when approaching a deep crevasse in the snow field, as you lose all sense of reason; even the protective emotion of 'fear' is dulled. Colin looked at the crevasse, backed off, then without hesitation began to run at it, well, it was more of a stumble really in the thick snow.

'Stop!' I shouted, but to no avail.

It was like a movie in slow motion, as he plodded along and jumped. It was a feeble effort but fortunately he landed on the edge at the other side, then leant forward and staggered on.

That was enough for me, I realised what he was suffering from and hurried towards him. It was no use saying anything, as he was way out of it by this time, so I just grabbed the sling around his waist, whipped a karabiner onto it with another sling, and gently led him down the snow field to eventually arrive at the café at the top of the cable car station. I ordered a large lemon tea, laced with six spoonfuls of sugar, stirred it up well, and sat there until he drank the lot!

'I thoroughly enjoyed that,' he said, smiling. 'I think I could manage another one!'

With that, we ordered two more drinks and relaxed; within minutes we were both back on planet earth!

37

They Came, They Climbed, They Conquered

The Zermatt's guide office is a simple, unpretentious place. In the window are notices about rates and recreational mountain walks offered to the general public. Inside, on the counter, a coffee pot was brewing thick black liquid. Near the counter, conversing in low tones, were some of the local men, who weren't wearing the correct apparel identifying them as guides, but were certainly a tough looking bunch. They had broad shoulders, thick necks and weather-beaten faces. The initial feeling was that we were interlopers; an unknown quantity. That feeling soon disappeared though, as the questions were fired at us fast and furious. They were very serious. They wanted to know what we had done since we arrived in Zermatt, and what other climbing experience we had. Finally they were satisfied by our background and our experience in mountain climbing techniques, and it was agreed that we would meet our guides at the Hornlihutte in a couple of days time. Colin thought he would like to leave it a bit longer, but I knew we would need at least two days to recover after the climb, before travelling home.

The following day we went to the climbing shop recommended by the Head Guide and were measured and fitted for crampons suitable for the ice field at the top of the Matterhorn.

The time had come for my date with this peak of my childhood dreams.

We left in the afternoon, of the day before our attempt was to take place. As we trudged along the 7,000 feet ridge, we climbed over boulders, upwards ever upwards, towards the Swiss Alpine Club Hut. We were already twice as high as Snowdon in North Wales and still had another 3,000 feet to go. Looking down we could see the hotels and matchbox size chalets clustered around the railway station.

We passed a small mountain lake, which unbeknown to us, we would most certainly remember on the way back!

As we approached the Hornilhutte we were both surprised to see a vertical steel ladder attached to the wall leading up to a first floor window. Above the window was a large painted sign; 'WINTER ENTRANCE – Altitude 3260 Metres.'

The light was fading fast and there was a bitterly cold wind blowing. As we opened the heavy oak door, we were met with a blast of warm air from the old wood-burning stove inside. We greeted our two burly looking guides who suggested that we had an early night as the climb would start at 3.30 a.m. and the warden would wake us up at 2.30 a.m. for a very early breakfast of hot muesli and instant oatmeal.

I was dying for the toilet and went to investigate the facilities. The toilets consisted of a long board with holes at six foot intervals, capped by a round lid which fitted and screwed down with a bayonet cap. I lifted the lid and peered cautiously down into a very deep crevasse; the wind howled up and nearly blew my head off.

'Nein! Nein!' shouted a German chap perched on one of the holes at the end. 'You must lift the lid, and sit down very quickly, or you will get a face full of my shit!'

Believe me, I didn't need telling twice!

Just before we went up to the dormitory, Colin and I went outside to look at the clouds swirling around the black menacing mountain top. The moonlight gave the mountain an unrealistic effect, as it seemed to be leaning over, as if it was about to topple down on top of us. It certainly had a sobering effect on our high spirits. It looked nothing like the pretty postcards you could buy from the village shops below.

Back in the dormitory we tried to make ourselves comfortable on the hard, wooden bunk beds. We had no trouble awakening at 2.30 a.m. as neither of us had slept a wink the entire night; probably the combination of excitement, uncertainty and the usual difficulty of getting any sleep at high altitude. Colin appeared in his warm, white, thick cricket trousers and jersey for breakfast. His guide looked him up and down.

'Hey Colin! I thought you had come to climb the Matterhorn, not paint it!' he remarked.

On the 25th July 1979, we left the hut at exactly 3.30 a.m. The guides had torches and we headed for the 200 foot shear wall of rock. Before I started I had told my guide that it was my ambition to climb the Matterhorn, not be hauled up on a tight rope. He was quite impressed, and promised me he would keep a slack rope at all times, even on the notorious ice pitch where disaster overtook Edward Whyper on his eighth successful attempt to reach the peak of this mighty mountain.

Originally, seventeen unsuccessful attempts had been made to conquer the Matterhorn (eight of them by Whyper himself) before, at last, the Englishman managed to pull it off.

Now Jean-Antoine Carrel was born in Breuil, the Italian hamlet below the peak's south face. He was one of the Alp's first mountain guides and the first man possessed with the vision and the will to climb the Matterhorn. His initial attempt was in 1857. He tried again in 1858 and 1861, followed by three more attempts in 1862 – two of these were with Whymper; they were friends and rivals, as both had the burning desire to be the first to reach the 'tiger's tooth', that had been pronounced 'unclimbable'. It was a battle of egos and shifting loyalties.

Whimper believed Carrel to be the best climber in the Alps, and had actually arranged to hire him for what turned out to be his successful attempt. Bad weather intervened and Carrel secretly agreed to guide a four-man all Italian team, leaving Whymper out in the cold. When the Englishman discovered that Carrel was already attempting the mountain from the Italian side he quickly put together a seven man team in Zermatt, to make an attempt from the Swiss side up the Hornli Ridge – the one we would be climbing. When Whymper and his team stood on the summit they could see Carrel and his men just 600 feet below them on the Italian side; the Englishman rolled a few stones to get their attention. Devastated, the native guide turned back, only to return three days later with a new team, to successfully complete the first ascent from the Italian Ridge and the second ascent of the Matterhorn.

Whymper's victory came at great cost; during the decent, four members of his group fell to their deaths. One man, Douglas Hadow, slipped on the ice pitch below the peak, pulling off three others. Whymper and his two guides, Peter Taugwalder and his son, also Peter, caught the fall, but the rope snapped and Michel Croz, a Chamonix guide, and the English climbers Charles Hudson, Douglas Hadlow and Francis Douglas, fell 4000 feet on to the Matterhorn Glacier below. The bodies of all but Douglas were later found and are buried in the Zermatt cemetery.

I believe there are fixed ropes nearly all the way up on the difficult pitches these days, but then I only found two fixed ropes and one was at the start of this 200 foot face.

My guide, Perren, disappeared up into the darkness. No problem, I thought, and I followed with one hand on the fixed rope and the other feeling for holes in the dark. I was about half way up when a sudden powerful gust of wind tore me off the rock face and hurled me out into space. I hung on to the loose rope for dear life. Then, bang, I was flung straight back on to the rock face, taking the full force on my right shoulder and arm. Crickey! I nearly wet myself. Then I managed to face the rock and finish the pitch in a more dignified manner, with the words that someone had scratched on the back of my bunk in the dormitory ringing in my ears; "He who hesitates will not conquer."

The climb is relentless and unforgiving. For the entire climb there is never anything resembling a path or route. If you stop you can only perch and you are always looking for hand holes or foot holes, always up, up and up. Speed is essential. As the day wears on the sun melts the snow and ice making it unsafe to climb on. The aim is to get to the top as soon as possible after daybreak and be off the mountain by noon. The air was cold and crisp and the skies were absolutely crystal clear despite the early hours.

We made good time, and within several hours we had made it up to the Solvayhutte, (a high altitude mountain ridge at 13,143 feet), which is small but provides excellent emergency shelter. After a short rest for food, banana, chocolate and a full bar of Kendal Mint Cake, followed by coffee from the flask I had hidden away in my rucksack, and some sober gazing at the absolutely sheer drop on all sides, my guide shouted over to me.

'Come on, the worst is still to come'

Oh great, I thought! I knew we still had to step out on to the ice where the Whymper disaster had occurred and, believe me, I didn't cherish the idea of hanging about on that pitch. I checked my crampons were firmly attached to my boots; they seemed to be firmly fixed with no slack. We started to head up once more, and the moment of truth was upon me, as we veered over to the right and stepped onto the steep iced East Face of the Matterhorn.

We zigzagged up and up, jamming our crampons into the slippery surface with every step. I briefly glanced down the 4000 foot sheer drop below me to the glacier, and quickly decided I had just better concentrate on the matter in hand.

The bitterly cold wind whipped across the icy surface. Isn't it funny, when you start to concentrate you start to notice the smaller details; as I jammed my crampons into the ice small icicles spattered out, some slithered down over the vast drop below, whilst the majority of them were being blown horizontally across the East Face. I had to refocus and concentrate on the route ahead.

It wasn't long before we climbed off the ice and onto the permanent snowfield that covers the Dachel (summit roof). Just below us, Colin and his guide were climbing up the ice field. It was then I had a vision of how Whymper and the two guides must have felt seeing their fellow climbers being swept over the edge of the nasty looking escarpment lip. I don't know whether it was a good idea to have read the detailed account of their climb before tackling it myself! At least Colin, who was taking it all in his stride with great confidence, was unaware of the tragic details of the first party to conquer this mighty mountain.

By now the skies were starting to get quite light. We trekked up the Dachel's icy snowfield using crampons to get a firm grim, and up we went to the final summit.

As we reached the top, I looked at my watch and the time was exactly 8.48 a.m. The sense one has at this point of being perched absurdly high up in the sky, with nothing above you, and the ground falling away below on all sides, is quite breathtaking. I paused as I stood in the snow on top of the

South Summit to reflect momentarily on the drama which eternally embroiled Whymper and his fellow Victorian climbers in historic climbing speculation on that day way back in 1865. I could now vividly imagine what it must have felt like for them and it left me with a chilled sense of awe and wonder at their marvellous achievement.

Colin and I then left the guides on the South Summit and scrambled along to the true North Summit, which is at the far end of a rocky spine with icy patches in the perpetually frozen crannies of the summit rocks.

The true high point of the Matterhorn is adorned with a filigree iron cross. The cross commemorates the lives of all those who have been killed attempting to do what we had successfully done, and is a product of the deep beliefs of the devoted Catholic people who live in the high alpine hamlets of this region.

It took a few minutes to realise what I had done; I had made it to the top of the Matterhorn.

Finally I had made it to the summit of my life-long dream. Here I was standing on the doorstep of heaven. It was indeed heaven to me, and as the first party to make the ascent that beautiful day, from the base to the top, we had quite a few moments of peace and quiet in which to absorb and appreciate the singular beauty that this high and historic individual mountain offers.

Colin's guide took the Isle of Wight Round Table plaque and jammed it firmly in the snow. I placed a picture of all my family taken at The Briars, placed in a waterproof bag, with a 1928 one shilling piece (my birth year) and buried it at arms length in the snow.

I was leading the descent down the steep notorious East Face ice field, when, much to my utter dismay, I saw my camera fall out of my rucksack. It sped down the ice and hurtled out into space, over the 4000 foot sheer drop to the glacier below. It had nearly all our photos taken on the summit on it. Fortunately, I had a couple left on a film which was tucked safely away in my pocket. (So, if any of you kind folk attempt the Matterhorn, please keep a look out for my cold and weary little camera which must still be lying on the Matterhorn glacier).

Now according to statistics, it is on the descent that most mountaineering accidents occur, due to fatigue and a somewhat lessened state of focus and concentration. I can understand the reasoning behind that. Having achieved your goal, what is next? All you want to do after five hours of solid climbing without a decent break is to sit down and rest. But oh no! There is still another five hours of climbing down that awaits your weary muscles and sore feet. The guides want to be off the mountain before the sun starts to melt the ice and snow.

Just below the Solvayhutte I crossed over a snow filled gully, belayed myself and took the rope in as Perren stepped onto a boulder in the centre of the gully. The boulder dislodged and disappeared down the gully, and I'm afraid Perren would have done the same, closely followed by me, if I hadn't been on a good stance and well belayed. Cor! It was the first time I've had to hold a sixteen stone giant of a man, on the end of a rope. I couldn't pull him up.

'Hold on, Derek!' he shouted, as he proceeded to haul himself up the rope. As he stepped on to the ledge he patted me on the back and shook my hand. 'Thanks, partner. You are a true and trustworthy alpine climber!'

It was all over in just a few minutes, but I could still feel that rope biting into my neck and left shoulder for sometime afterwards. However, that little bit of praise, from one of the best guides in Switzerland certainly made me feel good, and the rest of the climb down didn't seem too bad after all.

Arriving at the Hornlihutte both Colin and I were absolutely shattered and exhausted. We climbed the wooden stairs to the dormitory, staggered over to our bunk bed and collapsed, sprawled across the beds.

An hour later the warden woke us up to announce the guides had finished their dinner and would like their fee before leaving. We managed to stagger downstairs and meet our trustworthy guides, thanking them for helping us to fulfil our dreams. We shook their hands and they were off, walking briskly down the ridge heading for home, after just another days work.

With that, Colin and I also decided to also make a move and head down the ridge. Our boots felt as though they were full of drawing pins; every time I put my foot down, thousands of needle-like pains shot up into the soles of my feet. We arrived at the small lake and disregarded the advice of the warden, about not to take our boots off as our feet would swell up and we wouldn't be able to get them on again. So, off came my boots and I plunged my feet into the icy cold water. Heavenly bliss! Colin decided to do what he was told, and didn't take off his boots, but walked into the water right up to his knees and stood there in a daze. After about half an hour the pain had eased, or maybe the icy water had numbed all our feelings. Anyway, we headed back down to the village and made our way along the high street to our small friendly hotel.

I ran a hot bath and told Colin to get in and have a good soak, then I would do the same. Waiting for Colin to finish, I laid down on the bed and immediately fell into a deep sleep. I had no idea how long I had been asleep, but when I awoke there was no sign of Colin. I glanced into the bathroom, and there was Colin, laid out, with arms hanging limply over the sides of the old Victorian enamelled cast-iron bath, fast asleep, snoring away as if there was no tomorrow. The water was icy cold by this time, but it obviously didn't seem to bother him. It took quite a bit of shaking and shouting, before he slowly opened up just one eye, and looked up at me.

'We did it!' he said, smiling. 'We climbed the Matterhorn!' Then he closed his eye again, and drifted peacefully back to land of nod.

I yanked him out; I was ready for my nice hot bath. Then we slept for the rest of the afternoon. We eventually got dressed and went down in time for the evening meal. The proprietor's son was a mountain guide and told his father of our achievement. When we entered the dining room everybody stood up and clapped.

'Bravo! Bravo!' echoed around the room. Then all the guests and staff proceeded to shake our hands and pat us on the back.

Well, we didn't know where to put ourselves, so we just nodded and thanked them, and then sat down to a well-earned roast dinner – the first real meal of the day! After dinner it was straight back to bed and a good night's sleep.

After breakfast the next morning, we ambled along to the first Café Bar we came to and had a coffee, followed by a beer, then another beer, then another; we were so thirsty and dehydrated. I must say, we felt great as we entered the mountain guides office to receive our Certificates of Achievement, with a picture of the Matterhorn and signed by the Head Guide of Zermatt. He handed us the coveted gold badge depicting the Matterhorn. You can only receive this once you have been officially recorded in the guide's diary as having reached the peak of the Matterhorn.

Even today, this badge is proudly displayed on my ice axe, above a large picture of the Matterhorn, hanging at the top of our staircase. Many times if I am feeling a bit low or off colour, I will stop and look at that little badge and think what Perren had said, 'You are a true and trustworthy alpine climber'.

What had started as a picture, discovered in a comic box, and the reading of Edward Whymper's "Scrambles amongst the Alps", had now culminated in finally fulfilling a personal, enriching dream that had been an important part of my whole life – a figurative milestone had now been reached; an accomplishment of no small personal meaning.

But nothing, nothing, can compare with the silent glory of standing up there on the roof of the world, listening to the chill, keen wind howling with stories of climbers long gone and relishing that moment of personal triumph, which for me, will remain long in my memory until the day I die… standing there on the doorstep of heaven and thinking, this I have done!

* * * * *

5th August 2007 –

I have just celebrated my 79th birthday and Nyle, my fourteen year old grandson, who reflects my enthusiasm for the outdoors, has just finished reading my first book, The Spirit of Adventure, again; he must have read it at least half a dozen times by now! For my birthday he made me a card with two drawings of realistic ice axes on it.

Jordan, my youngest grandson, aged nine, has been doing "Albert and the Lion" at school, and so I gave him my original copy of the Lancashire Poem about Mr and Mrs Ramsbottom, and their young son Albert, and their trip to Blackpool. He produced a birthday card for me, based on the poem, about the adventures I had as a young lad, again taken from The Spirit of Adventure. The verse is written in old Lancashire!

I thought you might like to read it.

There's a lovely granddad called Derek

Who likes 'is fresh air 'an fun.
When 'e was young, Mr an' Mrs Feldon
'Ad their 'ands full, with their young son.
'E got up t' all sorts o' mischief –
Like talking t' pieces o' coal,
An' scrumping apples from t' orchard –
But 'e was always a 'appy old soul.
Today is 'is 79th birthday
An' we're all 'ere t' celebrate this day -
(An' make sure 'e keeps OUT o' mischief!)
So 'APPY BIRTHDAY, DEE DEE, we say!

As a matter of interest, I've also just been informed by email from the Matterhorn's mountain museum in Zermatt, that our name have been recorded, as climbers who have successfully reached the peak of the famous Matterhorn!

What a lovely birthday!

* * * * *

An amazing thing happened to me whilst standing on the summit of the Matterhorn. The moment I touched the wrought-iron cross denoting the ultimate peak, I had a new feeling of freedom, my mind became crystal clear. I knew that it was time to discard the old coat of frustration and fear and to throw away the shackles of despair, and step out into new challenges, to take the path of uncertainty, to step forth into a new awakening and to embrace all that life has to offer. I suddenly realised that in my life I was slowly but surely being ground down by people and situations beyond my control. Without knowing it I was falling into the trap of the teaching profession and living in the 'comfort zone'. Hang in there another 10 or 15 years and you can enjoy a good pension!

At that moment I had no idea what I would do, but I felt confident that when the time was right some opportunity would present itself and it would be up to me to grasp it with both hands, and step once more into the unknown!

The idea was really scary at first, but looking back on my life so far, I had always stepped into the path of the unknown and emerged eventually at the other side, after a few adventures along the way. I may be battered and bruised a little but always safe and in one piece.

Blow me down, on my return home, a job came up for a Craft and Technology Advisor for the County. Well, could this be it? I put in an application form and waited for an acknowledgement. Nothing. Strange, I thought, so I called into County Hall and asked one of the girls what was going on.

She informed me that my application had been withdrawn, as my Headmaster had been in touch and requested that the application was refused, as without me at the helm of the Technology Department, that I had created, he felt that it would collapse and close down. No-one else had the knowledge or enthusiasm to maintain the momentum of such a forward thinking department! Well, that was a kick in the pants.

A young arty girl got the County Advisors post, and came to see me and suggested that the 'new-thinking' was to miniaturise the workshops, and instead of the wonderful equipment, like lathes, milling machines and pillar drills that British Hovercraft had kindly donated to us, (they had even sent their electricians over to wire them up for us over a weekend), she suggested that they were to be replaced with tiny sewing machine size lathes that she had seen in a model makers catalogue!

To me this idea was absolutely ridiculous, bearing in mind that Keith Simmonds, my Deputy Head of Department at Cowes High School, had won the Young Engineers award over the last three years with his student's projects. The awards being presented by none other than Prince Charles himself! (Just in passing, Keith is now, an Education Officer, a deserving achievement for a very hard working and innovated young chap).

This unbelievable suggestion was the final straw, when out of the blue , a new work opportunity and challenge came from, none other than, Peter Hewitt, who many years ago at the age of 14 had stayed with us at The Briars and helped me with all my building work.

* * * * *

But before I go into that, I must just tell you about a strange, spiritual encounter I have just had with my elder sister Barbara.

A funny thing happened the other night. I was fast asleep when I felt somebody tapping me on my foot. I thought it was Glenys needing help so I sat up sharply and opened my eyes. To my surprise it was my sister Barbara, who appeared to be still in her forties, with black hair and a smiling face. She looked me straight in the eyes.

'I thought I'd let you know, our Derek, I'm going on Friday at 9 o'clock,' she said.

'Oh right,' I replied. 'Have a good journey and I'll see you later.'

She nodded, smiled and just faded away in front of my eyes.

I sat there for a few minutes. Well, I thought to myself, that's a strange how do you do! Then I got out of bed and went to the toilet, half expecting to see her on the landing, but no. Now this had happened Wednesday night.

In the morning I told Glenys about it.

'Was it 9 o'clock in the morning or evening?' she asked calmly.

Barbara was currently in a Nursing Home in Worthing and was in her late 80's. Well, 9 o'clock on Friady morning came – and nothing. Then at half past nine, Kenneth her son phoned to say that he had just been informed by the home that his mum had passed away about half an hour earlier, and they had to get the confirmation from the doctor before letting anyone know.

Spooky? No! The amazing thing is that it appeared to be quite normal, as if it was how it should be.

* * * * *

I think you have got to make the most of this life, as unfortunately nobody ever gets out alive!

It's the old saying, 'When one door closes another always opens' – and that is exactly what happened to me when my teaching career came to an end, and I was lead into a completely new world of adventure.

THE END?

"Nothing in life has any meaning
Except the meaning you give it."

Best wishes,

Derek

Glenys and Derek on their Wedding Day.

GLENYS'S MUM AND DAD. THE NEWLY WEDS. MY MUM AND DAD.

Now this is interesting! Our Wedding Day 9th JUNE 1951.

My Mum and Dads Wedding Day. 9th JUNE 1920.

Petra and Philips Wedding Day. 9th JUNE 1990

GLENYS AND DEREK WITH 'OUR' PRIDE AND JOY!

THE 1935 MORRIS VAN.

"We're off, we're off. we're off in a motor car!"

(Chapter 3)

WINTON BOYS ADVENTURE CLUB.

THE FAMOUS LIGHTWEIGHT SLEDGE.

THE PEAK DISTRICT.

"We threw ourselves to the ground as the monstrous bird swept down upon us!"

"Oh! Jolly Dee, Jolly Dee Fella's!"

(Chapter 7)

ALBUM 3.

TWELVE BRIDESMAIDS AND NOT A GIRL IN SIGHT!

WINTON BOYS SCHOOL.
RUDDIGORE. **(Chapter 9)**

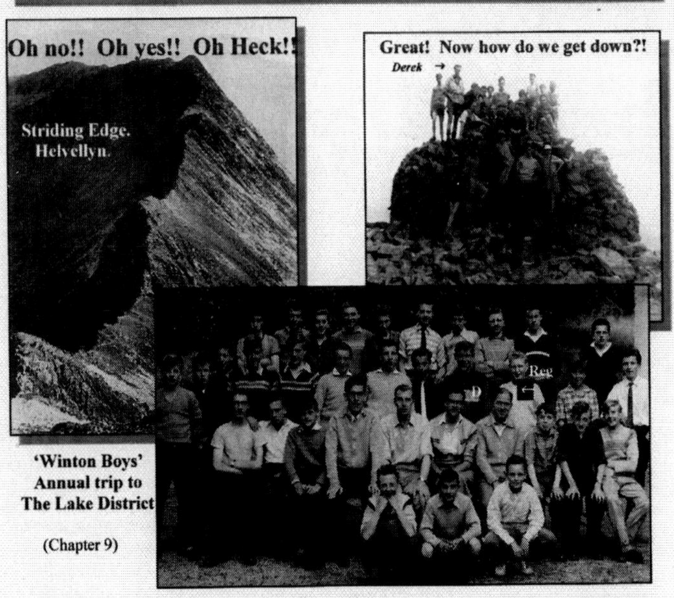

'Winton Boys' Annual trip to The Lake District

(Chapter 9)

__THE__
CARAVAN!
Derek, Glenys & Graham.

4, WINGATE ROAD,
LITTLE HULTON, WALKDEN,
NEAR MANCHESTER.
Tele. WALkden 3082.

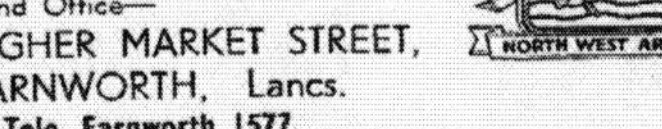

Showroom and Office—
39, HIGHER MARKET STREET,
FARNWORTH, Lancs.
Tele. Farnworth 1577.

FEDERATION OF PLUMBERS & DOMESTIC ENGINEERS
NORTH WEST AREA

Dr. to . .

DEREK FELDON & CO.,

PLUMBING & BUILDING CONTRACTORS

WE WERE VERY PROUD WHEN THE OWNERS MOVED IN.
THEY WERE ABSOLUTELY DELIGHTED WITH THEIR NEW HOME!

(Chapter 3)

BE CAREFUL WHAT YOU WISH FOR, AS IT MAY JUST COME TRUE! *Album 5.*

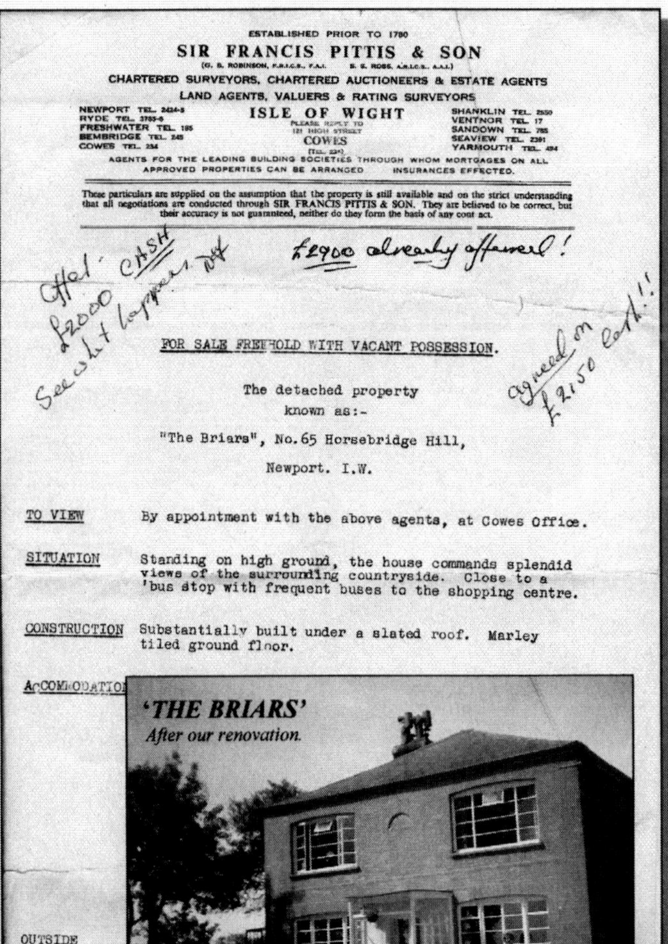
ESTABLISHED PRIOR TO 1790

SIR FRANCIS PITTIS & SON

CHARTERED SURVEYORS, CHARTERED AUCTIONEERS & ESTATE AGENTS

LAND AGENTS, VALUERS & RATING SURVEYORS

ISLE OF WIGHT

NEWPORT · RYDE · FRESHWATER · BEMBRIDGE · COWES

SHANKLIN · VENTNOR · SANDOWN · SEAVIEW · YARMOUTH

PLEASE REPLY TO 121 HIGH STREET COWES

AGENTS FOR THE LEADING BUILDING SOCIETIES THROUGH WHOM MORTGAGES ON ALL APPROVED PROPERTIES CAN BE ARRANGED   INSURANCES EFFECTED.

These particulars are supplied on the assumption that the property is still available and on the strict understanding that all negotiations are conducted through SIR FRANCIS PITTIS & SON. They are believed to be correct, but their accuracy is not guaranteed, neither do they form the basis of any contract.

£2900 already offered!

Offer: CASH £2000 See what happens, DA

FOR SALE FREEHOLD WITH VACANT POSSESSION.

agreed on £2150 cash!!

The detached property known as:-

"The Briars", No.65 Horsebridge Hill,

Newport. I.W.

TO VIEW — By appointment with the above agents, at Cowes Office.

SITUATION — Standing on high ground, the house commands splendid views of the surrounding countryside. Close to a 'bus stop with frequent buses to the shopping centre.

CONSTRUCTION — Substantially built under a slated roof. Marley tiled ground floor.

ACCOMMODATION

OUTSIDE

SERVICES

'THE BRIARS'

After our renovation.

WOW! IT'S REALLY OURS! (Chapter10)

ISLE OF WHITE !!!

WHIPPINGHAM. _Winter_ *1961.*

(Chapter 13)

WOOTTON CREEK. ***FROZEN OVER. 1961.***

Mountaineering at Cowes

Our first glimpse of SNOWDON!

Album 7.

Cor, Sir! Do we need oxygen?

(Chapter 17)

TRYFAN.

Tony and Dad. (Then)!! (Chapter 17)

Derek shows the way!!

Tony & Mate to follow!

Dad and Tony (Now) !!

Lew makes a rapid descent!

Capel Curig.

They survive after a cold night alone on the mountain!!

SNOWDON.

Come on lad's we're all for a bit of that !

Album 9.

Cough! Cough! ***The giant raised himself with a Noisy, Angry, Roar!***
Dave panicked and grabbed the giant in an attempt to hold him down.

This was the moment our Hovercraft was born! (Chapter 19)

Ted's Moment of Glory!

Bembridge Air Show Display..

Album 10.

SCIENCE AND TECHNOLOGY 1972 PROJECT COMPETITION.

OVERALL WINNERS :- **THE TECHNOLOGY DEPARTMENT.**
COWES HIGH SCHOOL. ISLE OF WIGHT.

THE TECHNOLOGY BLOCK.

OUR WINNING ENTRY!

SINGLE SEATER 'HOVER' SCOOTER.

Cowes High School.

Mr Brown Keith

Keith (My Deputy) and Mr Brown (Judge) Outside the Guild Hall Southampton.

"Mr Feldon, tell the boys they can bring it inside now"
"What! You must be joking!"

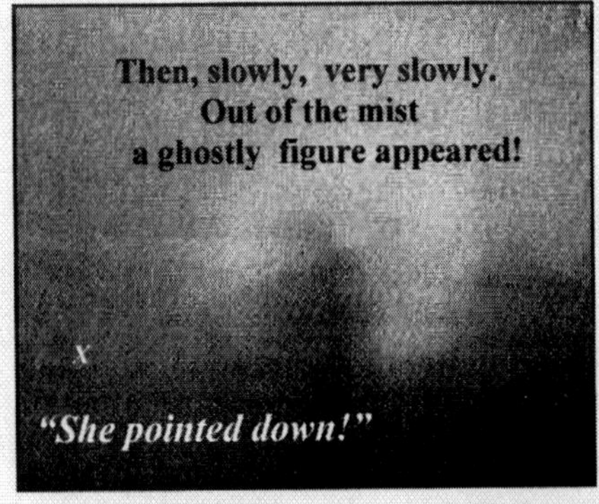

NEWPORT I.O.W. 1811.

Lying there was this pretty Filigree fastener!

(Chapter 33) *Album 12.*

Woolverton was a thriving little towne!

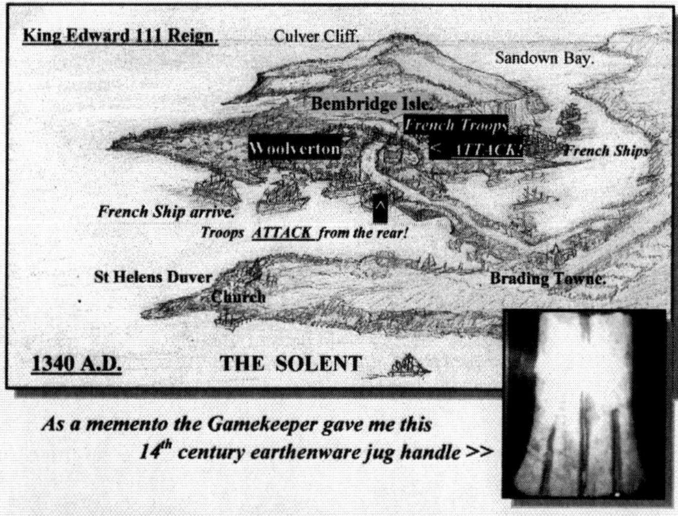

As a memento the Gamekeeper gave me this 14th century earthenware jug handle >>

It's birthday time! Tony was hurtled into the fresh icy cold water !
Woosh! >>>>> He shot out like a rocket!!!!

Yachtsman Uffa Fox launches one of the Cowes High Schools new sailing boats. — Photo: Rogar Smith, Cowes.

Uffa. Christening Snowhite and the Dwarfs.

5 boats named in one go

"ECHO" STAFF REPORTER

VETERAN yachtsman Mr. Uffa Fox officiated at a five-boat christening ceremony at Cowes yesterday. The boats, three dinghies, a sail trainer and a safety boat, are to form the nucleus of a small fleet attached to Cowes High School.

Mr. Fox christened all five craft at the National Sailing Centre, where they are to be based. The three dinghies, all Mirrors, were given the names of Sleep, Dopey and Sneezy.

Headmaster of the school, Mr. W. E. P. Winder, told the large crowd attending the event that the boats were paid for from about £1,400 raised over a number of years by the Parent Teacher Association.

Mr. Fox said it was "marvellous" for a school to establish such a fleet of boats.

MONEY SAVED

Mr. Garth Freeman, head of the school's English department, said that not only were the boats built at the school, but also their trailers, resulting in a lot of money being saved.

Their construction, by boys at the school, was under the supervision of woodwork teacher Mr. Tony Wyeth.

Anoraks worn by pupils at the ceremony were also made at the school by needlework teacher Mrs. Jean Catton, who was able to do them for £1.50 each.

Mr. Wyeth said: "We aim to add more boats to the fleet later. We already have three more Mirror kits at the school. We are also hoping to build a different type of basic trainer and an International Moth."

COST £49

The trainer launched yesterday, an overall 16 feet, was built at the cost of £49. It has a plywood haul and the sails were also made at the school.

The safety craft is a 16ft. 6in. semi-inflatable powered by a 40 hp engine. The wooden hull was designed and built at the school with the help of advice from the director of the National Sailing Centre, Mr. "Bert" Keeble and the Royal National Lifeboat Institution.

Ready made, the boat excluding engine would probably have cost about £600. But the school were able to construct it for £200.

For the christening, the boats flew the burgee of the newly formed sailing club at the school.

*Uffa (swaying quite a bit himself) turned to the dignitaries and smiled, "Well, what are we waiting for? Let's get down to some **serious** drinking!" and promptly headed off to the bar!*

(Chapter 24)

The Jolly 'Cowes' Sailors!

COWES HIGH SCHOOL
COWES, ISLE OF WIGHT
PO31 8HB
ISLE OF WIGHT EDUCATION AUTHORITY

From: Mr. D. FELDON
Dip. S.M., M.I.I.S.M.
Head of
DEPARTMENT OF
APPLIED TECHNOLOGY
Ext. 8

Headmaster:
E. P. WINDER, M.A.

Tel.: Cowes 3491 and 3437

Playground for handicapped children.

Our 'Jewellery' Design Centre.

(Chapter 24)

Our Engineering Centre.

Our Drawing & Design Centre.

Our family at 'The Briars' **1960.**

ALBUM 15.

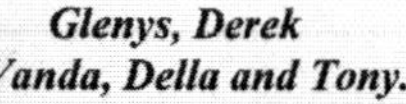

Glenys, Derek Vanda, Della and Tony.

Grandpa & Grandma Jones with the children.

Della and Vanda with their 'famous' 3 wheeler cars!

"Hi ya! Baby. I'm your dad!" ***ALBUM 16.***

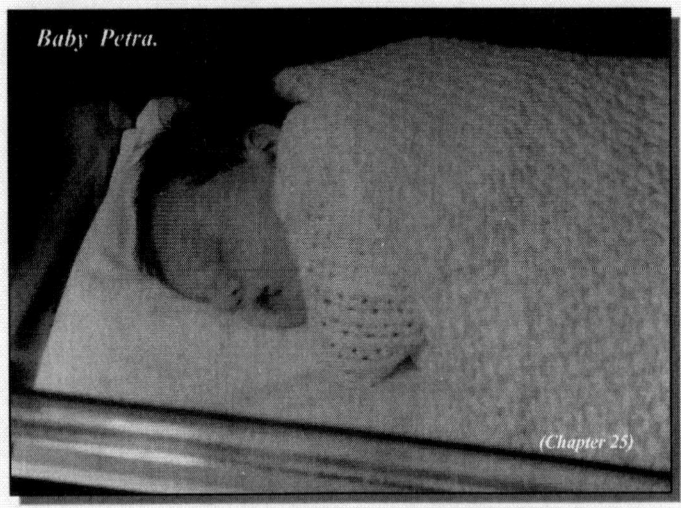
Baby Petra.

(Chapter 25)

I have three loving, supporting, fantastic children, and now a beautiful newborn baby girl, and a wonderful wife and mother. What more could I ask for?

FIVE DAYS THAT SHOOK THE WORLD!

ALBUM 17.

Gerry, Della, Vanda, Tony and David.

"Oh yes! - We were there!"

(Chapter 28)

Afton Down. 1970.

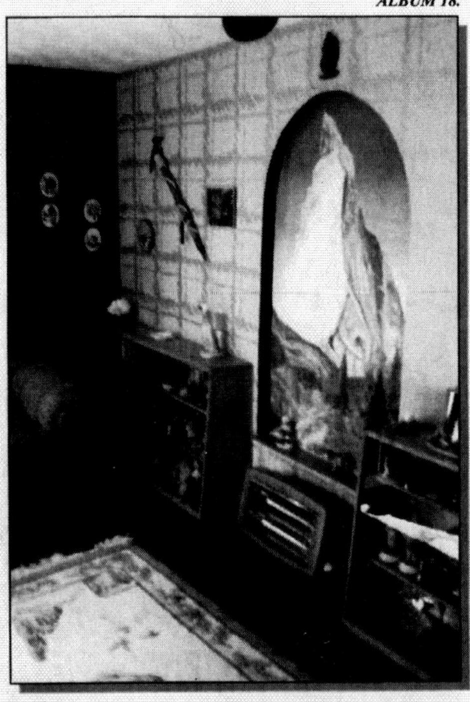

My eyes slowly drifted across the room and rested on the large oil painting of my dream mountain.

' The Matterhorn'

Would I still have the nerve to step out on that final ice pitch?!

"I had this boyhood dream!" **Album 19.**

"Climb if you will, but remember courage and strength is nought without prudence, and that a momentary negligence may destroy the happiness of a lifetime. Do nothing in haste, look well to each step and from the beginning think what may be the end." *Edward Whymper. 1865.* (Chapter36)

Album 20.

THEY CAME, THEY CLIMBED AND THEY CONQUERED!

Colin.

The Matterhorn
(Chapter 36)

Derek.

Perren (My Guide)

Derek.

Album 21.

STANDING ON THE DOORSTEP OF HEAVEN!

I had made it to the summit of my life-long dream!

Finally we had conquered the mighty Matterhorn !

Peak of success

The sky was the limit for two men who decided to have a joint celebration — 15,000 feet above sea level. Mr. Derek Feldon, a teacher at Cowes High School, and Mr. Colin Ward, a member of Ryde Round Table, both achieved a life ambition by reaching the summit of the Matterhorn.

Mr. Feldon (left), climbing since he was 12, has made several attempts on the Matterhorn. However, he was determined to conquer the mountain to celebrate his 50th birthday.

Mr. Ward, on reaching the top, fixed a wooden plaque of the Island with the Ryde Round Table crest inscribed on it to commemorate the Table's 50th anniversary.

The pair set off from the village of Zermatt and reached the hut at the foot of the mountain on July 24. The following morning at 3.30 a.m. they set off with torches. At 8.48 a.m. they were standing on top of the Matterhorn.

Life must be a great adventure, or it's nothing! ***Album 22.***

(Chapter 36)

This is to certify that

Mr. Derek Feldon **Mr Derek Feldon**

has climbed the Matterhorn

on the 25. Juli 1979 ***25 July 1979***

The Guide Association of Zermatt

Kioug E. The President:

PerrenWerner. The Guide:

Kioug E.

Perren Werner

Some climb mountains-

Whilst others just sit and dream!

"No thank you, I've just had a cup of tea!"

Chapter 26.

Safely notching up a first

COWES teacher Mr Derek Feldon has a most unusual qualification — he has just been awarded the Diploma in Safety Management, Britain's top professional qualification for safety men.

He is the first and, so far, the only school teacher to get this qualification, which is awarded after a number of courses and a written examination. Although one or two university lecturers have it, it is mainly a diploma sought in industry.

Mr Feldon, head of applied technology at Cowes High School, Isle of Wight, explained: "The Health and Safety at Work Act now covers schools, and I could see this was going to happen."

He has had an interest in safety for some years, and points out that it has a real relevance to the classroom, which in practical subjects now includes foundrys, workshops and laboratories.

He has been surveying local schools, and finds a lot of room for improvement.

There is a second aspect to his safety work — teaching school children about the importance of the subject. "Many of them will be going into industry," he told *Soundings*, "and the biggest accident rate is in the younger generation."

The picture shows Mr Feldon (right) receiving his diploma from Mr James Tye, director-general of the British Safety Council.

The Teacher February 27, 1976

The Teacher

International Institute of Risk and Safety Management

This is to certify that

DEREK FELDON

has been accepted as a member of the International Institute of Risk and Safety Management, established to advance public education in accident prevention and occupational health in industry.

Chairman
Board of Governors

Vice Chairman
Board of Governors

Date 31/1/1976

Album 24.

INGLEWOOD.

(Chapter 30)

The Porch before!

Petra.

The Imposing Archway. *(My handiwork)*

Job completed!

INGLEWOOD. ***My Loft Conversion.*** ***Album 25.***

Dean and Karen on holiday.

(Chapter 30)

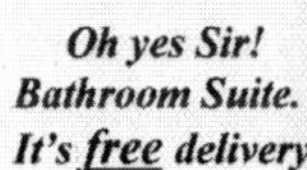

Oh yes Sir!
Bathroom Suite.
It's free delivery!

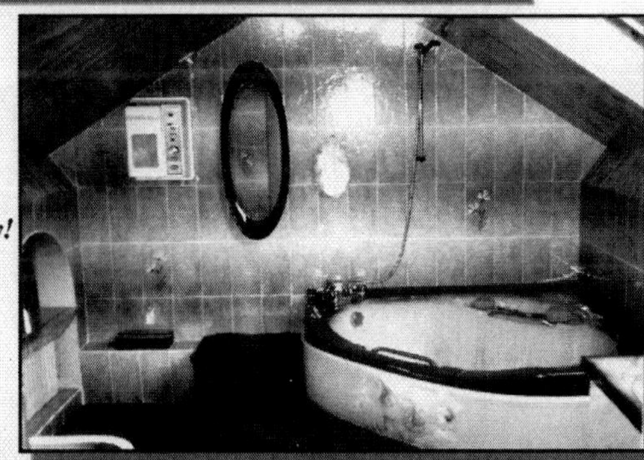

The Fantastic Heated IndoorPool!

INGLEWOOD.

Album 26.

(Chapter 30)

~FELDON~

COAT OF ARMS.

~ VIRTUTIS PRAEMIUM, HONOR ~
'First Bravery, then Honour'

~ COGITARE EST AGERE ~
'To Think is to Act'

The Crest ~ 'The Wild Man Proper'

My Personal Statement.

I do not choose to be a common man.

It is my right to be uncommon if I can.

I seek opportunities and enlightenment not security.

I want and will always take calculated risks!

I want to dream and to build.

Sometimes I may fall, but eventually I will succeed.

I will not trade my freedom for benefits or my dignity for handouts.

I will not cower before any master nor bend to any threat.

I will not be afraid to take one step beyond into the unknown.

It is my heritage to be proud and stand erect, to be proud and unafraid to think and to act for myself and my family and my friends.

To enjoy the benefits of my creation and to face the world boldly and say;

" THIS I HAVE DONE!"

Derek Feldon.

Acknowledgements

Please acknowledge my indebtedness to the websites and information consulted for extracts and photographs.

Aldo Scarpa Kaag www.pbs.ch/eng/tell.html
IoW Festivalrook4.freeserve.co.uk/afton1970
www.bbc.co.uk/Hampshire/iowfestival
www.geocities.com/sunsetstrip/wight
www.bigmagic.com/pages/black
Picturewww.underview.com/movies/messagetolove.html
QuotesIsle of Wight Rock Archives
Matterhorn www.outside.away.com
www.lanset.com
www.earthstation1.com
www.wikipedia.org
Tryfansandysaunders@ www.thewalkzone.co.uk
www.needlesports.com
Hovercraft www.jameshovercraft.co.uk

I apologise if I have omitted any other source of reference.

ISBN 142517671-2

9 781425 176716